Jim Heidinger helps us focus on our historic theological struggles. This b serious conversation about a way for

Southeastern Jurisdiction
The United Methodist Church

This book explores the roots of the UMC conflict and takes the reader past symptoms to root causes. Having a historical context for this current reality breeds great clarity. You owe it to yourself, your church, and your pastor to have the whole story.

—**Carolyn Moore**
Founding Pastor, Mosiac United Methodist Church
Evans, Georgia

Jim Heidinger, a leader of church renewal for twenty-five years, recalls the story of Methodism's theological trajectory into liberalism. He reminds us that Methodism's spiritual confusion is not recent but institutionally began more than one hundred years ago.

—**Mark Tooley**
Institute on Religion and Democracy
Washington, DC

As formerly faithful mainline denominations abandon the gospel of Jesus Christ for lesser gospels, they find their lifeblood drained and the pews emptying. Jim Heidinger, a friend and colleague across denominational lines in renewal work for some four decades, unmasks the clear connection between the rise and spread of theological liberalism and the precipitous decline and loss of vitality of the Methodist denomination.

—**Carmen Fowler LaBerge, President**
Presbyterian Lay Committee
Presbyterian Church USA

James Heidinger's masterful analysis of the decline of United Methodism appears one century after the rise of modern liberal theology, the movement that triggered Methodism's steep decline. The timely appearance of this important study comes in the critical hour when United Methodism is tottering in the face of its greatest crisis of faith, with historic Christian orthodoxy hanging in the balance.

—**Steve O'Malley**
J. T. Seamands Professor of Methodist Holiness History
Asbury Theological Seminary

James Heidinger's book offers a clear and convincing analysis of the church's primary problem, which is theological liberalism. As a winsome evangelical, he speaks the truth in love. His grasp of Methodism's history in America is profound. For every United Methodist who longs for a renewed and revived denomination, this book is a vital guide.

—**Rev. Dr. Bill Bouknight**
United Methodist Pastor, Retired
Columbia, South Carolina

In *The Rise of Theological Liberalism and the Decline of American Methodism* James Heidinger has put together a comprehensive work that is both scholarly in its breadth and depth and at the same time imminently accessible and interesting to those who have little or no formal theological training. Heidinger describes in compelling fashion not only the deficiencies of Protestant liberalism but why and how it undermines the historic Christian faith. Those who feel called to "defend the faith once and for all delivered to the saints" in the first part of the twenty-first century will find this book not only helpful, but indispensable.

—**Rev. Rob Renfroe**
President and Publisher of *Good News*
Pastor of Adult Discipleship, The Woodlands United Methodist Church
The Woodlands, Texas

This book is a must-read for anyone seeking to understand the current agitation roiling the United Methodist Church and other mainline denominations in America. With penetrating analyses but loyal mien, Dr. Heidinger uncovers a deep divide that has resulted from the early twentieth century embrace of theological liberalism by a relatively small but influential group of academics and other leaders intent on accommodating the church to secular intellectual trends. One can only hope that all parties in the current debates will seriously ponder Heidinger's work.

—**Wallace Thornton Jr.**
Author of *When the Fire Fell* and *Radical Righteousness*

The Protestant liberal theological tradition captivated American Methodism for a century—much to the detriment of the United Methodist Church and her predecessor church bodies. Jim Heidinger's account of that captivation and the evangelical resistance to it provides a perspectival history that is essential reading for anyone interested in the future of Wesleyan Methodism.

—**Andrew C. Thompson, ThD**
Senior Pastor, First United Methodist Church
Springdale, Arkansas

James Heidinger has done his historical and theological labor with thoroughness and has written the results with clarity. As this book makes clear, Heidinger is not one voice alone crying in the wilderness. There are many others who desire a reformation of our UM Church's historic faith. Dr. Heidinger's book will make that reformation, if not more probable, at least more possible. Strongly recommended. Perfect for study in church–school classes and covenant groups.

—**Rev. Paul T. Stallsworth**
Pastor of Whiteville United Methodist Church
Whiteville, North Carolina
Editor/President of *Lifewatch*

Jim Heidinger explores the recent past of Methodism in America and demonstrates quite clearly how "the faith once delivered to the saints" was compromised and in the end undermined by the shift from the supernatural to the natural, from divine revelation to merely human teaching, and from a Christ who sets the captives free to a Christ who is merely an example to be imitated. This is a deeply honest and faithful account of a very troubled history. Its abundant wisdom displayed throughout helps us all to chart the way forward.

—**Kenneth J. Collins, PhD**
Professor of Historical Theology and Wesley Studies
Asbury Theological Seminary

THE RISE OF THEOLOGICAL LIBERALISM

AND

THE DECLINE OF AMERICAN METHODISM

James V. Heidinger II

 Seedbed

About the cover: City United Methodist Church in Gary, Indiana, was established in 1906 when Gary was in the midst of a steel industry boom. Its massive tower and 950-seat Gothic sanctuary has been a landmark in the city ever since its completion in 1926. It would ultimately gain a membership of more than three thousand in the 1950s, but declined to the point that it was closed in 1975. This beautiful and majestic building was eventually abandoned and left to decay. The cover photograph was taken in 2013 and shows the extent of its deterioration and serves as a visual reminder of the subject of this book.

Copyright 2017 by James V. Heidinger II

Unless otherwise indicated, Scripture quotations are taken from the Holy Bible, New International Version®, NIV® Copyright ©1973, 1978, 1984, 2011 by Biblica, Inc.® Used by permission. All rights reserved worldwide.

Scripture quotations marked NKJV are taken from the New King James Version®. Copyright © 1982 by Thomas Nelson. Used by permission. All rights reserved.

Scripture quotations marked NRSV are taken from the New Revised Standard Version Bible, copyright © 1989 the Division of Christian Education of the National Council of the Churches of Christ in the United States of America. Used by permission. All rights reserved.

Printed in the United States of America

Front cover photo by Mike Boening (www.mikeboening.com)
Cover design by Strange Last Name
Page design by PerfecType, Nashville, Tennessee

Heidinger, James V., II.
   The rise of theological liberalism and the decline of American Methodism / James V. Heidinger II. – Frankin, Tennessee : Seedbed Publishing, ©2017.

      xvi, 272 pages ; 21 cm.

      Includes bibliographical references (pages 249-272)
      ISBN 9781628244021 (paperback : alk. paper)
      ISBN 9781628244038 (Mobi)
      ISBN 9781628244045 (ePub)
      ISBN 9781628244052 (uPDF)

      1. United Methodist Church (U.S.)--Doctrines. 2. Methodist Church--United States--History. 3. Liberalism (Religion)--United Methodist Church (U.S.) 4. Church attendance--United States.   I. Title.

BX8331.3 .H45 2017   230/.7   2017932483

SEEDBED PUBLISHING
Franklin, Tennessee
seedbed.com

To my wife,
Joanne,
who has helped with this endeavor
more than she will ever know.

Contents

Foreword

THIS BOOK CONSTITUTES a pivotal intervention in the current debates about the nature and future of United Methodism. It should be read and pondered across the denomination. It will be seen by historians as an invaluable source for understanding what has happened over the last generation.

James Heidinger II has been a quiet but extremely influential figure in the recent history of United Methodism. He makes no pretension of being an academic historian. However, this is one reason why this work is so important. He has been deeply involved in the life of the church as an agent who has sought to renew United Methodism across a lifetime of ministry and service. This is not a role that anyone in his position can relish because it entails being a lightning rod for all sorts of fantasies and anxieties about the church. However, he has borne years of criticism with incredible dignity and fortitude, plugging away as a master of ceremonies in both high and low places. The result is a personal take on what has happened from an agent of change and hope. He has operated from the trenches and his analysis must be taken seriously precisely because his observations represent a crucial but neglected stream within United Methodism as a whole. We cannot understand where we have come from or where we are headed without this clearheaded and gracious testimony.

I find it astonishing that so few have devoted attention to providing serious historical narrative of Methodism in the United

States across the last generation. Maybe we are still too close to events to venture forth. Maybe the truth about our recent past is too painful to record openly. Maybe we are too confused to know how to orient our narratives. Whatever the case, we have here a hang glider account that provides grist for all future historical mills that may operate. No doubt in time there will be other narratives; however, this narrative must be given a privileged place in the resources that are available. We have here an insider's account of the first importance.

Heidinger's passion has long been the scriptural and doctrinal reinvigoration of United Methodism. He has, to be sure, also been heavily involved as a key leader of the Good News movement in the ecclesial events of the last half-century. Because of this latter identity it is easy to dismiss his work as that of a political operator. I recently heard of one leading bishop who dismissed the evangelical and orthodox wing of United Methodism as an incarnation of Machiavelli. I doubt if he knows anything of substance about Machiavelli and the recent scholarly revision of his work. It was enough to dismiss the conservative wing of the church he was called to lead as a power-hungry cabal. More moderate assessments have taken a softer line, dismissing this stream of United Methodism as a front for the Republican Party at prayer. It is a sorry sight when the Council of Bishops not only fails to come to terms with this crucial sector of the church, but fails to provide the natural courtesy of responding to letters representing their concerns. Other features of the caricature fit with this kind of inaction. Thus, it is commonly thought that evangelicalism in United Methodism is obsessed with issues related to sexuality, even though they were not the first to bring this to the table. Or it is accused of being a monolithic group bent on leaving or dividing the church. Anyone remotely acquainted with the inner tensions and debates knows how misleading these descriptions are. Above all, they miss the theological passion that undergirds folk like James Heidinger II. It is precisely this dimension that he has chosen to take up and explore in this volume.

There are, of course, other dimensions to evangelicalism that are not treated in any great detail here. How does this wing of the church fit into the wider evangelical constituency in North America? What role do class factors play in the identity and content of evangelical Methodism? What contribution have evangelicals made to piety and spirituality over the last generation? Why do so many evangelicals become progressives? How have evangelicals handled the challenges of the last generation? How do we map the relation between the Wesleyan version of evangelicalism and wider political and social developments? Heidinger has wisely decided to focus on a theological reading of the recent past and how that affects the decline that everyone readily recognizes. The content is decidedly his own. Other evangelicals may want to draw up a different bill of particulars. They may balk at the sharp disjunction between liberal and conservative in play here. However, the great virtue of the approach adopted is that it is clear and substantial. Other narratives will have to reckon with this one if we are to make progress in understanding and action. In fact, this is no mere propaganda piece in favor of Good News and other Renewal movements in the neighborhood. Heidinger has his own searching critique of his own tribe and team. Even so, he has never been prone to jeremiad; he has been resilient in working for civil dialogue and constructive change.

It is patently clear that we now stand at a crossroads as far as the future of United Methodism is concerned. Folk are moving beyond anxiety toward the development of what Professor David Watson has aptly called "the Next Methodism." Rest assured there will be a next Methodism and it will have a stormy relationship with the United Methodism put together by a complex hero of many evangelicals, Albert Cook Outler, of blessed memory. Outler shifted his ground in later years, although few know the details as yet. He had a stormy relationship with evangelicals, as he did with everyone. I would dearly love to get his take on where we are. Whatever he might be thinking on the other side, we are headed for a new day. It would be great to sit in on a seminar with Outler and Wesley and other great heroes and heroines of our tradition. The workers die but the work goes on, as Wesley once noted. There are eighty-two million descendants of John Wesley across the globe so Methodism is not going to disappear any day soon. The big question is what place United Methodism will have in that future. This book is a must-read for those pondering that question.

William J. Abraham
Albert Cook Outler Professor of Wesley Studies
Perkins School of Theology, Southern Methodist University

Introduction

THE UNITED METHODIST Church in America is in the midst of a struggle to recover its vitality and relevance. It seeks to extract itself from the malaise of membership decline, financial crises, and a loss of identity.

During the 2009–2012 quadrennium, the United Methodist Council of Bishops organized a task force to propose changes that might help bring a restoration of vitality to our languishing denomination. The resulting Call to Action Committee brought recommendations based on a massive Congregational Vitality research project, led by the New York–based consulting firm Towers Watson.[1] The study was launched in an effort to address United Methodism's forty-three consecutive years of membership decline, with losses totaling more than three million members.

This loss is not something to be glossed over or seen as insignificant. By any measure, such a loss is staggering and tragic. In addition to critical membership loss, the research project showed that only five thousand of our more than thirty thousand United Methodist congregations would be considered highly vital. The fact that United Methodism is doing such an in-depth evaluation reflects an important admission by church leadership that United Methodism is in trouble. Thankfully, our leaders clearly understand that it is past time to get serious about the cause of the denomination's tragic, long-term decline. Our spiritual health, vitality, and our very future are at risk.

We must ask, What happened to United Methodism? How did we get into this downward spiral? How could an American denomination that once was so vital, grew so rapidly, won the lost to Christ, and established new churches end up with forty-four consecutive years of membership decline?

As we face this question, it is important to realize that all of the historic mainline denominations in North America are facing the same challenge. All have been infected by the same virus, with familiar feverish symptoms: membership loss, lack of spiritual vitality, loss of the authority of Scripture, doctrinal confusion and even abdication, bureaucratic domination, pro-homosexual activism, and the embracing of trendy, nonorthodox theologies. Sadly, all of America's mainline Protestant churches have somehow succeeded in *trivializing* the great truths of the historic gospel, while *absolutizing* a very liberal, left-wing social and political set of opinions.

If United Methodism is to find its way out of its present malaise, I am convinced we need to understand just where we went wrong and when we lost our way. It is my conviction that the problems we struggle with today are not primarily matters of structure or organization, nor are we looking at something that happened just in the past forty to fifty years. The seeds of our present decline go back to the early 1900s.

This was an era in which America experienced incredible social and intellectual ferment, something for which the historic Protestant churches were unprepared. This period saw the emergence of what is known historically as "theological liberalism," a movement that touched not only American Methodism but also every major denomination in America. At the same time, the period saw the emergence of what became known as the "social gospel," an attempt by American churches to meet the crushing social needs of the fast-growing urban areas and the related challenges of industrialization, immigration, and issues associated with manufacturing and labor. It would be difficult to overstate the impact of these two movements on the churches in America.

When we speak of theological liberalism, we are not talking about a spirit of openness, graciousness, or liberal-mindedness. We are speaking of a movement during the early 1900s that challenged and soon displaced the very substance of the church's classical doctrine and teaching. J. I. Packer, eminent Anglican theologian, gave an indication of the sweeping impact of theological liberalism on the evangelical faith of that era when he wrote, "Liberalism swept away entirely the gospel of the supernatural redemption of sinners. . . . It reduced grace to nature, divine revelation to human reflection, faith in Christ to following His example, and receiving new life to turning over a new leaf."[2] His summary has breathtaking implications, which we shall see in more detail later.

In the chapters that follow, I will look first at what could be called our "forgotten past" in terms of our Wesleyan theological heritage. We need to consider the possibility that in the aftermath of theological liberalism, we have lost touch with the substance of our rich Methodist doctrinal heritage. I will briefly look at the intellectual climate of the 1900s era that gave birth to theological liberalism and the rise of the social gospel; I will document the account of Wesleyan theology in serious transition as a result of those movements; I will note serious attempts by prominent Methodists in the early 1900s to halt the theological drift away from historic Wesleyan doctrine; and finally, I will offer concluding evaluations of theological liberalism and the social gospel, including how these movements have influenced United Methodism today.

I believe that the experience of the Methodist Church in the critical and turbulent era of the early 1900s does, indeed, continue to have an impact on the United Methodist Church today (and on all of the mainline American denominations as well). To understand our present dilemma, we must understand this historical period during which so much of the substance of Methodist thought and teaching changed.

It is my prayer that this book will help us understand the nature, influence, and legacy of theological liberalism on Methodism in America. The current lack of trust within the denomination, identified as a significant problem for United Methodism today by the Call to Action research, is a part of liberalism's ongoing legacy.

We know there are deep and critical differences in what our United Methodist pastors believe, preach, and teach, as we shall see in later chapters. When I say critical differences in belief, I am not referring to secondary or nonessential doctrinal opinions. I mean major doctrinal tenets that are at the core of the Christian faith. For years, evangelicals have realized that a number of United Methodist leaders have avoided discussing or writing about the creeds and doctrines of the church. We have suspected that it is because they have either become unsure about them or perhaps have ceased believing them.

Looking at the legacy of theological liberalism has helped me understand why for decades there has been such an aversion to theological discussion within United Methodism. Some of our denominational clergy have acknowledged quietly (and usually privately) that they are unable to be candid with their congregations about doctrinal tenets they do not, or no longer, believe. They know their members would be outraged and likely stop giving—and probably end up looking for a new church home. For obvious reasons, those clergy are reluctant to engage in serious conversation about the historic doctrines of the Christian faith. For them, the major focus of the church's teaching should be simply upon the ethical teachings of Jesus. They would urge us to refocus the church's attention to simply following His example and abiding by His moral teachings. To do so would leave us with something less than the classic Christian faith.

At the same time, there are encouraging signs that United Methodism may be in the process of focusing its attention once again on its rich Wesleyan doctrinal heritage. Perhaps United Methodism is in the process of rediscovering Wesley and his relevance for our day. But first we must understand the impact that theological liberalism has had on our church. I pray such a rediscovery of our Wesleyan theological heritage is happening, and I hope this book might help us understand why that desperately needs to happen.

Chapter 1

United Methodism's Forgotten Past

FOR MORE THAN four decades, the United Methodist Church and the other mainline/old-line denominations in America have found themselves in serious decline. Three of these—the Episcopal Church, the Presbyterian Church USA, and the Evangelical Lutheran Church in America—in addition to suffering sharp membership loss, are now in the throes of schism. The turmoil these denominations are experiencing is the result of deep cleavages in doctrinal matters, questions of scriptural authority, and long-standing controversies about moral issues such as homosexuality, same-sex marriage, and abortion.

Likewise, United Methodism and the other mainline denominations in America have all experienced the rise of unofficial renewal movements in their respective communions. These are organized efforts to challenge doctrinal error and to seek reform and renewal in those communions. For more than three decades, I have been part of a ministry called Good News, known officially as a Forum for Scriptural Christianity, Inc. It is a national renewal movement within the United Methodist Church, founded in 1967. It is one of the oldest of the various renewal ministries in the historic mainline denominations, with the Presbyterian Lay Committee, founded in 1966, being the oldest. For more than thirty years, I participated in a

1

fellowship of renewal leaders from these movements, which included all of the mainline communions in the United States and Canada. We met at least annually to share strategies, pray together, and seek better understanding of the challenges facing our respective denominations, challenges brought about by the impact of theological liberalism.

All of these renewal ministries have had, as a major goal, efforts to bring doctrinal and spiritual *revitalization* as well as ecclesial *reform* to their denominations. More recently, some of them have had to alter their mission to include navigating through denominational division—helping local congregations engage in discernment about their future and whether to remain within or leave their struggling denominations. Thankfully, that has not happened yet within United Methodism.

In their study of United Methodism, the Towers Watson consultants interviewed hundreds of our church officials and leaders. In their report, *Operational Assessment of the Connectional Church*, they told the Call to Action group that a "general lack of trust within the Church was a pervasive and recurring theme in the majority of interviews." The study went on to say this lack of trust is a "root cause for under-functioning structures and processes of the Church."[1]

This finding is highly significant. What are the reasons for this "general lack of trust" within United Methodism? I have both observed and experienced this lack of trust during my more than four decades of ministry in the denomination. Across the years, I have thought that major corporate giants such as General Electric or the Ford Motor Company might well have experienced more camaraderie than we had in the United Methodist Church.

During my years of ministry, I became convinced that a serious problem facing United Methodism is that we have lost our theological identity. We, like most of the other mainline Protestant churches in America, have been tragically negligent of our foundational doctrines. In United Methodism, we have ignored or denied our rich Wesleyan theological heritage and the historical creeds of apostolic Christianity.

We have been reluctant to ask, Why has this happened? It was a symptom of our longtime aversion to doing serious theological reflection that our recent denominational self-study chose, amazingly, *not* to consider matters of doctrine or theology as it searched for what might lead United Methodism to congregational revitalization. It would appear that United Methodism is unsure whether matters of doctrine and theology are related to renewal and revitalization.

One might argue that United Methodism has two broad religious streams functioning under one large ecclesiastical tent. One stream would be a traditional, Wesleyan Christianity consistent with the historic Christian faith as it has been passed down across the centuries. Those affirming this tradition, however, being a part of a church that has not always valued doctrinal study, may not articulate that faith well, reflecting more often doctrinal incoherence than solid biblical teaching. Nevertheless, their basic instinct is to believe the authoritative message of the Bible. The other stream would be some combination of theological liberalism, an acculturated folk Protestantism, various blends of pop spirituality and New Age themes, and a postmodern inclusivism that attributes validity to all of the world's major religions. I purposefully said "some combination" as one would find a wide variety in the latter stream. These two religious expressions, not always clearly defined and sometimes having areas of overlap, provide a glimpse of our present, often-confusing doctrinal milieu.

For a number of years, we tried to conceal our theological differences under the cloak of diversity and even gave it the sophisticated name of "theological pluralism." The church officially affirmed theological pluralism from 1972 until 1988, when the General Conference intentionally removed the troublesome phrase. A theological commission, appointed by the 1984 General Conference and chaired by the late Bishop Earl G. Hunt Jr., brought a new theological statement to the 1988 General Conference, and it was approved overwhelmingly. Theological pluralism was out, and the much-improved corrective was the concept of "the primacy of Scripture," an emphasis found repeatedly in the *Book of Discipline*'s new statement "Our Theological Task."[2]

Sadly, during those years when we embraced theological pluralism, United Methodism was seen as the denomination in which one could believe about anything one wanted to believe theologically. We were told repeatedly that we were not a doctrinal church. Some even claimed that this was, in fact, one of our great strengths, something to be celebrated.

The late Bishop Mack B. Stokes expressed what many of us felt about the inadequacy of theological pluralism, writing in 1979: "Pluralism is not a theological or doctrinal principle. How can it be? . . . Do we not all agree that there are certain doctrinal emphases that have come to us through the Wesleyan heritage? Are we pluralists on these? Of course not."[3] Many evangelical United Methodists were deeply troubled by theological pluralism from the moment it was affirmed at the 1972 General Conference.[4]

I still recall vividly an incident years ago that illustrated clearly why pluralism was unacceptable to most all evangelicals in the denomination. A young evangelical pastor in the East Ohio Conference had learned about a professor at one of our United Methodist seminaries who in his teaching had denied the bodily resurrection of our Lord. Upset by what he had learned, the young pastor wrote an article in his church newsletter that was critical of the professor. His district superintendent saw the article in his young pastor's church newsletter. In a letter of chastisement and pastoral scolding, the superintendent reminded the young pastor that he must remember that he was ministering in a denomination that affirmed theological pluralism.

For that district superintendent, and unfortunately many others as well, theological pluralism meant that one could deny the bodily resurrection of Jesus Christ and still be a good United Methodist. The real problem, according to the superintendent, was not with a professor who denied a central tenet of the Christian faith. The problem was with an idealistic, overly zealous young pastor who took doctrine too seriously and appeared to be intolerant. Why? Because he would not affirm a seminary professor whose teaching was seriously in error and which contradicted our United Methodist doctrinal standards.

The above exchange illustrates, I believe, some of the dynamics that have helped create the lack of trust that was discovered in our recent denominational self-study. Some of our pastors, theologians, and leaders often embrace and teach doctrines and beliefs that are contrary to the historic doctrines of the church. I am not talking about marginal, nonessential items or what Wesley referred to as "opinion." I am talking about major doctrines—the central tenets of the Christian message, such as original sin, the deity of Christ, His atoning death for our sins, His bodily resurrection, and the promised return of Christ.

I was ordained an elder in the East Ohio Conference of the United Methodist Church in 1969. Soon afterward, I began hearing the revisionist themes from fellow clergy and read about them in various denominational publications and journal articles. These revisionist themes have changed little across the years. They include claims such as: the Scriptures are of human origin, not divine; Jesus was not born of a virgin, nor was He raised from the dead; Jesus never really claimed divinity for Himself and was, therefore, no different than you or me; Jesus did not ascend into heaven, and thus will not be coming again; and finally, humankind is basically good, not sinful, and all that is needed is education and the opportunity for our inherent goodness to blossom and flourish. These views have been far more widespread than we might know or want to admit.

Reflecting on these claims, I recall a message I heard a number of years ago by the pastor of one of our largest United Methodist churches at a sizable Lenten luncheon. The pastor made a stunning claim about his disdain for the doctrines of the church, particularly the Apostles' Creed. To a mostly lay audience, he said, "I can affirm the opening phrase of the Apostles' Creed about 'God the Father Almighty,' but the rest just sticks in my throat." What he said was phrased in a warm and folksy way that sounded spiritual and sophisticated, not at all heretical. However, this prominent United Methodist pastor was expressing a dismissive attitude toward most of the major doctrines of historic Christianity as expressed in one of the Christian church's most ancient creeds.

The tragic thing about such a denial is that a number of our United Methodist clergy would not have a major problem with it. In fact, many of our clergy probably know ministerial colleagues who would, in a moment of personal candor, admit the same thing. Now, while we no longer affirm theological pluralism in our *Book of Discipline*, it still exists de facto in the life of the United Methodist Church and serves as a cloak for doctrinal unfaithfulness.

Such a stance by United Methodist clergy does, indeed, raise problems of trust, along with questions of integrity. Those of us ordained to ministry within the United Methodist Church pledged publicly at our ordinations that we had studied the doctrines of the church and believed them to be true. In the "Historic Examination for Admission," candidates for ordination are asked a series of questions, including: "Have you studied the doctrines of The United Methodist Church? After full examination, do you believe that our doctrines are in harmony with the Holy Scriptures? Will you preach and maintain them?"[5] For pastors to deny major doctrines of the Christian faith that we promised faithfully to preach and teach raises serious issues about professional and personal integrity. It also helps us understand why the consultants reported a persistent lack of trust across the denomination. Clergy are well aware of these doctrinal differences in the United Methodist family, though there is little discussion about them.

If we are ever to recover our theological identity, we must first understand *what* we have lost, *when* we lost it, and *how* we lost it. If we have turned from our basic Wesleyan theological heritage and, for that matter, from the doctrines of the historic creeds of the church, we need to know exactly what happened and when it happened, and whether corrections have been made since it happened.

It is the thesis of this book that the era of the early 1900s in American Methodism was the critical period in which Methodism experienced major doctrinal transition, revision, defection, and even denial of her Wesleyan doctrinal heritage. It was this era that saw the rise of theological liberalism accompanied by the emergence of the social gospel. The two are not the same thing, it should be noted, but they are closely related.

The doctrinal changes taking place during this era would soon be accepted and institutionalized by the leadership, bureaucracy, and educational institutions of the Methodist Episcopal Church. They were not, however, understood or affirmed by the preponderance of Methodist members in local churches across the land.

Unfortunately, many of our pastors have developed quiet and subtle ways of concealing these theological realities from their laity lest they become upset and decide to protest, either by withholding their giving or simply choosing to leave. Among the three million members we have lost since 1968 are thousands of astute, biblically grounded laypersons who have realized what has happened and have opted for a more biblically grounded church home elsewhere.

It is critical that we understand what transpired in the early 1900s in American Methodism. In his inaugural address at Cambridge University in 1954, C. S. Lewis said that it is the forgotten past that makes slaves of us. The era of the early 1900s seems far removed from us today. This is especially so in an age that has little time for or interest in history. But we must not let that critical time in our Methodist history *become our forgotten past.* It was a period of enormous upheaval and change for the Methodist churches in America, as well as for all of the historic mainline Protestant denominations. It is my conviction that the long shadow of influence cast from this period is still being felt by all of us today.[6]

Unfortunately, most United Methodists know very little about the early 1900s. They are unaware that our church did not emerge from the first third of the twentieth century in good shape theologically.

If we are to fully understand the nature of our present struggles and institutional malaise, we must understand this critical period in our denominational history and the lessons it has for us today.

During this era Edwin Lewis, eminent Methodist professor of theology at Drew University School of Theology, penned a scathing journal article entitled "The Fatal Apostasy of the Modern Church."[7] Reflect on his title. Consider those strong, almost acidic, words coming from a respected theology professor at one of our official Methodist seminaries. And Lewis was not the only prominent Methodist of that period speaking in such draconian terms.

During my ministry, I have heard United Methodists speak with appreciation about the many contributions of the social gospel, which emerged during the same period as did theological liberalism. To this day, we take pride in our involvement in it and in Methodism's insistence that Christian holiness must include social holiness. In fact, Wesley's life and ministry were a model of exactly that. However, the nature of the social gospel is also something about which most United Methodists today know little, including those of an evangelical persuasion.

The social gospel was a time-specific movement of the churches as they struggled to address and deal adequately with the enormous social problems resulting from urbanization and industrialization. It was also a movement about which even some of its early sympathizers and enthusiastic adherents became concerned, believing that something of the substance of the gospel was being lost in the popular, new social emphases. It was not simply a discovery of the social implications of the gospel. It was much more than that.

While the social gospel awakened new sensitivities to urban working conditions, shameful child labor practices, and critical needs among America's large immigrant population and the urban and rural poor, it did much more. It incorporated major new interpretations, emphases, and even revisions of the basic Christian message. All of this did not happen without major, and one would add justified, controversy.

Theological Amnesia among American Evangelicals

Not only are we United Methodists unaware of the impact of the early 1900s in American Christianity, evangelicals in general are less and less aware of the issues that created such controversy at the time. Dean C. Curry, longtime professor at Messiah College, wrote about the evangelical amnesia he has seen in his more than three decades of teaching young evangelical college students.

Curry expressed concern about gradual dimming of any knowledge about the great modernist-fundamentalist controversy of the early 1900s in his students ("modernism" being another name for theological liberalism). He pointed out that apart from just a superficial awareness of distinctive denominational and liturgical features, "most young evangelicals know little about theology and, worse, see no reason theology should be an issue." Curry said a large majority of his evangelical students would have difficulty articulating the theological differences between, say, radically liberal Episcopal presiding bishop Katharine Jefferts Schori and megachurch evangelical pastor Rick Warren. Professor Curry believes most would describe the differences as just a matter of "differing priorities." They would generalize that "liberals call attention to the social side of Christianity, whereas evangelicals are more likely to highlight the centrality of individual pietism." Many of us have heard those same generalizations before and find such a caricature both troublesome and inadequate.

Without theological grounding, Curry warned, young evangelicals have no guiding spiritual rudder and are at the mercy of the "prevailing winds of personal feelings and the cultural *zeitgeist* [spirit of the times]." The result is a new way of "doing church." Unfortunately, this new way finds its focus "in the postmodern holy grails of tolerance, diversity, generosity, openness, inclusion, anti-dogmatism, and subjectivity."[8]

Traditionally understood, Christian theology is about drawing lines between truth and error. But Curry claimed that this is something today's young evangelicals are reluctant to do. Being steeped in an ethos of tolerance, they have little interest in a robust defense of orthodox Christian doctrine. A new generation of United Methodist clergy has not escaped this trend either. There is far more interest in church growth and church planting but, unfortunately, little interest in carefully understanding and defending orthodox Christian doctrine.

Professor Curry recalled in particular the controversy when prominent Protestant pastor Harry Emerson Fosdick publicly accused the fundamentalists in 1922 of bitter intolerance toward those of more liberal persuasion. Fosdick was a gifted, eloquent theological liberal and was angry at conservatives who questioned his theology. John Gresham Machen, a Presbyterian professor at Princeton Theological Seminary, responded to Fosdick's charge a year later with his magisterial defense of orthodox Christian theology in his book *Christianity and Liberalism*. In it Machen (who did not identify himself as a fundamentalist) warned that the Christian church "is battling against a totally diverse type of religious belief, which is only the more destructive of the Christian faith because it makes use of traditional Christian terminology."[9] It was Machen's conviction that theological liberalism was a different religion than historic Christianity.

I want to be clear at this point. Seeking to understand the issues of this historic period is not a call to return to fundamentalism, though the standard portrayal of it is often an extreme and unfair caricature. It is, however, vital to realize that core theological issues were at stake during those years, and we need to understand just what those issues were.

True, the controversies in which Fosdick and Machen were key players are long past. But it is a history we must not forget regardless of our denominational background. Professor Curry rightly warned that the same battle between two Christianities rages on today. It is a battle "between a historic faith grounded in a supernatural biblical record and two thousand years of church tradition, [versus] a modern Christianity redefined by the assumptions of Enlightenment antisupernaturalism."[10] This is a struggle serious believers must not ignore.

What troubles me about our fading memory of the theological controversies of the early 1900s is that it is a sign that the American Protestant churches have become more theologically shallow and less discerning in matters of Christian doctrine. And for us United Methodists, at the very time we are involved in the comprehensive Call to Action initiative in an effort to restore vitality to our denomination and find ways to halt our staggering membership decline, the consultants for the study (perhaps encouraged by denominational leaders) put aside theological issues, indicating they would not be considered as a factor in our effort to develop more vital congregations. That decision astounded many of us!

One wonders, *How can we not be focusing on theological issues?* John Lawson, a former professor of history at United Methodism's Candler School of Theology at Emory University, made the important point some years ago that lasting renewal within the church is *necessarily linked* to theological renewal. He wrote:

> While there have been revivals of Christian devotion that have been revivals of simpleminded and unreflective enthusiasm only, the great and constructive revivals always have been revivals of sound, balanced, and scriptural theology, as well as of "the heart strangely warmed." The evangelical renewal of the church cannot arise apart from a renewal of her historic and scriptural evangelical theology.[11]

Lawson was right in noting the necessary linkage between spiritual renewal and theological renewal. I recall reading a similar word from Alister McGrath of Oxford University, who said that inattention to doctrine "robs the Church of her reason for existence and opens the way to enslavement and oppression by the world." He went on to say that a church that despises or neglects doctrine "comes perilously close to losing its reason for existence and may simply lapse into a comfortable conformity with the world."[12] His words are timely for us United Methodists.

Unless we are informed with sound, scriptural doctrine, we will be something less than the body of Christ. Such a church will be in danger of becoming little more than a religious expression of the Red Cross, the United Nations, or a local fraternal organization with a few folksy religious sentiments. Such a neutered church will lack the power and self-confidence to call the peoples of the world to be reconciled to God and become lifelong disciples of Jesus Christ.

United Methodism must not continue its inattention to doctrine. If great periods of revival come, as Lawson noted, with a recovery of "sound, balanced, and scriptural theology," we need desperately to understand what has made ours unsound and unbalanced today. In order to understand the rise of theological liberalism in America in the early 1900s, we must begin by taking a close look at the turbulent, changing intellectual climate in which it emerged.

Chapter 2

The Early 1900s: An Era of Great Intellectual Ferment

THE RISE OF theological liberalism within Methodism and Protestant America cannot be understood apart from an understanding of the socioeconomic changes that took place in America during the last half of the nineteenth century. No one event alone can explain the change as America was being transformed from a predominantly agrarian to an industrialized society.

In this chapter we will consider some of the forces that converged at this time to provide the social, economic, and intellectual setting out of which came theological liberalism as well as the accompanying social gospel movement.

A brief look at the intellectual currents of this period risks oversimplification. However, I hope it will, without belaboring the matter, provide the needed context to understand the turbulent era and intellectual ferment out of which these ideas were emerged.

Industrial Revolution

The Industrial Revolution, which took place in the late eighteenth and early nineteenth centuries, brought a profound change in the lives of men and women in America. It brought about the dominance of power-driven machinery so that the work of many skilled hands could be done much more rapidly and more cheaply by steam-driven machines.[1] The morale of the nation was affected. Formerly, a craft or trade gave people status and security with no great hostility toward the employer. But gradually the center of emphasis moved from the worker to equipment and capital, and the individual worker was in danger of feeling like a mere accessory.[2] Thus, a divide between owner and worker appeared and steadily deepened. Household labor shifted to factory labor with not only the tools, but often the workers' homes being owned by industry, while the worker remained a mere tenant. For many workers, an open and inviting frontier had vanished, to be replaced by the routine of factory work, and the moral and spiritual results were devastating.

One of the problems of this revolution is that it was unforeseen in America, so there was little preparation. George Vincent wrote early in the twentieth century:

> This movement has not been spectacular; it has been for the most part unforeseen, unplanned, and only slightly guided by human reason; it has radically changed the conditions of life, has redistributed populations, drawn all mankind together, and raised problems many and complex . . . The family, the state, science, education, morality, and religion are often baffled in trying to maintain vital and fruitful relations with the new order of things.[3]

Growth of Cities

One of the most immediate results of industrialization was the growth of the cities in America. Industrialization and the factory system inevitably drew people to the industrial centers, where employment was to be found. Also the labor-saving machinery manufactured in towns and cities was sent out to the farms to take the place of field hands. This resulted in a redistribution of labor and a drawing of the populace into the industrial towns.[4]

Charles H. Hopkins brought into perspective the rate of urban growth by pointing out that during the decades of the 1880s, Chicago's population increased more than 100 percent![5] This mushrooming of large cities destroyed the almost undisputed supremacy of the rural regions that had characterized America until this time. The severity and complexity of urban problems are difficult to appreciate fully. Aaron I. Abell described this sweeping phenomenon that was taking place:

> During the forty-year period, 1860–1900, the number of cities of eight thousand or more inhabitants increased from 141 to 547, and the proportion of townsfolk from a sixth to nearly a third. . . . The city was the hot-house of every cancerous growth—of new evils like industrial war and class hatred and of the older evils of pauperism and crime, of intemperance and vice.[6]

Closely related to this growth of cities was the rapid diffusion of new ideas and standards as the cities became centers of change. Moral standards, which had been adjusted to earlier, moral rural conditions, were yielding to new situations, and the entire nation was affected. "Half the people live in cities and the other half are powerfully influenced by urban ideals," wrote George Vincent. Noting how rapidly the rural areas were being caught up in the change, he wrote, "There was a time when the garments rejected by a fickle city fashion could be sold to confiding rural people, but nowadays the country subscribers to daily papers . . . are as exacting as city shoppers."[7]

This shifting of population and the new concentration of the populace brought great changes to two of the most important American institutions: the family and the church. The former closeness of family and community ties was broken amid the flow of humanity to the cities. These ties were replaced by the new and less-secure experience of living in a highly transient society surrounded by a crowd of aliens and strangers. The slums, dark tenements, factories, long hours, low wages, lawlessness, and delinquency were a tragic discovery for eager migrants moving into the "opportunities" of the metropolitan areas.

Immigration

Another factor in the social turbulence of the latter part of the nineteenth century was the mass immigration to America of Europeans, who were viewed as a threat to the plans and dreams that most Protestants held for America. From the end of the Civil War until 1900, some 14 million immigrants came to the United States. In 1900, one-third of the nation's population of 75 million people were either foreign-born or the children of those who were foreign-born.[8]

This great influx of people to America compounded the growing problem of the cities by creating even more barriers between the city and rural populace. The more recent immigrants came from southern and eastern Europe, bringing greater linguistic, cultural, educational, and religious differences than the earlier immigrants. A majority of these new Americans-to-be were Roman Catholics. They tended to settle in the large cities, near the port areas, and provided some of the toughest, low-paid, unskilled labor for the factories.[9] The religious, sociological, and psychological barriers between these people and most American Protestants, especially Methodists, were profound.

American Protestants were deeply apprehensive about the immigrants who had been flooding onto American soil. The latter were charged with bringing new and unhealthy views about the use of liquor and Sabbath observance. American Protestantism, Methodists not excepted, felt strongly that these newcomers to American society composed a real and immediate threat to America's Christian civilization.

The New Science and Social Darwinism

Another critical ingredient in the forces influencing American thought in the early 1900s was the thought of the new science and social Darwinism. These two factors were an important part of the general incoming tide of more secular intellectual and social thought eroding traditional American ideas.

First, a widespread and growing acceptance of the scientific or empirical method brought new stress on observation and experimentation in the determination of truth. Customary appeals to authority or normally accepted tradition were challenged in nearly every discipline. A new worldview was developing that was mechanistic in nature, with heavy reliance on the search for cause and effect.[10] It would be impossible to overstate the impact of this development. The enthusiasm and excitement about the new scientific methodology were sweeping the country, and it was devastating for Christian theology and the orthodoxy of the day.

With growing emphasis on natural causation, there was little or no room for special divine act or revelation. The idea of miracles and the supernatural were brought into question in a way they had never been before. The new scientific approach challenged the Bible as a whole and proved to be devastating to theological orthodoxy in America. The new science left virtually no room for such biblical themes as miracles, a virgin birth, a bodily resurrection, or a second coming of Christ to culminate history. Thomas C. Reeves, in his book *The Empty Church: The Suicide of Liberal Christianity*, wrote aptly that "science tends to stress the all-sufficiency of the human intellect, to be scornful of the past, and to dismiss or at least distrust the value of anything beyond its rigorous examination, including the supernatural."[11]

Coupled with the rising popularity of scientific methodology was the powerful penetration into American intellectual life of Darwinian evolution in all of its different manifestations. C. H. Hopkins noted the broad sweep of this influence: "The last decade of the nineteenth century witnessed the wholehearted acceptance of the Darwinian theory of evolution by progressive American theologians."[12] Those of the Darwinian school held that since humans were developing from more elementary to more complex forms of life and thought, that early or primitive Christianity—which served an earlier age of humanity adequately—could be put aside for the more advanced views of scientific empiricism.

Many writers believe that Darwin's evolutionary thought is the key to understanding religious liberalism as it developed during this period. The doctrine of evolution, along with the emphasis on scientific methodology, helped to narrow the gap between man and nature, emphasizing that the whole natural world was characterized by a unity of process and development.[13] Lloyd Averill, in fact, pointed out that this concept is the main thrust of Daniel Day Williams's definition of liberal theology and quoted Williams, who said:

> By liberal theology I mean the movement in modern Protestantism which during the nineteenth century tried to bring Christian thought into organic unity with the evolutionary world view, the movements for social reconstruction, and the expectations of "a better world" which dominated the general mind.[14]

Averill added further emphasis to the influence of Darwinism, noting that in the profile of religious liberalism, every characteristic has an evolutionary reference, either direct or indirect. He concluded that "the formative influence of the evolutionary outlook was such that, before the impact of Darwinism, theological liberalism cannot properly be said to have appeared, however much other elements in the liberal profile may be present."[15]

Without question there were various types and variations of liberal theology. Yet characteristics found in nearly all of these variations included the continuity of all life, the immanence of God, optimism about man and society, a modified (or denied) supernaturalism, ethicized religion, and a rational test for religious doctrine. All of these characteristics can be related in one way or another to Darwinian theories. We will discuss the substance of theological liberalism in a later chapter, but the point here is simply to understand something of the widespread acceptance of Darwinian evolutionary thought and the new science and its impact on America's intellectual life as well as on the Christian churches in America.

German Thought

Another influence on the social and religious thought of the early 1900s was the growing number of American religious leaders who were traveling to Germany to study in the universities under German philosophers. It has been noted that of the seven hundred scholars listed in America's *Who's Who* in 1900, more than three hundred had studied in Germany.[16] Many who went to Germany were theologians who would return to challenge and change the traditional views of the evangelical church in America. The German approach was to study religion from a rational and scientific worldview, reinterpreting it according to modern scientific perspectives.

In 1891, Walter Rauschenbusch, usually considered the leading exponent of the social gospel in America, went to Germany for the second time and studied under Adolf von Harnack, one of the leading spokesmen of the Ritschlian school of theology.[17] Ritschlian thought strongly influenced Rauschenbusch at the point of a solidaristic view of sin and of the ethical importance of the kingdom of God.[18]

Though critical of Ritschl at the point of his sociology, Rauschenbusch became a forceful expositor of the Ritschlian theology, which during his lifetime was at the height of its influence throughout the Protestant world.[19]

Methodist theologians were also influenced by German thought. Increased acceptance of the historical-critical study of the Bible and the discovery of the Jesus of history gave new impetus to the already emerging liberal theology and the growing social gospel movement, with the attempt in both to build the kingdom of God on earth, based on the social teachings of Jesus.[20]

With German influence came a very different understanding and approach to reading and understanding the Bible. Reeves noted that "higher criticism sought to trace the literary methods and sources used by biblical authors."[21] What made the approach so destructive for the church was that the *underlying assumption* of these scholars was that "the Bible was another piece of ancient literature, the product of many different people over many centuries, reflecting myths and folklore current at the time of authorship."[22] Reeves added that "the miraculous in Scripture was, of course, minimized or eliminated altogether in this process . . . Reason and experience decreed that miracles did not happen and thus had never happened."[23]

The influx of German thought into Methodism during this era was strong enough that John Alfred Faulkner, professor of church history at Drew Theological Seminary, in his book *Modernism and the Christian Faith*, titled one of his chapters "Ritschl or Wesley?"[24] In it he asks rhetorically: "But why do we bring Wesley and Ritschl together? For the best of reasons. The latter is threatening to drive the former out of business."[25]

It needs to be said that Faulkner did not consider himself a fundamentalist, but rather would have referred to himself as an orthodox believer or an essentialist. He was a respected professor at a Methodist seminary but was deeply concerned about the influence of German thought upon his beloved Methodist Church. He spoke of "a sea-change in the beliefs of evangelical ministers" and the threat of teaching that he believed would "emasculate evangelical Christianity, especially the Methodist branch of it."[26] His words reflect a concern about major substantive changes taking place due to these various influences upon American society.

Clearly, the social and intellectual forces at work in American society during this era mark the emergence of a new era, one that was challenging the traditional and the established, posing new questions and bringing about a very different worldview. It was, indeed, an era of dramatic and unprecedented change, more so than most of us would imagine. And as was noted earlier by Professor Faulkner, it was a time of significant change in Methodist theology, and for that matter, for all of Protestant theology in America. We turn now to the transition that took place in Methodist thought during this period. Important questions to keep in mind as we look further at this era are: How, exactly, did Methodist doctrine and theology change during this period? How was this change received across the church? Was this change widely accepted among the people called Methodists?

Chapter 3

Methodist Theology in Transition

AS THE NATION was experiencing profound socioeconomic change during the late nineteenth and early twentieth centuries, so also was America's Protestant churches. The Methodist Church in America was a part of that change, in ways most of us would not fully understand.

In this chapter we will look at the theological and philosophical transitions that were taking place during this period. We will look at Methodism's lack of emphasis on theology and critical inquiry and the impact this had during the intellectual ferment of the early twentieth century. This diminished emphasis on matters of doctrine and theology made Methodism vulnerable to accommodate its teaching to the new themes being expressed in theological liberalism, or modernism, as it was sometimes called. We will consider the popular claim emerging at the turn of the century that Methodism was not a doctrinal church and then consider John Wesley's view about the importance and place of doctrine.

What is critical for United Methodists today is that we understand what American Methodism was going through at the beginning of the twentieth century and to appreciate the theological struggles that were taking place. This era holds a key to our present-day, diminished interest in theology. This includes the claim still made today that Methodism is not a doctrinal church, as well as our tendency in recent decades to indulge in theological accommodation and revisionism.

Crisis and Change at the Turn of the Century

In his study on "Methodist Theology in America in the Nineteenth Century," Leland H. Scott made the important observation that Methodists generally have not submitted their nineteenth-century theological background to careful study or evaluation.[1] He gave several reasons for what he saw as a general lack of critical study of Methodist attitudes regarding theological inquiry. For one thing, there has been a lack of concern in America in general about the elements in our own intellectual past. But another reason he cited has been the belief among many Methodists that we are not a doctrinal church. This claim has become a mantra that has come to be repeated so often that it is a part of the narrative of American Methodism. It is a perfect and useful theme to emphasize if one is interested in relegating theology to a subordinate position in one's church.

Scott also suggested that Methodism has been more concerned with evangelical experience than with problems of theological reflection. There is truth to the claim that Methodism was busy evangelizing and building churches during this era, especially as it was growing and following the expansion of the American frontier. It is also true that with a diminished interest in theology, Methodism would understandably gravitate to a focus on Christian experience."[2]

Scott went on to say that the most evident characteristic of nineteenth-century Methodism was the gradual decline in emphasis on the Wesleyan doctrines, which stressed the personally related themes of redemptive grace. Part of the reason for this phenomenon was uncertainty over religious authority. American Methodists at that time were simply not able to clarify "the respective authority of scripture, reason, and evangelical experience."[3] More simply, Methodist theologians and theology were not prepared to deal critically with the new social, theological, and philosophical challenges brought by the intellectual turbulence at the end of the nineteenth century. Scott concluded that this "rendered it [Methodism] susceptible to such revisionist views as (for instance) came to characterize the Ritschlian school."[4]

Gerald McCulloh noted how the numerous and turbulent forces of this period began to come to play upon Methodism:

> Rapid and far-reaching change in belief and practice was in store for the Methodist people as they entered the last quarter of the nineteenth century. Within forty years the reliance upon revelation as man's sole source of the knowledge of God was challenged by the appeal to reason in the quest for religious knowledge. Man's understanding of himself was expanded through the insights of psychology. The strongly pietistic legacy of the revival movement was confronted by a growing ethical interest in the nature of the good and man's moral obligation.[5]

During this turbulent period, new views were being presented concerning revelation, the nature of man, sin, salvation, and eschatology and the world, all of which helped create a serious crisis within Methodism. Methodism was merely one of the numerous participants in this broad reorientation of American Protestant thought. Other communions were experiencing similar changes. The oft-quoted sentence of Frank Foster in his work *A Genetic History of the New England Theology* reflects how drastic and thorough this reorientation was. He wrote concerning the New England theology, "It had endured more than 150 years; it had become dominant in a great ecclesiastical denomination; it had founded every Congregational seminary; and, as it were, in a night, it perished from off the face of the earth.[6]

It is difficult to envision such a sudden, sweeping change in a denomination's theological history, but Foster's statement reflected the kind of major changes that were taking place. One might not make such a sweeping claim about changes within Methodism, as we shall see later. However, a major reorientation was also taking place within Methodism, according to Robert Chiles:

> The last fifteen years of the nineteenth century saw the theological leadership of American Methodism change hands almost completely. The shift signaled the end of one theological era and the beginning of another. "Liberal evangelicalism" had prevailed in Whedon, Warren, Curry, Foster, and Miley. The new generation of Terry, Tillett, Curtis, Sheldon, Rall, and Knudson was dedicated to something different—"evangelical liberalism."[7]

Leland Scott concurred, adding that these changes did not happen quietly or unnoticed, "Indeed, the period marking the turn of the century witnessed an increasing spirit of contention within American Methodism regarding the doctrinal tendencies of those in positions of leadership."[8] Scott's words there are important. He wrote of the tendencies of those "in positions of leadership," which reflects one important aspect about the doctrinal changes that took place in Methodist theology at the time: it was not a popular movement, but rather was a trend to be found in denominational seminaries and colleges, in their professors, among church bureaucrats and leaders, and among those involved with church publishing.

Gerald McCulloh also referred to the "sweeping changes in Methodist theology" during this period, adding that they were achieved only with much criticism and controversy.[9] It is imperative that we understand more fully the nature of the controversy that did, indeed, take place within Methodism as her theology was being changed, modified, and sometimes denied.

The Role and Importance of Doctrine
for American Methodists

We saw earlier that Methodism at the turn of the century placed little emphasis on the importance of theological inquiry. S. Paul Schilling wrote that in the opinion of many, Methodists have only a marginal interest in doctrine and theology.[10] Many even claim that Methodism is nontheological, insisting that the main emphases have always been practical and evangelical. Such a claim was often made at the turn of the century. It found growing acceptance and enabled Methodists to give more attention to the new disciplines of sociology, psychology, and the philosophy of religion. It also helped them focus on addressing the overwhelming social challenges they faced in the festering urban areas. Furthermore, new scientific methodology and the historical-critical approach to Scripture left traditional doctrinal formulations appearing archaic. This was, of course, consistent with the mood of America as we saw earlier, which was away from the traditional, orthodox, and accepted, toward a discovery of the new, which was believed to be evolving.

Clearly, this was not Methodism's finest hour in terms of her doctrinal history. For that matter, neither was it for the rest of the nation's Protestant churches. It was probably with these trends in mind that historian Henry Steele Commager said, "During the nineteenth century and well into the twentieth, religion prospered while theology went slowly bankrupt."[11]

It is remarkable that in their diminution of theological interest and doctrinal study, Methodists would often refer to Wesley as the *ground for their indifference*. This claim, however, simply cannot be justified, though many at the time voiced it and perhaps wanted it to be true. Robert Chiles rightly noted:

> There is now little inclination in scholarly circles to dispute
> that Wesley was theologically informed and deeply concerned

to maintain a sound foundation for the Methodist movement. Though his catholicity of spirit and his stress on the experiential aspects of Christianity made it easier for later Methodism to relegate theology to a secondary role, such a devaluation is widely recognized to be untrue both to Wesley's intention and to his practice.[12]

Unfortunately, many modern-day United Methodists have bought into the idea of a non-doctrinal, non-creedal denomination that has never been seriously interested in doctrine but always focused primarily on the centrality of Christian experience. This claim has provided a handy justification for our denomination's neglect of attention to doctrine and theology to the present day.

S. Paul Schilling wrote, "There are important and convincing indications that the major beliefs of ecumenical Christianity are normative for Methodists."[13] The truth is that Methodism in America has always had certain definite theological distinctives, though these have not always been expressed identically or consistently by theologians.

Gerald McCulloh, for example, defined these distinctives as the universality of sin, free salvation for all, the witness of the spirit, and the call to Christian perfection.[14] Leland Scott included in his list of essentially Wesleyan doctrines the following: radical conversion, the spirit's witness, the moment of entire sanctification, and the eschatological urgency of salvation.[15]

Citing Colin Williams, Robert Chiles listed as the doctrines that Wesley insisted on at various times in his ministry: original sin, the deity of Christ, the atonement, justification by faith alone, the work of the Holy Spirit (including new birth and holiness), and the Trinity.[16]

An important key to understanding Wesley's views about theology is the distinction he made, though perhaps not always with precision and consistency, between "opinions" and "essential doctrines" or between "grand, fundamental doctrines" and mere "opinions."[17] His idea of opinions dealt with forms of church government, modes of worship, and some doctrinal positions that may have been intellectually objectionable, yet held by people with definite Christian experience. It was regarding such views as did not "strike at the root of Christianity" that Wesley declared "we think and let think."

For years we have heard the revisionist claim made by United Methodists that there was great theological latitude in John Wesley as he graciously allowed his Methodists to "think and let think." However, that is a classic misquote. What usually gets omitted is the qualification at the beginning of the statement, from his tract "The Character of a Methodist," in which he said, "As to all opinions *which do not strike at the root of Christianity*, we think and let think" (emphasis mine). There is a world of difference between the partial quotation and the full statement.

Another famously misquoted statement from Wesley is the statement from his sermon on "Catholic Spirit," which is based on Jehu's question to Jehonadab, from 2 Kings 10:15, "Is thine heart right, as my heart is with thy heart? . . . If it be, give me thine hand."[18] Of all of Wesley's sermons, this may be the one most notoriously abused. In this sermon, Wesley reflected his gracious and nondogmatic view toward opinion, which would include, again, such things as modes of worship, forms of church government, and forms of baptism and prayer, for example. Wesley was not expressing this graciousness and openness of heart about basic, core doctrines of the faith. In fact, he went on to explain what he meant by the question, "Is thine heart right, as my heart is with thy heart?" He spent some seven lengthy paragraphs asking, "Do you believe . . . Do you believe . . . Have you the divine evidence . . . ?" For Wesley, right doctrine was a vital ingredient for a right heart. Your heart could scarcely be "right" in Wesley's terms if you denied, for example, the deity of Jesus Christ or His bodily resurrection.

United Methodist theologian Thomas C. Oden, in his *Doctrinal Standards in the Wesleyan Tradition*, addressed the issue of taking Wesley's sermon on "Catholic Spirit" as a justification for doctrinal latitudinarianism or indifferentism. He pointed out that Wesley stated his doctrinal core right in the sermon, not in "propositional statements" but rather, "in candid, simple questions asked from the heart." And Oden noted, insightfully, that they are organized in a Trinitarian frame in paragraphs 12–18.[19] The doctrines addressed in Wesley's questions focus on God's existence and attributes, Christ, justification by grace through faith, and the Holy Spirit and the Christian life. Oden saw each question "as a window to a major point of systematic theological reasoning addressed to the heart."[20]

Wesley insisted in his sermon that a catholic spirit is not *speculative latitudinarianism* (emphasis his).[21] After decrying an "unsettledness of thought, this being 'driven to and fro, and tossed about with every wind of doctrine,'" he went on to make his great clarion charge that remains relevant for United Methodists today: "A man of a truly catholic spirit has not now his religion to seek. He is fixed as the sun in his judgment concerning the main branches of Christian doctrine."[22] Clearly, one cannot go to John Wesley to find corroboration for mushy, vapid, and unorthodox theology, or for that matter, even for inattention to doctrine. He would have none of it.

A further indication of Wesley's insistence on faithfulness to sound and scriptural doctrine is seen in his provisions governing the purchase of "preaching houses." In 1763, Wesley drafted a Model Deed, which stipulated that the pulpits of the Methodist chapels were to be used by those individuals who preached only those doctrines contained in Wesley's New Testament notes and his four volumes of sermons.[23] The provision stated that if a majority of the trustees felt that any preacher was not conforming to these standards in either doctrine or practice, then another preacher was to be brought in within three months.[24]

American Methodism, in 1808, gave further prominence and importance to doctrinal standards. At the General Conference of that year, the first "Restrictive Rule" adopted provided that "the general conference shall not revoke, alter, or change our articles of religion, nor establishing any new standards or rules of doctrine contrary to our present existing and established standards of doctrine."[25]

Unfortunately, the Methodist Church at the beginning of the twentieth century was not as emphatic as Wesley about the importance of doctrine and clarity of belief. As Methodism in America was growing rapidly throughout the nineteenth century, more attention was given to problems of church growth and an expanding American frontier. Precision in theological formulation and doctrine was not a major focus during that period of activism and growth. The significance of this did not become apparent until the last quarter of the century and the beginning of the twentieth, as Methodism encountered the flood of secular thought and the intellectual challenge of German philosophy. It was simply not prepared for those challenges.

Methodism learned at the turn of the century that there are real dangers that accompany theological uncertainty. Paul Schilling wrote candidly about these dangers, reflecting specifically about the Methodist Church and its legacy of uncertainty:

> Its doctrinal indefiniteness has sometimes encouraged shallowness. Critical and constructive thinking is hard work, and any suggestion that it is less important than Christian living is readily taken by some as an excuse for avoiding it. Too frequently Methodists, content to let theology remain obscure to them, do not know what they really believe, and quality of life as well as thought has been impaired. Or they unwittingly embrace a "theology" very different from that represented officially by their church.[26]

These words are an apt description of how Methodism has handled its theological heritage, both at the beginning of the twentieth century and later throughout that century. We began back in the early 1900s, as we shall see later, the disturbing trend of relegating matters of theological substance to a subordinate role in the life of our church. The result was that Methodism became vulnerable to serious doctrinal revisionism and error.

Amazingly, Robert Chiles wrote that "by the turn of the century, the references to John Wesley in Methodist theological literature were infrequent. When they did appear, more often than not their purpose was to correct rather than to find corroboration in Wesley."[27] I was stunned when I first read that. Here the people called Methodists were, at the beginning of the twentieth century, referring only infrequently to the writings of their founder, and when they did, it was usually *to disagree or correct him.* How could that be? Chiles added that a new set of determinative and widely accepted views had appeared, which were drawn "chiefly from the surrounding culture." What were these new intellectual forces? They were "science and its evolutionary world view, the critical study of the Bible, and philosophy as set forth by Ritschl, Lotze, and Schleiermacher."[28]

With the rise of these new forces, Methodism began to experience serious theological convulsions. Alarm was expressed in theological journals and books, between ministers as well as theological professors, that serious modifications or worse were taking place within Methodism. Some hailed the new emphases as a great improvement over the dated traditionalism and orthodoxy of the day. However, for others, it was seen as nothing less than the abandonment of historic Christian doctrine and Methodism's Wesleyan doctrinal distinctives.

We move now to look more specifically at some of the charges and expressions of alarm and concern that were being made within the Methodist family during this era.

Chapter 4

Charges of Theological Modification and Doctrinal Revision

IN THE LAST quarter of the nineteenth century, Methodist theologians in America were still basically traditional and orthodox in their theology. However, they were also aware of the major developments in critical and scientific thought. Some insisted that Methodism must achieve intellectual respectability during this time of transition, while others were more concerned with sustaining the basics of evangelical orthodoxy. At the turn of the century, the tension between the *adaptive* and *conservative* elements became more intense. It was a season of transitional tendencies that, said Leland Scott, led to "the preparation of Methodism's leading thinkers for the assimilation of certain non-evangelical developments in philosophical theology."[1]

We shall consider in more detail later the widespread influence of German philosophy on American Methodist theologians during this period. But first, it is important to know of the voices from within Methodism that were expressing deep concern that fundamental and basic doctrines in Methodism were being neglected, modified, and even abandoned. The tensions and conflicts of this era remain a part of Methodism's "forgotten history."

33

One of the earlier works published amid the turmoil taking place was a volume titled *Methodist Theology vs. Methodist Theologians* by George W. Wilson. The title itself is telling. The work is a review of some of the major writings of three controversial Methodist theologians of the day—including Borden Parker Bowne and Wilbur Fisk Tillett.

Bowne was a gifted and popular professor at Boston University and was made professor of philosophy in 1888. He served as head of the department and was made dean of the graduate school. The extent of his influence on future Methodist leaders cannot be overstated. Wilbur Fisk Tillett was the dean of the theological school at Vanderbilt University and, as a member of the Methodist Episcopal Church, South, was a popular and influential figure much like Borden Parker Bowne.

Wilson wrote from a pro-academia stance affirming the importance of scholarship, the university, and the danger of an unhealthy negativism. He also guarded against employing certain naive clichés, such as "back to Pentecost" or "back to the Bible." However, early in his book, Wilson indicated that certain important doctrines were under attack:

> Of recent years Methodist Book Concerns have published several volumes in which the authors assail doctrines which are fundamental to the spirituality, growth, and perpetuity of her institutions. . . . Their aim is to correct well-established beliefs, under the plea of giving us a more reasonable, philosophical, and a sounder theology and terminology. Under the charge of an unsound interpretation of the scriptures, a false psychology, limited intellectuality, lack of scientific acumen. . . , the writers of these volumes hurl from them testimonies, doctrines, and teachings concerning every vital truth which has made us a distinctive people.[2]

He summarized his concern by writing that "everything fundamental to Methodism is being assailed."[3]

Wilson's volume is given increased significance by the fact that the introduction of the book is by Methodist bishop W. F. Mallalieu of Auburndale, Massachusetts, who wrote:

> It is clear also that the time has come when there is need of such a book as this, and it is to be hoped that it will be read with candor and its truths accepted, and our Methodism become more Wesleyan and Scriptural as the years go on, rather than yield to the un-evangelical, un-Wesleyan, and un-Scriptural tendency of the present times.[4]

This work was published in 1904.

Reference will be made later to Wilson's response to Bowne's theology and teaching. However, his critique and conclusions regarding W. F. Tillett touched on important Wesleyan teachings. He charged:

> Sin is being treated as "un-evolved animalism." Repentance is a mere change of one's thinking. Regeneration is displaced by "evolution." The witness of the Spirit is called "misguided emotion," inspired by a legal and not a moral idea. . . . Everything distinctively Methodistic is being questioned and the system of theology which cleared the moral sky of thousands of Christians in other folds, is being declared not self-consistent by its own teachers. A spiritual dearth has come over us which can not be removed by liberal giving, nor explained away by the theory that this is a "transitional age," or that we are "cleaning up the Church records," or that the "trend of the times is towards ethics and sociology."[5]

Wilson's summary of Tillett's teaching gives us a glimpse into some of the issues of controversy at the time. It is evident that for Wilson and the Methodist bishop from Massachusetts that the new teachings being introduced into Methodism at the time were definitely contrary to the historic Wesleyan doctrinal standards.

Another voice raised in protest against the new thought emerging in Methodism was that of John Alfred Faulkner, professor of church history at the School of Theology at Drew University. Faulkner served Methodist pastorates for fourteen years and was then appointed to the faculty at Drew in 1897. His career there spanned the first quarter of the twentieth century and his voice was heard frequently through his books and in Methodist periodicals.

Faulkner looked back to 1879 as the year in which momentum picked up significantly in the shattering of Methodist doctrinal standards:

> The new theory of atonement by Dr. Miley in 1879, the revolutionary series of little books by Dr. Bowne in 1898–1900 . . . the almost complete passing of the emphasis on holiness and perfect love. . . . the substitution of the "liberal" Baptist divine's book on theology (Dr. W. N. Clarke) for our own Dr. Curtis' in 1916 in the Course of Study for Preachers, and the many recent books and articles by Methodists of a radical or Unitarian trend—these are signs of a disintegration of that solidarity of testimony which was at once our glory and the spring of our world-wide conquests.[6]

Faulkner was convinced that Methodism had a role to play in the theological debate of the day, but felt it first needed to clarify and redefine those doctrines of belief essential to its message. He also was clear in his denial that he was a fundamentalist in doctrine or mentality. Conservative Methodists at the time referred to themselves as traditionalists, or orthodox, and sometimes as essentialists, but they did not consider themselves fundamentalists.

Faulkner also expressed concerns in 1917 in an article in the *Methodist Review* on the theology of William Newton Clarke. The previous year, Clarke's *Outlines of Christian Theology* had been placed on the Course of Study for Methodist Ministers. During this period, more clergy trained for the Methodist ministry through the Course of Study than by attending seminary. Though Baptist, Clarke's work in systematic theology was warmly received among evangelical Protestants in America. Faulkner praised the work for its "clarity," its "reasonableness," and its "quiet moderation of argument," and for the spirit in which it was written, particularly its lack of sectarianism.[7]

On the other hand, he was critical of Clarke's theology at the points of his doctrine of Scripture, of the atonement, of justification, and of eschatology. Faulkner claimed that Clarke was Ritschlian in his view of Scripture, with his doctrine only loosely attached to the sacred text.[8] He believed Clarke had explained away the biblical idea of the atonement, ending finally with a weak moral influence theory.[9] He interpreted Clarke's concept of justification as based on both Schleiermacher and Catholic tradition, leaving justification dependent on the new life in Christ and even subsequent to it.[10] Finally, he found in Clarke a denial of the second coming of Christ as well as any possibility of eternal punishment.[11] He concluded that Clarke might have studied the Greek Testament and biblical commentaries more, and liberal theologians and philosophers less.[12]

Faulkner's most important work on the theology of the day was his *Modernism and the Christian Faith*, published in 1921. In this volume he accented the impact of the German philosopher Albrecht Ritschl on Methodism. We noted earlier that Faulkner believed that Ritschl was threatening to drive Wesley out of business. He wrote of his concern in this extended quotation, which is worth careful reading:

> Since about 1890, the ideas of Ritschl have been slowly penetrating English-speaking lands and modifying former beliefs. . . . There can be no doubt that one cause for the tremendous liberalizing influence which since the last twenty-five years has wrought a sea-change in the beliefs of evangelical ministers has been the trend which has gone forth from the potent name of Ritschl. Not only so, theological seminaries in America are filled with professors who have either sat in the Ritschlian lecture rooms in Berlin, Marburg, Gottingen,

etc., and have come back devotees of the faith, or they have imbibed at Ritschlian springs nearer home. Now, as a thorough carrying out of Ritschl's principles would emasculate evangelical Christianity, especially the Methodist branch of it, it is not without reason that I have asked the question, Shall we leave Wesley for Ritschl?[13]

These are stunning words from this respected professor at Drew. He was not writing about subtle differences or minor nuances. He spoke of "a sea-change in the belief of evangelical ministers" and principles that would "emasculate evangelical Christianity." This was a deep cry of alarm.

While professor Faulkner recognized Ritschl's significant stature and contribution to philosophy and admitted that Methodists might carefully select that which was true, still, he was deeply concerned about the impact Ritschl's philosophy was having on the church.

In the Methodist sense there is no such thing as salvation in Ritschl; neither the word nor thing hardly occurs in his writings. Forgiveness occurs, and it means bringing home to a man the fact that God loves him, so that unburdened of any feeling of guilt he may mount up to an independent position in the kingdom of God.[14]

He could scarcely have used stronger words in warning the church about Ritschlian thought.

The Methodist League for Faith and Life

Another major voice protesting changes taking place in Methodist doctrine during this period was that of Harold Paul Sloan, a prominent pastor in the New Jersey Conference. He was a graduate of the theological school at Drew University and moved quickly as a bright young minister into positions of leadership in the conference. By the mid-1920s, he was pastoring the largest church in the conference in Haddonfield, New Jersey. He was also a member of the Committee on Education, which was the entity responsible for the commission on the Course of Study for Methodist Clergy. In the several years before the 1920 General Conference, Sloan and other pastors had been networking to raise their voices in protest against the theological content of the books that had been introduced into the Course of Study. Sloan claimed that some thirty-one annual conferences had petitioned the General Conference for some check on the commission that was selecting the books for the Course of Study.

In early 1920, Sloan summarized the New Jersey Conference's position as it addressed the issue. The conference's objection was "to certain current theological theories destructive to the very foundation truths of the gospel that are being pressed upon the young ministers of the Church."[15] Numerous other annual conferences joined the New Jersey Conference in protesting the liberal content of the Course of Study. At the 1920 General Conference, Sloan brought a minority report that the books in the Course of Study be "in full and hearty accord" with traditional Methodist doctrine as stated in the denomination's Articles of Religion. It also gave the bishops the right to make changes in the course after it had been prepared by the commission. The report was approved but little seemed to have changed.

In 1921, Sloan found a wider outlet for his message of reform through the pages of *Pentecostal Herald*, edited by H. C. Morrison, a Methodist leader who would go on to found Asbury Theological Seminary in Wilmore, Kentucky. Morrison published in serial form Sloan's extensive critique of theological liberalism within Methodism. Sloan's major focus was on the "Course of Study question," and he warned early in the series that if a "majority of the preachers of Methodism are taught contrary to the established standards of their church and Historic Christianity . . . it will be a matter but of a few years before the Church's standards will be completely undermined."[16]

As more annual conferences raised voices of protest, Sloan and his colleagues felt they were poised to have an even greater influence on the 1924 General Conference. However, their liberal opposition was more organized, and they saw little progress.

By fall of 1924, Sloan met in Philadelphia with twenty of his fellow evangelicals from what was a growing number of like-minded clergy across the church. They planned their next course of action, and on November 12, three of them met with the Board of Bishops, which was meeting in Atlantic City, New Jersey, and expressed their protest against six books in the Course of Study they believed unacceptable theologically. Only one was dropped as a result of the meeting, and the conservative community felt frustrated by the lack of Episcopal action.

In February of 1925, Sloan and a group of clergy and laity met in Wilmington, Delaware, and founded the Methodist League for Faith and Life, an organization whose purpose was to "meet this Modernist current and drive which is threatening Methodism as the Unitarian drive did Congregationalism a hundred years ago."[17] Sloan was elected president of the League, and within twelve months it claimed a membership of some two thousand coming from sixty-two annual conferences of the Methodist Episcopal Church.[18] An additional stated purpose was to seek the "complete reorganization of the Commission on Courses of Study, to bring it into harmony with the entire mind and spirit of the Church."[19]

Sloan was a respected church leader and a delegate to General Conferences beginning in 1920 and on for many years. He directed his criticism at the inadequate Christology of Methodist leaders who he felt were taking the church toward an "insipid Unitarianism."[20]

Sloan and members of his League knew how to network in their efforts to influence the direction of the church. One of Sloan's most significant efforts was during the General Conference of 1928. It was there he delivered a petition with ten thousand signatures from 522 Methodist churches in forty-one states, charging growing disloyalty to Methodist doctrinal standards in Methodist seminaries, pulpits, and literature, including the Course of Study. Sadly, while making his appeal that the investigation committee report back, the delegates drowned out his voice and refused to give consideration to his concerns in any of the remaining sessions.[21]

In his unpublished doctoral dissertation on Sloan's Methodist League (see note 17), now-retired Bishop William B. Lewis told of Sloan's efforts to enlist Episcopal support for his Methodist League. One of the disappointing discoveries was to see the Methodist bishops refuse to take a stand during the heated doctrinal controversy of the 1920s, even though a number of them agreed strongly with Sloan. The following vignette tells the disturbing story.

In April 1926, Bishop Adna W. Leonard preached a sermon at Paterson, New Jersey, calling himself an "Essentialist" in theology. He meant by this that he was neither fundamentalist nor a modernist but essentially an evangelical conservative. His sermon evoked strong commendation from the conservative Methodists. Sloan especially liked it. And Bishop Leonard was pleased with the burst of enthusiasm and responded favorably to Sloan's compliments.

From that time on Bishop Leonard's correspondence reflected a growing warmth toward Sloan's League. Shortly thereafter, Bishop Leonard met with Sloan, Bishop Joseph F. Berry, and Clarence Antrim at Wannamaker's Department Store in Philadelphia and discussed plans to help advance the interests of the League. The plans included an agreement between Bishops Leonard and Berry that *they would unite* with the League if Bishop Frederick D. Leete would agree to accompany them in the action.

In May 1926, the very next month, Bishop Leonard visited Sloan in his home in Haddonfield and helped him lay plans for League strategy. Throughout the rest of the year, Leonard was constant in his advice and support of Sloan and his Methodist League. He agreed with Sloan and helped him with his plans.

In January 1927, Bishop Leonard accepted an invitation to attend a League meeting in Philadelphia. He entered wholeheartedly into the discussion and spoke at length on the League's cause as being in the best interests of evangelical Christianity. Taking their cue from Leonard's earlier sermon, members voted to change the name of their publication from the *Call to Colors* to the *Essentialist*. At that meeting, Leonard indicated that a number of bishops might soon unite with the League. Momentum seemed to be building. The February 1927 issue of the *Essentialist* was to carry an article by Bishop Leonard endorsing the League and identifying himself and his colleagues with its cause. Sloan was elated. On February 11, Sloan reminded Bishop Leonard that the February issue of the *Essentialist* was ready to go to press as soon as his article arrived.

Then just a few days later, on February 17, Sloan received a letter with devastating news. Bishop Leonard wrote to him, saying: "In view of all the matters involved, I feel under the necessity of saying that it will not be possible for me to identify myself with The League for Faith and Life as one of its members." At the same time, Leonard sent an article to Halford Luccock of the *New York Christian Advocate* in which he disclaimed any association with the movement and denied any credit for the naming of the *Essentialist*.

Sloan was crushed. The leaders who had attended the January meeting, which Bishop Leonard had attended, were utterly astounded. They knew what he believed and how he felt. It was incomprehensible that he would so suddenly reverse course.

In the months that followed, Sloan said little about Leonard's betrayal, keeping it in close confidence. But he was devastated. The Board of Bishops continued to present a united front in its relationship to the Modernist/Liberalism controversy within the church, even though some bishops were aware of, and distressed by, the church's doctrinal unfaithfulness. Many of the bishops had talked about the problem and written articles and books about it. But when challenged and urged to act on behalf of doctrinal faithfulness and confront the matter head-on, they opted instead for a facade of unity as a Board of Bishops rather than choosing to contend for the faith that was under attack.

On at least four occasions, representatives of the League brought their concerns before the Board of Bishops, but to no avail. The bishops responded once with a statement saying, "We exhort ourselves and all of our brethren to avoid controversial agitation." On another occasion, a bishop replied by letter to Sloan, "I appreciate the sincerity of your purpose in defending the standards of our Methodism but I question the wisdom of your methods in organizing the League for Faith and Life and the promotional plans proposed."

Sloan was convinced that the bishops needed to assert themselves in light of the theological crisis the church was facing. He wrote to Bishop Raymond Wade, saying "I am profoundly convinced that the Methodist Church is waiting for the leadership of the Board of Bishops. . . . We can have no revival unless the Bishops aggressively proclaim their undeviating confidence in the deity, virgin birth, and bodily resurrection of Jesus Christ." By March 1930, Sloan had concluded sadly, "The Board of Bishops is dominated by a desire to avoid division."

Sloan's efforts through his Methodist League was by any measure an impressive grassroots effort at major doctrinal reform and renewal in the Methodist Church. Interestingly, his movement has been compared to the national Good News movement today, with which I have been associated for more than three decades. It, too, has been and is a grassroots effort to bring spiritual and doctrinal renewal to the United Methodist Church. One sees many similarities in the denomination's response to these renewal ministries.

Allow me to digress for a moment. For many years, since Good News's founding in 1967, the bishops of the church have for the most part opted for unity and collegiality rather than addressing the serious theological issues the church has regularly encountered. There seems to be an unwritten understanding among our bishops that doctrinal oversight and correction is not a part of the Episcopal task. A number have affirmed their belief that doctrine is not a matter over which the church should argue. Most especially, it is not a matter that should be a subject for a formal complaint, though the *Book of Discipline* identifies it as such. Though the United Methodist Church has experienced forty-four consecutive years of declining membership, I cannot remember a time when an active Episcopal leader voiced major concern that perhaps the United Methodist Church is not being faithful to its historic Wesleyan doctrine. (I say "active" bishops because I do recall several retired bishops expressing such concerns.) Our shortcomings have nearly always been attributed to structural or programmatic issues, but *never* theological matters. And evangelical United Methodists who today are part of the Evangelical Renewal Coalition have also heard and seen in print the retort that Sloan heard many years ago: "We appreciate what you are trying to do, but we question the methods you are using."

Nonetheless, what one must conclude from these voices in our forgotten Methodist history is that there were serious theological issues at stake during this period and real tensions and conflict experienced in the church. It could be argued that trends set during this period charted a course of action for Methodism for decades to come.

At the heart of many of these charges was the transition that Methodism was experiencing in its membership standards, membership vows, and the place and importance of creeds in the life of the church. These changes are an important part of this era of transition.

Chapter 5

Transition in Membership Standards and the Diminished Place of Doctrine and Creeds

THERE ARE A number of reasons why Methodism was not significantly affected by the fundamentalist-modernist upheaval of the mid-1920s as were other denominations. In Methodist literature of this period, Methodist leaders often boasted that such serious upheaval had not taken place in the Methodist Church. Several reasons are understandable.

First, Methodist leadership seemed determined to avoid the ugliness of bitter controversy and heresy-hunting that they saw taking place in other major denominations. After Harold Paul Sloan's delegation met with the Board of Bishops in November 1925 to express concerns about the books in the Course of Study, the bishops removed only one of the six problematic books and chose to stay the course otherwise. In addition, however, the bishops urged all Methodists "to avoid controversial agitation."[1]

Second, the most serious outbreak of controversy came in 1925, which was just one year *after* the General Conference of 1924, leaving three more years before the main governing body of Methodism convened again.

A third factor, however, was that within Methodism there was a distinct relaxation on the importance and value of creedal formulation, membership standards, and baptismal vows. The mood was one of transition away from careful creedal and doctrinal precision. The new mood was one of openness, tolerance, and Christian love in action.

There was a feeling at the turn of the century that with so many pressing social ills and the challenges they presented to the churches, to delve too deeply into theology was to risk controversy and division. This was seen as wasted time and energy when so many critical social problems were crying out for attention, especially in the urban areas.

Behind such sentiments lurked the painful memory of the divisions that Methodism experienced from 1894 well on into the 1900s over the Holiness Movement. The controversy and painful divisions it brought resulted in scores of new churches, associations, and independent bodies, including the Church of the Nazarene and the Church of God, Anderson, among others. At a time when Methodism was facing serious doctrinal challenges, its recent memory of doctrinal upheaval and division from the Holiness controversy left doctrinal dispute and theological debate in bad company. Rather than deal with the serious theological challenges facing the church, it was much easier for Methodist leaders to say, "We must not get involved in doctrinal controversy. We have more important tasks to be done." We will look more closely at the Holiness Movement in a later chapter, but I am convinced that the reticence to wrestle with serious theological questions that were emerging was partly the result of the earlier Holiness upheaval and division.

The antipathy toward creeds and doctrinal formulations is very obvious in the periodical literature from this period. Quite often, the titles tell the story. Ernest F. Tittle's article in the *Methodist Review* was entitled "The Use and Abuse of Creeds."[2] In his article, Tittle cautioned against an overemphasis upon creedal formulation. However, he also expressed his alarm over the uncritical tendency by many Methodists of the day to emphasize *action* at the expense of *belief.* One senses something of an uneasy conscience in his article that something important was being neglected. He insisted that "it is a matter of very considerable importance what a man's creed is. . . . For what a man believes will eventually influence what he does."[3] Unfortunately, many did not share his concern.

At the same time there was a tendency for church leaders to blame the sluggish awakening to social needs on a preoccupation with systems of theology. The call and emphasis of the day was shifting from creeds to human needs. Kenneth E. Barnhart cited a series of periodical articles sounding this same note. One gasps at the seeming readiness to dismiss the churches' creeds. Consider this writer in the *Methodist Review* in 1910:

> Creeds have had their day. They are no longer effective. Without doubt, they were well intended. Possibly they have done some good—they certainly have done much harm. The church has been loyal to her creeds, and has spent much good blood and splendid brains in the defense of them. All this was considered the very essence of Christianity. It was child's play, as we now see it, and in some instances paganism. The revolt against creeds began in the lifetime of many now active in the work. The creeds are retired to the museums and labeled "Obsolete."[4]

One is astonished by the audacity of this dismissive attitude toward the great creeds of the church. The Apostles' Creed, the Nicene Creed, just "child's play," perhaps "paganism," and thus thankfully, the creeds are now "retired" and labeled "Obsolete." Barnhart referred to a "series" of periodical articles that sounded this note. It is difficult for most of us today to imagine such a mood in the denomination that produced such an antipathy toward the church's historic creedal formulations.

The title of Harris Franklin Rall's article, "Not Intellectual Credence but Personal Trust," is telling.[5] Rall sounded the note of the great need for unity in light of the division and strife already seen in many churches. His attack upon the place and importance of creeds is amazingly comprehensive:

> And what creed would it be today that would be accepted by Christendom? The Nicene Creed, with its abstractions so remote from the actualities of life? The Athanasian Creed, damning all who do not believe its definitions? . . . Can we accept as adequate even the Apostles' Creed, overleaping as it does all our Lord's life between the cradle and the cross, omitting all reference to our supreme hope of the coming of the Kingdom of God?[6]

It was almost with a sense of exhilaration that New York pastor Philip Frick wrote an article entitled "Why the Methodist Church Is So Little Disturbed by the Fundamentalist Controversy," in which he gives his answer—it is the lack of dogmatic creedal assertion.[7]

The results of this pronounced antipathy toward creeds and doctrine can be seen clearly in the changes taking place during this period in the membership standards and baptismal vows. Gerald McCulloh wrote of a definite change in the doctrine of sin, which was strongly expressed in the opening exhortation by the minister in the ritual for Baptism to infants. In 1884, it began, "All men are conceived and born in sin."[8] By 1919, the opening words for the baptism of infants read, "God in his great mercy hath entered into covenant relation with man, wherein he hath included children as partakers of its gracious benefits."[9] The language, mood, and doctrinal emphasis had changed greatly.

Another indication of these changes and of creedal antipathy can be seen in the change of the requirements for membership. In 1864, the Methodist Episcopal Church first provided a form for use in the reception of members. One of the tests for membership was one's subscription to the Articles of Religion. With the new mood in the church, this requirement came under frequent criticism. Despite conservative resistance, it was removed in 1916.[10] Belief in the Apostles'

Creed continued to be required after 1924, as it was included in the baptismal ritual, but it, too, was dropped in 1932.[11]

It may well have been in response to this General Conference action in 1932, as well as to the popular preference for the new Social Creed rather than the historic theological creeds that led Drew University's Edwin Lewis to protest these developments in the strongest of terms. His article, mentioned earlier, was like a trumpet blast and expressed his alarm by his almost apocalyptic title, "The Fatal Apostasy of the Modern Church." He lifted his voice sharply, writing:

> But what does the modern church believe? The church is becoming creedless as rapidly as the innovators can have their way. The "Confession of Faith"—what is happening to it? Or what about the "new" confessions that one sees and hears—suitable enough, one imagines, for, say, a fraternal order. And as for the Apostles' Creed—"our people will not say it any more": which means, apparently, that "our people, having some difficulties over the Virgin Birth and the resurrection of the body, have elected the easy way of believing in nothing at all—certainly not in 'the Holy Catholic Church.'" So we are going to allow them to be satisfied with "The Social Creed of the Churches," quite forgetful of the fact that unless the church has a "religious" creed besides a "social" creed the church as such will cease to exist long before it has had time to make its "social" creed effective in the life of the world. . . . The church has set itself to do more at the very time that it is lessening its power to do anything.[12]

It is clear from Lewis's statement that in 1933, the year he penned his notable journal article, a significant number of Methodists were having difficulty affirming the historic creeds of the church; were no longer affirming key doctrinal themes, such as the virgin birth and bodily resurrection of Christ; and instead, were opting for the new

Social Creed of the Churches, which had been adopted at the 1908 General Conference.[13] What Lewis saw clearly was that the church was not built upon a Social Creed, as timely and helpful as that may have been. It was and is built upon the historic Christian faith of the apostles and martyrs.

What makes Lewis's protest even more significant is that in his earlier years at Drew, Lewis was one of the theologians under fire from other conservatives for his doctrinal weakness. This period marked an important "theological conversion" in Lewis's life.[14]

Lewis's article provided a helpful glimpse of the transition that was taking place in Methodism during the first third of the twentieth century—a transition away from doctrinal formulation and theological concerns to the new and "more relevant" interest in social ministry. The mood was away from emphasis on the content of belief and doctrinal articulation, and focused rather on the necessity of Christian love in action.

Methodist Theology vs. the Philosophy of Religion

The antipathy within Methodism toward theology during this period may have been partially responsible for the susceptibility within Methodism to the influence of German philosophy mentioned earlier. At the turn of the century, Methodist seminaries had numerous professors who had either sat in the lecture rooms in Berlin, Gottingen, and Marburg or had studied under those who had. Those studying abroad brought back not only German biblical research, but also the philosophies of Schleiermacher and Ritschl. One of the most significant leaders in Methodism at this time and perhaps one whose thought influenced more Methodist leaders in succeeding generations was Borden Parker Bowne (1847–1910).

Bowne came to Boston University as a professor of ethics in 1876 after having studied at Paris, Halle, and Gottingen. In 1888, already known as an able and brilliant thinker, he was made professor of philosophy and became dean of the graduate school of theology. He brought to Methodism what would become known as the philosophy of personal idealism. His thinking was influential on many of the new figures in Methodist theology at the turn of the century, including his colleagues Olin A. Curtis and Henry C. Sheldon at Boston.[15] Numerous others of his students became important teachers and writers, including Frances McConnell, Edgar Sheffield Brightman, and Albert Knudson. Again, it is difficult to overstate the impact Bowne had upon Methodist theology. When a survey was made in 1949 for the Commission of College Teachers of Religion of the Methodist Conference on Christian Education, it was learned that of 144 graduate degrees reported among teachers at Methodist colleges, 48 (exactly one-third) were from Boston University. The next largest contributors, Drew and Garrett seminaries, combined had only 24.[16] Clearly, the outreach of Bowne's "personal theism" from Boston has been unprecedented.

In his important book *Evangelical and Methodist: A Popular History*, longtime pastor, historian, and renewal leader Riley Case noted that Bowne and other theological liberals were following German liberals and rationalists Schleiermacher and Ritschl by redirecting the "essence" of religion "from Scripture and creeds and conceptual truth to religious experience." He added that Methodists were particularly vulnerable at this point since "Wesleyans had always held experience in high regard, whether the new birth, or assurance, or sanctification."[17] Case gave this succinct summary of Bowne's thought:

> What Bowne . . . did was to associate revelation with the human mind rather than with the Scriptures, define gospel more as the coming kingdom of God (a sort of politicized Christian democracy) rather than the news that Christ died for our sins, emphasize philosophy of religion rather than of theology, understand the human problem more as ignorance

than as sin, shift the essence of faith from doctrine to "values," and see the church as a human institution for change rather than as the mystical body of Christ.[18]

Bowne's career at Boston, however, was not without controversy and opposition. In his teaching and thought, Bowne vigorously moved against the more traditional expressions of theology. In his *Methodist Theology vs. Methodist Theologians*, cited earlier, George W. Wilson, after a lengthy critique of Bowne, summarized:

> Everything distinctively Methodistic is negated or denied in these pages. Sin, repentance, regeneration, the witness of the Spirit, testimony to conscious spiritual experiences, etc. All distinctions go down before this "new conception." Wesley, Clarke, Watson, Fletcher, Pope, Miley, and all others who have taught us in the past go for naught, and clouded statements of an undefined theory take their place.[19]

In recounting the importance of German philosophers upon American theologians during this period, Robert Chiles claimed that the distinctive trait of this period within Methodism was the "displacement of theology by philosophy of religion."[20] As a response to this change taking place, between 1894 and 1918, volumes were written by Methodist scholars and leaders such as G. L. Curtis, E. R. Hendrix, H. M. DuBose, H. Wheeler, and T. B. Neely, trying to direct Methodism back to what they felt were its historic and legally binding standards.[21] Unfortunately, they received little hearing. Case captured the mood of the church well, writing:

> At the time, many believed the Church needed to choose between exciting new thought and dead orthodoxy. Whatever the doctrinal standards had been in the past, "standards" ought not now stand in the way of progress. A new ruling class in Methodism had come on the scene and essentially had decreed

that the essentials were no longer essential. The core did not hold. Christian truth was at the mercy of modern thought.[22]

An interesting reaction to the ferment within Methodism came from a voice outside the church's tradition. In 1902, in an obvious reference to Bowne's writing, eminent philosopher William James wrote:

> When I read in a religious paper words like these: "Perhaps the best thing we can say of God is that he is the Inevitable Inference," I recognize the tendency to let religion evaporate in intellectual terms. Would martyrs have sung in the flames for a mere inference, however inevitable it might be? Original religious men, like Saint Francis, Luther, Behmen, have usually been enemies of the intellect's pretension to meddle with religious things. Yet the intellect, everywhere invasive, shows everywhere its shallowing effect. See how the ancient spirit of Methodism evaporates under those wonderfully able rationalistic booklets . . . of a philosopher like Professor Bowne.[23]

Obviously, with the influx of the new philosophy in the church, one of two things was happening. Either those churchmen uninitiated in the popular new philosophical views were simply unable to understand and adjust their thought-world and theology to the new philosophy, or else they were able to so sufficiently do so as to be convinced that serious theological and doctrinal change was taking place in the church's doctrine and teaching. Curtis K. Jones made a stinging critique and severe judgment against the new personalistic philosophy, arguing that it "neither begins nor really ends with Christianity. It begins with some speculations about the self and the world and ends with an hypothesis about God."[24]

Another critique of the new theology comes from Robert Chiles in his reflections on Albert Knudson, a student of Bowne and probably the preeminent theologian of the second generation of Boston personalists. He observed that in Methodist theologians Watson and

Miley, basic philosophical loyalties were occasionally reflected but only in hurried appearances. However, he wrote:

> In Knudson . . . philosophy is neither preliminary nor incidental to some special problems. It dictates the setting and tools as well as the method of justification and mode of expression for Christian theology. Although philosophical influence on theological formulation before Knudson was not new to American Methodism, never before had it been so extensive and comprehensive, and rarely had its modifications of the tradition been so drastic.[25]

Bowne taught at Boston University from 1876 until his death in 1910. Over the course of those thirty-four years, he wrote seventeen books and penned more than 130 articles. He was a teacher of future pastors, educators, bureaucrats, and bishops of the Methodist Church. His influence can scarcely be measured.

Heresy Trials of Bowne and Mitchell

The extent of concern among some students at Boston regarding what they considered attacks on traditional Methodist theology was seen in the two famous charges of doctrinal heresy between 1895 and 1905. The first heresy trial to take place was that of Professor Bowne in 1904.

The trial was held with Bowne's full consent, with the hopes that when the charges were cleared up, the accusatory mood would be cleared from the air.[26] The charge against Bowne was broad and included denying the atonement, the Trinity, and the existence of miracles, and teaching doctrines contrary to the Articles of Religion and to the established standards of doctrine of the Methodist Church.[27] The trial was held before fifteen members of the New York East Conference and ended in a complete vindication of the accused by a unanimous vote. Bowne confided to a friend after the trial, "The decisive and unanimous declaration of my doctrinal soundness is a great gain."[28]

Riley Case reflected that the charges against Bowne were probably brought about fifteen years too late. By 1904, the brilliant and popular professor had been at his post for twenty-eight years. Many of the leading pastors in Northeastern Methodism, including those who were assigned to sit in judgment of his teaching, had been his students. Furthermore, the Methodist Church was well on its way toward theological liberalism, or modernism.[29]

Case summed up his reflections, writing poignantly:

> If Bowne could not be convicted of denying the doctrines of the Church, then no one could be convicted. After Bowne, there was nothing that could be taught or denied by seminary professors that would make them unacceptable as teachers in Methodist seminaries. Heresy trials would cease to exist not because of an absence of heresy, but because of the lack of will to take doctrine seriously.[30]

The second trial, held in 1905, actually had a history beginning in 1895, with accusations made against Hinckley G. Mitchell, professor of Hebrew and Old Testament exegesis at Boston University School of Theology.[31] This incident received more publicity, perhaps because it was more bitter than was Bowne's trial.

Mitchell was accused of sympathy toward the new biblical criticism. The charges were made again in 1900 and once again in 1905. In 1905, the bishops refused to endorse Professor Mitchell. He, in turn, asked to be tried by the Central New York Conference, of which he was a member. The conference refused to give him a formal trial, but it did pass a resolution of censure for teachings that were contrary to the Holy Scriptures and to the doctrinal standards of Methodism. However, in 1908, the General Conference held that this action had been illegal and put it aside. Also, the Judiciary Committee of that General Conference ruled that the bishops had no jurisdiction or authority to investigate charges of erroneous teaching in Methodist seminaries.

Though Professor Mitchell was officially vindicated, his teaching services had been lost to Methodism. In the interim that he was without Episcopal approval, he had transferred from Boston University to teach at the Theological School at Tufts College.[32] It is not without significance that Tufts was a Unitarian-Universalist institution. The fact that he would find a vocational home there suggests that he probably had, indeed, moved away from the doctrines of Wesley and historic Christianity.

What is clear from the previous chapters is that there were real tensions within Methodism during this period between those who were traditionalists and a small but influential group of professors and leaders who were accommodationists—believing passionately that the gospel must be changed, revised, and reinterpreted to make it relevant and more appealing to modern, scientific man. Some were exuberant that a new day had dawned for intelligent Christianity. They affirmed a new mood of openness and freedom from earlier established doctrinal standards. Others, however, were not at all optimistic, as we have seen. They raised their voices and engaged their pens in protest. They feared that dangerous neglect, serious changes, and perhaps even a denial of Wesleyan doctrine was taking place—and not only Wesleyan doctrine, but a denial of the essential doctrines of historic Christianity.

So, the question needs to be asked, What, exactly, was this theological liberalism—or modernism, as it was also called—that was bringing about such change in the Methodist Church? Many mistakenly believe that liberalism was mainly referring to a new attitude of openness, tolerance, and graciousness in the church as opposed to a harsh, unloving, and rigid attitude on the part of those more traditional or orthodox. Again, some today may see theological liberalism as representing those in the church who place their emphasis in ministry on actions of social ministry and compassion while the orthodox or evangelicals are those who focus primarily on evangelism and mission outreach to find and win the lost.

The latter understanding is an unhelpful caricature that is unfair to the rich heritage of Methodist evangelicalism, which has always had a vibrant social dimension from the very start in the Wesleyan Revival. It is true that there was an unfortunate response by some later fundamentalists who responded to the social gospel movement (which we will consider in a later chapter) with an attitude that said, "Okay, you go ahead and focus on meeting the social needs of our society, and we will focus on saving souls." This, of course, was a tragic rending asunder of what the gospel has always joined together, and what had always characterized Methodism since its founding—warm-hearted personal faith and vital social ministry.

Admittedly, there could sometimes be a harshness of attitude or an uncharitable spirit among those who were trying to challenge and turn back the theological revisionism of the period. At the same time, a similar problem developed among theological liberals. Some of them began to look with a dismissive condescension on those clergy who were not seminary trained but who had entered the ministry through the Course of Study. These pastors were serving faithfully across the church, many in rural and small-town settings, and they were not able to engage the new liberal theology that was heavily influenced by German rationalism and the new disciplines of psychology, sociology, and the philosophy of religion. A yawning gap developed between these two camps of Methodism. It is also a strategic part of Methodism's forgotten history that we need to understand today.

However, even more important than these attitudinal tensions, we must understand that theological liberalism (modernism) was characterized by specific doctrinal claims and inferences (though never systematized) that made it far more than simply an attitude of openness, graciousness, and kindness. No doubt many of the seminary professors who embraced theological liberalism were warm, winsome, unselfish, and kind individuals. They were popular and related warmly to their students, and this, no doubt, made their doctrinal denials and controversies more difficult to challenge.

In the next chapter I will try to answer the important question, Just what was theological liberalism? I say "was" purposefully, as I want to define carefully what was going on historically during the early 1900s so we can understand what some liberal professors, theologians, and church leaders were affirming doctrinally and teaching their students—and what they were abandoning. This becomes even more important when we realize that theological liberalism, the "new theology" as it was sometimes called, would eventually be accepted in all of Methodism's official theological seminaries and also incorporated into many of the Courses of Study, the route into ministry by those clergy who did not attend seminary.

Chapter 6

Just What Was Theological Liberalism?

SOME YEARS AGO a pastor writing in one of our United Methodist annual conference papers gave a warm defense and affirmation of United Methodism's being a "liberal" denomination. He insisted that the "L-word" was not something bad. For support he cited *Webster's Dictionary*, which defined liberal as "generous, openhanded, broad-minded, etc." Of course, if that is all that theological liberalism were, there would be no concern. A genial and benign spirit like that would not have brought such controversy and radical change. Such a simplistic view, however, reminds us why we need to look more carefully at what exactly we mean by theological liberalism. And in defense of the writer mentioned, theological liberalism is not widely understood, nor is it something easily defined or much discussed today. The term "liberalism" is often used to refer to the social and political views embraced by individuals and by some of our church boards and agencies. However, in this chapter, my focus will be on understanding clearly what the substance was of theological liberalism, which emerged during this period in our church's history. To understand what it affirmed—and did not affirm—helps one realize why it was so destructive to the health and vitality of the Methodist Churches (North and South), and other mainline Protestant churches as well.

Theological Liberalism—an Accommodation to the Age

In a word, theological liberalism was the religious system that blended with the new scientific and evolutionary worldview of the late nineteenth and early twentieth centuries that was sweeping across America. As noted earlier, the new science claimed that all events could be explained by universal laws of cause and effect. In addition, optimism spurred on by the popular new evolutionary theory led Americans to believe a new and better society was emerging, and it was inevitable. The exciting new intellectual currents discussed earlier left little room for unusual events such as miracles or divine revelation. Obviously, the popular intellectual current that was anti-supernatural at its core would be devastating to the Christian churches and their doctrinal claims.

Alister McGrath, former professor of theology at Oxford and recently the chair of theology, ministry, and education at King's College London, wrote this about theological liberalism:

> Perhaps the most distinctive feature of the movement is its accommodationism—that is, its insistence that traditional Christian doctrines should be restated or reinterpreted in order to render them harmonious with the spirit of the age. Considerable emphasis was placed on the need to be open to the new insights afforded by philosophical, social and religious advancement, rather than being tied to the dogmas of the past. Liberalism was especially hostile to any form of particularism, such as the notion of a special divine revelation.[1]

It is difficult for us today to appreciate fully just how much sweeping change this new anti-supernatural intellectual climate brought to the Christian churches. More specifically, the church faced the formidable challenge of how to defend its miraculous core doctrines, such as the fall of man, the incarnation, the deity of Christ, the resurrection, the promised return of Christ, and so forth. An awareness of this kind of intellectual climate helps us understand how clergy could suddenly become dismissive of the great creeds of the church, such as the Apostles' Creed, as we saw earlier.

Nevertheless, one is astounded at such an audacious trend among those charged with maintaining fidelity to the historic Christian faith. As we saw earlier, Drew University theological professor Edwin Lewis expressed astonishment—if not anger—when he lamented that Methodists were having difficulty using the Apostles' Creed because of its affirmations of the virgin birth and resurrection of Christ. This historic creed, with its supernatural doctrinal claims, was being put aside by a number of Methodists; in its place was the popular new Social Creed, which was being used warmly and enthusiastically across the church. Lewis believed this tragic exchange was one indicator of the "fatal apostasy" of the church in his day.

This was the challenge facing the church at the beginning of the twentieth century. The historic doctrines of the Christian faith looked quaint and even archaic, and most certainly not defensible before the widely accepted new scientific and evolutionary worldview.

Theological liberalism was essentially, then, the movement that accommodated the Christian faith to the new, anti-supernatural axioms that had quickly become widely accepted in American intellectual circles. While denying tenets basic to historic Christianity, liberalism believed it was helping preserve traditional Christianity by attempting to make it relevant for modern man. Or, in the words of theologian Kenneth Kantzer, former editor of the evangelical journal *Christianity Today*, theological liberalism was an attempt to update an old, beloved religion so it could survive in the modern world.

If theological liberalism describes the movement to accommodate the substance of the Christian faith to anti-supernatural axioms, the term "modernism" reflects the new or modern *cultural* mood of the day, though the term is often used interchangeably with "liberalism." And to describe it helps us understand how there could be such a sudden and sweeping rejection of the church's historic doctrines and teaching.

Alister McGrath said of the modernism that emerged in the early twentieth century that its fundamental theme was its desire to control through a sheer will-to-power. He described the cultural mood this way:

> Humanity needs only the will to achieve autonomous self-definition; it need not accept what has been given to it, whether in nature or tradition. . . . The rejection of tradition is an integral element of this demand to master, and to achieve emancipation from any form of intellectual or social bondage.[2]

He said that the emphasis that modernism placed on the autonomy of human reason "was a desire to liberate thought from what was seen as the oppression of the past." Therefore, the concepts of "authority" and "tradition," both so very important to historic Christian belief, were seen "as tantamount to the fettering of the present by a dead past."

McGrath concluded that for modernism then, "human reason was seen as holding the key to emancipation from the discredited political and social systems of the past."[3] Obviously, such a cultural mood promising emancipation from an inferior and deficient past would pose a formidable challenge to the Christian church and its teachings.

One major change during this period was the replacing of the central Christian theme of *revelation* with the new controlling concept of autonomous *human reason*. As we shall see, reason became the dominant trump card in what could or could not be affirmed as true for the Christian church of the day. Christian truth was thus to be determined by assumptions and presuppositions totally outside the Christian orbit. Tragically, this cut away entirely the church's appeal to Scripture, tradition, and the creeds.

The late Richard John Neuhaus, founding editor of *First Things* journal, often made this same point, writing that liberalism "cannot make the distinction between the authoritative and the authoritarian. Every appeal to authoritative truth—God's self revelation, Scripture, creed—is by definition authoritarian, because it threatens to cramp and limit the expressive self."[4] Or as Neuhaus often referred to it, the "autonomous self"—his definition of the liberal mind, which relativized or dismissed all authoritative truth claims in the name of open-mindedness.

Theological Liberalism: A Theological Critique

As we consider more closely what was and was not affirmed by theological liberalism, I will draw upon three major sources. The first is Edwin Lewis, whose article "The Fatal Apostasy of the Modern Church" we have cited earlier. After many affirming responses to his article, he expanded on the theme with a major book—*A Christian Manifesto,* published in 1934.[5] A second major source is the classic work *Christianity and Liberalism,* by J. Gresham Machen, published in 1923.[6] Machen was professor at Princeton Theological Seminary. After being forced out of the Presbyterian Church because of his commitment to orthodox theology, he became professor of New Testament at Westminster Theological Seminary in Philadelphia, a graduate school he helped found. Both Lewis and Machen wrote major works engaging theological liberalism at the point of its questionable doctrinal substance. A third source is Dr. J. I. Packer, British Anglican churchman, author, and theologian.[7]

In reading Lewis the Methodist and Machen the Presbyterian, one sees numerous common themes. Both believed that their church's attempts to accommodate their teachings to make them acceptable to modern man was doing violence to the essential substance of the Christian faith. It was, they both believed, creating a new religion. Professor Lewis charged that much Christian belief "has gone into discard." And when asked why, he said the answer was in the magic phrase "modern thought."

> We are told that one cannot be at one and the same time a modern man and a loyal adherent of the Christian faith in its original sense. If one would be alive to all the currents of

modernity, and still be a Christian, it can be only as one eliminates from traditional Christianity everything with which
the alleged modernity cannot be harmonized.[8]

What must be eliminated, of course, were the supernatural
events of the Christian message—divine revelation, the virgin birth
and incarnation, miracles, the resurrection, and the future return of
Christ. These supposedly could not be harmonized with modernity.

Lewis went on to say that if you want "a new religion," one that is
constructed "without scrupulous reference to the Great Tradition" or
with reference only to those things that agree with one's own presuppositions, there is nothing to prevent one from having it. But he added,
"Only, we ought to be quite frank with ourselves, and with others, and
admit what we have done—substituted the new for the old. In that
event, would not the next step be to give it a new *name* as well?"[9]
Lewis, of course, knew that when the supernatural doctrinal elements
of Christianity are removed or replaced or radically reinterpreted, you
have a new and different religion than historic Christianity.

Machen, the Presbyterian, voiced the same criticism. He acknowledged that liberalism was trying to reconcile science and Christianity,
and often used the term that it was trying to "rescue" Christianity
from being irrelevant to modern man. But early in his work, he stated
his thesis, writing: "We shall be interested in showing that despite the
liberal use of traditional phraseology modern liberalism not only is a
different religion from Christianity but belongs in a totally different
class of religions."[10]

Again, Machen wrote that what the liberal theologian has retained
"after abandoning . . . one Christian doctrine after another is not
Christianity at all, but a religion which is so entirely different from
Christianity as to belong in a distinct category."[11] Machen believed
that the liberal attempt to reconcile Christianity with modern science
had "really relinquished everything distinctive of Christianity."[12]

Edwin Lewis complained that theological liberalism, which took
its clues "from deterministic and naturalistic theories," had left no

place for the great truths that are at the heart of Christianity. Here is his assessment of the substance of liberalism as he asks his readers to consider what had happened:

> The Bible became nothing but "a great literature"; Jesus was looked upon as "the choicest blossom on the human stock"; man carried within himself the power of his own emancipation, and a properly controlled heredity, environment, and education would guarantee a perfect result.[13]

Lewis reflected the astonishment many of us would feel in reading about such doctrinal defection, writing: "It seems almost incredible now that Christian thinkers should have entertained and propagated such ideas without seeing where they must inevitably lead."[14] Clearly, theological liberalism was much more than simply a commitment to being generous, openhanded, and broad-minded.

Machen insisted that what empowered the early church to begin its mission and experience great growth was its belief that Jesus had, indeed, been raised from the dead. And such a belief, he noted, involved the acceptance of the supernatural, which was at the heart and soul of the Christian faith. He went on to say that the issue does not concern individual miracles, but rather *all* miracles. Furthermore, the question "concerning all miracles is simply the question of the acceptance or rejection of the Saviour that the New Testament presents." He added:

> *Reject the miracles* and you have in Jesus the fairest flower of humanity who made such an impression upon His followers that after His death they could not believe that He had perished but experienced hallucinations in which they thought they saw Him risen from the dead; *accept the miracles*, and you have a Saviour who came voluntarily into the world for our salvation, suffered for our sins upon the Cross, rose again from the dead by the power of God, and ever lives to make intercession for us.[15]

The difference between these two views "is the difference between two totally diverse religions," Machen wrote. It would not do to refer to these merely as differing interpretations. Throwing down the gauntlet, he wrote: "It is high time that the misleading use of traditional phrases should be abandoned. . . . Shall we accept the Jesus of the New Testament as our Saviour, or shall we reject Him with the liberal Church?"[16]

He insisted that this was the issue that must be faced.

Lewis, who wrote eleven years after Machen's work, would have agreed with Machen's either/or challenge. He was critical of the charge that traditional Christianity could not defend itself against the challenges of modernism, and he was equally distressed that the great truths of the faith were being denied by the church, itself:

> For certainly as respects the repudiation of the supernatural, the denial of such great truths as revelation, incarnation, atonement, regeneration, and the like and the rejection of the right of Jesus Christ to universal homage, it is no longer possible to say that the church stands on this side and the world on that.[17]

Lewis believed the church had allowed the world, and more specifically the academic world, to dictate the terms of what may or may not be believed about historic Christianity. The result of this tragic accommodation was what Lewis described as "a growing cleavage between what the Christian faith actually is and what a large section of the church supposes it to be." And this cleavage, he believed, threatened "the continuation of the faith itself."[18]

Machen used very similar terms in describing what he believed was much more than an academic concern but rather a direct attack upon the churches. He wrote:

> Modern liberalism in the Church . . . is at any rate no longer merely an academic matter. It is no longer a matter merely of theological seminaries or universities. On the contrary its

attack upon the fundamentals of the Christian faith is being carried on vigorously by Sunday School "lesson-helps," by the pulpit, and by the religious press.[19]

One begins to see that the issues at the heart of the controversy over theological liberalism were not tangential or insignificant. It was a serious struggle over the very substance of the Christian message. It was much more than just a spirit of openness, broad-mindedness, and tolerance. It was much more than matters of nuance in which liberal Christians affirmed the church's social witness while traditional Christians emphasized matters of personal salvation. While some denominations did face this unfortunate dichotomy, this simplistic, stereotypical description of the controversy is woefully inadequate and fails to deal with the substantive issues at the heart of the controversy. Both Lewis, the Methodist, and Machen, the Presbyterian, believed the matter dealt with two very different religions.

J. I. Packer wrote that liberalism was the product of academic theologians who were very much men of their times, who were highly critical of pre-Enlightenment thinking. He described six general features that characterized liberal theology wherever it appeared. Under just one of his six points was the belief that the Bible was simply "a fallible human record of religious thought and experience rather than a divine revelation of truth and reality." Liberalism embraced "doubts . . . about the historical facts on which Bible writers base Christianity"; it insisted that "the churches should be undogmatic in temper, tolerating a plurality of theologies, and seeing personal and social ethics as their main concern." Finally, it affirmed the belief that "seeking society's renewal rather than evangelizing individuals is the primary Christian task."[20]

One of the characteristics just noted was that the churches should make personal and social ethics their main concern. This was a core principle in theological liberalism, and understandably so. If one believed the supernatural aspects of the Christian faith were no longer defensible and thus had become irrelevant to modern man, one could still hold to the ethical teachings of Jesus as a fallback position and not abandon the entire enterprise.

Edwin Lewis was critical of liberalism at this very point, saying the church was left with "a Heroic Figure who went about doing good, who spoke words of profound wisdom, and who is an example of complete loyalty to what he believed the will of God to be—but no more." He lamented that for many Methodists, to say anything more than this about Jesus "can no longer command the assent of intelligent men." What, then, is the church left with according to liberalism's new faith? he asked. "We must keep silent about the more purely religious features of Christianity and have much more to say about its ethical and social features."[21] Lewis claimed that many teachers and preachers have "set themselves the task of re-establishing the church on the foundation of the Jesus-ethic alone, and of redefining the function of the church accordingly."[22]

Machen noted insightfully that according to the modern liberal view, Jesus differs from the rest of men only in degree and not in kind. He could be divine only if all men are divine. He went on to make the important assertion that "in the New Testament and in all true Christianity, Jesus is no mere example for faith, but the object of faith. The Christian . . . reposes confidence in Jesus in a way that would be out of place in the case of any other than God."[23] It cannot be said too strongly that there is a world of difference in viewing Jesus as simply an *example* for faith, rather than the *object* of our faith.

In another of his points about liberal theology, J. I. Packer cited what he calls a sub-Trinitarian idea of God, which includes "a non-incarnational Christology that conceives of Jesus as a religious pioneer and model, a man supremely full of God, rather than as a divine savior."[24]

The phrase "a non-incarnational Christology" can sound benign and perhaps merely a bit academic. However, both Machen and Lewis knew that the new Christology was a completely different way of understanding who Jesus was and why He came. It was as if nineteen centuries of Christian tradition were being put aside for a totally new understanding of Jesus of Nazareth. Lewis protested strongly about such a revisionist view, writing, "But you have no right to claim that you can refuse to believe that God was personally incarnate in and as Jesus Christ and at the same time be a witness to the world of the faith that originally gave birth to Christianity."[25] For Professor Lewis, no honest church leader could put aside belief in the incarnation and also claim faithfulness to historic Christian doctrine.

Machen also protested that liberal preachers and theologians might say "Jesus is God," but in doing so, they mean "something entirely different from that which the Christian means by the same word." He charged that God, for the modern liberal, was "not a person separate from the world, but merely the unity that pervades the world."[26] This was, he insisted, a view "diametrically opposed to the Christian belief in the Deity of Christ."[27] He added that in order to maintain themselves among their colleagues and quiet the fears of their conservative associates, the liberals would "resort constantly to a double use of language." The liberal may sincerely believe in his heart that "Jesus is God," but the trouble is that "he attaches to the words a different meaning from that which is attached to them by . . . persons to whom he is speaking. He offends, therefore, against the fundamental principle of truthfulness in language."[28] He added this stinging remark about such deceptive language: "Christian ethics do not abrogate common honesty; no possible desire of edifying the Church and of avoiding offence can excuse a lie."[29]

Packer mentioned another of liberalism's characteristics, that being "a denial that the fall of a primitive pair brought guilt, pollution and spiritual impotence upon our race, in favor of a vision of mankind moving spiritually upward." Thus, the liberal views God's plan as "perfecting an immature race rather than redeeming a fallen one."[30] Again, there is a vast difference between these two understandings of God's plan.

Both Machen and Lewis were also in agreement that theological liberalism had lost the consciousness of sin. It is clearly of great significance whether the church views humanity as sinful and fallen or merely as immature and in need only of education and a more wholesome environment. Many church leaders bought into the idea that all the church needed to do was fan the flame of the innate goodness of men and women.

Lewis asked rhetorically whether the church could recover the New Testament faith. His reply was, "We cannot recover it unless we can also recover the sense of sin . . . The Christian God is one from whom issue at one and the same time the judgment of condemnation upon our souls and the provision whereby that judgment may be lifted."[31] He acknowledged that such a doctrine is anathema to so-called modern man. He went on to explain why:

> He does not like it. It shocks his self-esteem. It clashes with his boasted principle of natural progress. It challenges his moral optimism. It asks him to believe that something needs to be done for him that he cannot do for himself: he must simply submit to its being done. In a word, it means supernaturalism. Yes, it means just that—supernaturalism, the thing we have been led by false reasoning to equate with superstition.[32]

Machen echoed Lewis's charge. He claimed the basic fault of the modern church was that it was "busily engaged in an absolutely impossible task—she is busily engaged in calling the righteous to repentance."[33] He said that modern preachers are trying to help people avoid the conviction of sin, resulting in shallow preaching, which he rebuked strongly:

> The preacher gets up into the pulpit, opens the Bible, and addresses the congregation somewhat as follows: "You people are very good . . . you respond to every appeal that looks toward the welfare of the community. Now we have in the Bible—especially in the life of Jesus—something so good that we believe it is good enough even for you good people." Such is modern preaching. It is heard every Sunday in thousands of

pulpits. But it is entirely futile. Even our Lord did not call the righteous to repentance, and probably we shall be no more successful than He.[34]

What one sees in theological liberalism is actually a pattern of denial of the historic doctrines of the classic Christian faith. Machen contended that the overwhelming majority of liberal churchmen who reject the virgin birth "reject also the whole supernatural content of the New Testament." He added that these people "make of the 'resurrection' just what the word 'resurrection' most emphatically did not mean—a permanence of the influence of Jesus or a mere spiritual existence of Jesus beyond the grave."[35] Machen and Lewis were both convinced that to give the doctrine of the resurrection of our Lord such a different meaning altogether was revisionist theology, and for that matter, it was also intellectual dishonesty. The early church believed that the body of Jesus had been raised from the tomb by the power of God, and that was the theme of early church preaching. Such a belief, of course, means accepting the reality of the supernatural.

There was one bit more of revisionist theology. Liberalism also denied the substitutionary view of the atonement, wrote J. I. Packer, "in favor of the moral-influence and representative-trailblazer accounts of Christ's death for us, and thoughts of God forgiving on the ground that penitence makes us forgivable." He went on to add, and this was a critical theme for liberalism, that it embraced "a denial of Christ's personal return, in favor of the hope that universal moral progress will establish the kingdom of God on earth."[36]

Theological liberalism, then, was that religious movement that arose in the early 1900s and was euphoric in its optimism, believing it was riding the new intellectual wave of the future, which indeed it was. It believed it could rid the Christian church of its restrictive, provincial, outdated worldview and help it survive in a new and intellectually sophisticated modern era. It was a strategy by well-meaning churchmen and theologians, many of them having done graduate studies abroad, which was determined to attract people to

Christianity by accommodating and adapting the Christian gospel to the wisdom and worldview of secular, scientific modern man. Liberal theologians and pastors believed that in such accommodation they would preserve and even strengthen Christianity. Some felt it would rescue the faith from pending oblivion.

Unfortunately, the impact of theological liberalism was just the opposite, as it succeeded in devastating the vitality of the Christian churches in America—including Methodism. Liberalism believed it could rid Christianity of its unscientific supernatural elements (miracles, incarnation, resurrection, ascension, etc.) that might cause a thoughtful inquirer embarrassment. By doing this, those embracing the new theology believed they were saving the most important and lasting part of the Christian message—the ethical and moral teachings of Jesus.

The first step in this accommodation was not to immediately deny certain doctrines but to qualify those considered problematic. Harvard dean Willard Sperry characterized liberalism as the "Yes, but" religion. It would say, "*Yes*, I believe in the deity of Christ, *but* the language of Chalcedon has become meaningless. We must redefine the doctrine so as to make it intelligible to us who live in the twentieth century. *Yes*, I believe in the virgin birth of Christ, *but* by that I mean . . ." And on it would go. While liberal theologians believed their motivation was good and noble, there was serious dishonesty emerging, of all places, right in the Christian church. Questions of integrity arose as it became clear that liberalism was either creating a new vocabulary or injecting traditional Christian terms with new and contradictory meanings much different from what the terms had meant to the church across the centuries.

Theological Liberalism: A Series of Negations

An important characteristic of theological liberalism was that its basic tenets were primarily *negations*—they were statements of what liberal theology *no longer believed about traditional orthodoxy*.[37] That is to say, of necessity, liberalism almost always defined itself *over against historic Christianity.* Consider, for example, several theological characteristics of liberalism as we have noted previously and what it was that they were, in fact, negating or denying.

First, liberalism viewed God's character as one of pure benevolence and thus without wrath. All people are His children, and sin separates no one from His love, thus none will be lost. Such a view affirmed the concept of universalism, the view that all people will be saved. Thus, *the need for salvation or redemption was denied.*

Second, liberalism believed there is a divine spark in every man and woman. All people, therefore, are good at heart and need only encouragement, nurture, and education. All that is needed is the opportunity for their natural goodness to express itself. Thus, *humanity is basically good, not sinful, and the doctrine of original sin was denied.*

Third, liberalism viewed Jesus Christ as Savior only in the sense that He was our perfect teacher and example. He was not divine in any unique sense nor did His life reflect anything miraculous. He was not born of a virgin, did not work miracles, and was not raised from the dead. Thus, Jesus was simply a man like other men and did not suffer and die as an atonement for our sins. In such a view, *Christ's virgin birth, deity, atoning death, resurrection, and ascension were denied.*

Fourth, liberalism believed that just as Christ differs from other men only comparatively and not absolutely or substantively, neither does Christianity differ from other religions. It is just one, perhaps one of the most important, among the world's various religions, all of which stem from the same basic source. Thus, the church's missionary effort should not aim to convert but rather to promote a cross-fertilization of ideas for mutual dialogue and enrichment. The Christian faith is neither unique nor intended to be universal. Thus, *the church's worldwide missionary mandate was denied.*

Finally, liberalism affirmed that the Bible was not a divine record of revelation, but merely a human record of the religious experiences of a nation and a people. Thus, few if any doctrinal statements or creeds are essential to Christianity. The things of lasting importance and worth salvaging in the Christian message were the moral and ethical teachings of Jesus. Here, the Bible is seen only as a collection of human writings. It is not the divinely revealed Word of God. It is merely a historical record, not a revelatory Word. Thus, *the authority of Scripture was denied.*

Having looked carefully at what theological liberalism affirmed and denied, we begin to understand why there was such upheaval and resistance to this "new theology," as it was called. This was no insignificant thing happening in the life of the Christian church. A frontal assault was taking place on the church's essential doctrines, an attack made all the more dangerous because it came from church leaders and, under the guise of intellectual sophistication, claimed to be helping Christianity survive the intellectual challenges it was facing. The new theology was using familiar Christian terminology, but they had been given new and different meanings.

Bonhoeffer's Reflections on American Theology

A fascinating glimpse of what was happening to American theology with the emergence of theological liberalism comes from the German pastor and martyr Dietrich Bonhoeffer, who came to America in September 1930 to study at Union Theological Seminary in New York City. Admittedly, Bonhoeffer was not your ordinary theological student. He had an earned doctorate from Berlin University and had studied under Adolf von Harnack, a renowned liberal theologian in Germany. While Bonhoeffer did not agree with many of Harnack's conclusions, he respected his serious scholarship.[38]

As he experienced things firsthand at Union, he found the theological situation worse than he had anticipated:

> There is no theology here. . . . They talk a blue streak without the slightest substantive foundation and with no evidence of any criteria. The students—on the average twenty-five to

thirty years old—are completely clueless with respect to what dogmatics is really about. They are unfamiliar with even the most basic questions. They become intoxicated with liberal and humanistic phrases, laugh at the fundamentalists, and yet basically are not even up to their level.[39]

What Bonhoeffer discovered was that he had come to Union at a time when the "bloody battle royale between the liberals and fundamentalists was in full swing in 1930."[40] Just eight years earlier, Harry Emerson Fosdick, America's most famous liberal preacher, preached his controversial sermon "Shall the Fundamentalists Win?" In that sermon, he had expressed his "serious doubts about most of the historic assertions of the Christian faith, including the virgin birth, the resurrection, the divinity of Christ, the atonement, miracles, and the Bible as the Word of God."[41] Bonhoeffer soon learned that Union Seminary was "on the side of Fosdick, Rockefeller, and Luce."[42] Rockefeller's millions had helped build the stunning and massive Riverside Church (adjacent to Union Seminary), modeled on Chartres Cathedral, and was to influence students in the liberal theological tradition for years to come. Henry Luce put Fosdick's face on the cover of his *Time* magazine, with a glowing cover story about him and the church.

While Bonhoeffer acknowledged that the students fell into several basic groups, he noted that "without doubt the most vigorous . . . have turned their back on all genuine theology and study many economic and political problems. Here, they feel, is the renewal of the Gospel for our time."[43] And while the students showed impressive personal sacrifice in providing food and lodging for some thirty unemployed people over the winter, still he said, "It must not, however, be left unmentioned that the theological education of this group is virtually nil, and the self-assurance which lightly makes mock of any specifically theological question is unwarranted and naïve."[44]

Bonhoeffer's observations about the American churches, especially in New York City, were also particularly critical. "The sermon has been reduced to parenthetical church remarks about newspaper events. As long as I've been here, I have heard only one sermon in which you could hear something like a genuine proclamation."[45] He went on to ask, "One big question continually attracting my attention in view of these facts is whether one here really can still speak about Christianity?"[46]

In a significant summary of his observations of the American churches he had witnessed, with the exception of several African-American churches that impressed him deeply, Bonhoeffer wrote, "In New York they preach about virtually everything, only one thing is not addressed, or is addressed so rarely that I have as yet been unable to hear it, namely, the gospel of Jesus Christ, the cross, sin and forgiveness, death and life."[47] Just what has taken the place of the Christian message? According to Bonhoeffer: "An ethical and social idealism borne by a faith in progress that—who knows how—claims the right to call itself 'Christian.' And in the place of the church as the congregation of believers in Christ there stands the church as a social corporation."[48]

Liberalism—a "New Form of the Christian Faith"

One of the clearest admissions by a liberal theologian about what theological liberalism did and did not affirm came from James Gordon Gilkey, a popular pastor of South Congregational Church in Springfield, Massachusetts. Gilkey was a graduate of Harvard College and Union Theological Seminary and was invited to be the main speaker at the Texas Pastors' School at Southern Methodist University in Dallas, Texas, in July 1944. Well-known evangelical Methodist pastor Robert P. Shuler protested the Gilkey invitation, saying Methodism was bringing into Methodist pastors' schools men who were experts in the denial of the basic doctrines of classic Christianity.[49]

Shuler called attention to Gilkey's theological admissions in the latter's book, *A Faith to Affirm*.[50] Gilkey was quite candid in stating the "new doctrine":

We Liberals believe five things about Jesus. First: He was a human being, like all the rest of us in quality. Second: He was born in the normal way, the eldest child of Joseph and Mary. Third: The miracles attributed to him are in reality legends which sprang up during and after his life. Fourth: His most important act was not to die on the cross, but to live and teach our race its most significant set of religious and ethical beliefs. Fifth: His soul or spirit, not his physical body, survived death. In some further realm of existence it still continues its endless life and growth.[51]

Gilkey went on to say about Christ's death: "We cannot think that by dying Jesus purchased for human beings forgiveness of sin: to us Jesus' death is tragedy, nothing more." He assured his readers, "Jesus' death did not alter God's attitude toward us, or make God any more willing to forgive us and help us . . . Jesus' death was sheer tragedy. It had not been arranged in advance, there is no way by which it can be justified."[52]

Concerning the resurrection, Gilkey wrote, "The probability is (we think) that Jesus' body remained in the ground, and eventually underwent the familiar process of disintegration and decay."[53] But we should not despair because "Jesus' soul or spirit lived on, surrounded by the love and care of the Eternal God . . . This is what Easter and 'the resurrection of Jesus' mean to us. . . . We picture it as the survival and endless growth of a priceless personality."[54]

Gilkey's views on the *teachings* of Jesus revealed clearly that they were all he had left of classic Christianity: "We Liberals regard them [the teachings of Jesus] as the most precious elements in Christianity; and we propose to take them, combine them with new truths and insights gained since Jesus' time, and then offer this combination of teachings to the modern world as *a new form of the Christian faith*"[55] (emphasis mine).

One gasps at such outright and bold theological assertions that present a totally revised view of Jesus, of His atoning death on the cross, of His resurrection from the dead, and then stated, incredibly, that "new truths and insights" will be combined with Jesus' teachings to bring about "a new form of the Christian faith." These were the views of a pastor steeped in theological liberalism who was invited to come and teach Methodist pastors about theology. One can be sure that those in leadership positions who were responsible for inviting Gilkey were in sympathy with his views. Clearly, the faith "once for all entrusted to the saints" (Jude 3 NRSV) was no longer adequate.

The withering critique of theological liberalism from the visiting German pastor and the candid admissions from this Congregational pastor help us understand more fully the significance of J. I. Packer's summary statement mentioned earlier about the devastating impact of liberalism on evangelical faith: "Liberalism swept away entirely the gospel of the supernatural redemption of sinners. . . . It reduced grace to nature, divine revelation to human reflection, faith in Christ to following his example, and receiving new life to turning over a new leaf."[56]

Liberalism was never systematized as a coherent body of doctrine, but rather was a religious system in reaction to the orthodox doctrines of the Christian faith, which many believed were no longer defensible to the modern mind. Certainly, not all of liberalism's adherents would have affirmed all of the doctrinal denials just mentioned. Certainly, some theologians and pastors wanted to be seen as liberal rather than as traditionalist or fundamentalist, but still held on to some traditional understandings of the Christian faith that remained dear to them. Since Methodism was supposedly not a doctrinally oriented denomination as many were claiming, then theological consistency would not have been a matter of major importance.

Nevertheless, what is sadly true is that theological liberalism in its various shades and understandings was a very different understanding of traditional or historic Christianity. It was the tragic result of church leaders who, in a search for academic relevance and social affirmation, acquiesced to the intellectual climate of the day—which was making mankind and human reason the measure of all things.

Theological liberalism urged the church to put aside the more troubling supernatural aspects of Christianity, such as Jesus' miracles, His deity, and His resurrection, and called the church to focus instead on the moral and ethical teachings of Jesus. People were encouraged to emulate the ethics and teachings of Jesus in all of their relationships, assured that by so doing, the church would help bring about the kingdom of God on earth.

It is no surprise, then, that emerging in tandem with liberalism was the movement known in American Protestantism as the "social gospel."

Chapter 7

Methodism and the Social Gospel

AS THE HURRICANE-FORCE winds of change blew across American society in the early 1900s, accompanying the emergence of theological liberalism was the rise of the social gospel. This movement affected not only Methodism, but also much of American Protestantism.

The social gospel has been defined as "a loosely organized movement in North America from roughly 1880 to the start of the Great Depression (1929) which attempted to formulate a Christian response to the rapid social changes of the period."[1] It arose partly as a result of the *internal* challenge of changing theology, which demanded that the concepts of the immanence of God, evolutionary progress, a solidaristic view of man and society, and an emphasis on the ethical teachings of Jesus be implemented in social action.[2] Added to that was the *external* challenge emphasized strongly by C. H. Hopkins, who saw the social demands of the newly industrialized age as forcing American Protestantism to defend and rethink its ideology and reform many of its methods. He wrote:

> Of the many perplexing issues growing out of industrialism, those that concerned the relations of labor and capital . . . so largely dominated the interests of socially minded clergymen . . . that the social gospel may without question be described

historically as the response of Protestantism to those specific situations. . . . The problems of an industrial civilization remained the central interest of social Christianity.[3]

Major pioneers in the social gospel included Washington Gladden (1836–1918), a Congregational minister in Springfield, Massachusetts, and then Columbus, Ohio. While in Ohio, he had parishioners who were mine owners whose laborers struck in the mid-1880s for better wages and working conditions. His belief in the justice of their demands "led to a more insistent appeal for the rights of labor and the application of the 'Golden Rule' to industrial organization."[4]

Perhaps the most important advocate for the social gospel was Walter Rauschenbusch (1861–1918), a German-American Baptist minister who served for ten years in New York City's "Hell's Kitchen" and then became professor of church history at Rochester Seminary in New York State. His "first-hand experience of industrial exploitation and governmental indifference to workers made him a convinced critic of the established order."[5]

Historian Mark Noll said that "the Social Gospel is often identified with theological liberalism, and with some justice."[6] Gladden, he pointed out, was a popularizer of biblical higher criticism, a major feature of theological liberalism; and Rauschenbusch, though much more realistic about the "intractably fallen character of human nature," yet also "reinterpreted some traditionally supernatural elements of Christian doctrine."[7] In doing so, he was a part of the theological trends in the graduate studies of his day. In fact, he was one of the leaders, as he went to Germany in 1891 and studied under Albrecht Ritschl and his followers. There he received insights from Ritschl for blending his evangelical faith with his passion for social concerns and the ethical teachings of Jesus.

What is important to understand about the social gospel is that it was intricately related to, and an outgrowth of, theological liberalism. It did not represent the beginning of social ministry among America's Protestant churches. Before the social gospel gained popularity, the

Institutional Church movement had begun ministries to the physical, social, cultural, and intellectual needs of the people in the cities. In the early 1890s, one of Methodism's early institutional churches was Wesley Chapel in Cincinnati, which was offering ministries such as a kindergarten, a day nursery, a young ladies' benevolent society, a bureau of justice in which lawyers gave services to the poor, a building association in which people were taught to save toward a home, and a visitation society.[8]

In New York City, Central Methodist Church was transformed into the Metropolitan Temple, with other Methodist churches in the neighborhood consolidating with the newly formed temple. It offered fifty different social ministries and services each week, using every means to reach people for Christ. Services included choral societies, reading rooms, an athletic association, an employment bureau, youth organizations, a kindergarten, a sewing school, and dressmaking classes.[9] By the end of the 1890s, in New York City alone, out of 488 Protestant churches, some 112 were carrying on direct institutional activities of some kind. So, the churches of this period were already aware that the gospel did, indeed, have social imperatives for their members. However, the social gospel was something more.

In the world of theological liberalism, ethics became the major determinant of religious truth. With a major focus on the ethical teachings of Jesus and an evolutionary optimism of a new day emerging in an American Christian society, for those who had embraced the new liberal thought, "concern for life here eclipsed interest in the life hereafter."[10] George Marsden and B. J. Longfield went on to say about the trend:

> The divinity of Jesus was commonly attributed to his ethical and religious perfection, and the church was understood to be an agency for moral action and development. Many liberals, insisting that the purpose of Christianity was to transform society into God's kingdom, became vocal proponents of the Social Gospel.[11]

As we shall see, a prominent theme of both theological liberalism and the social gospel was *the creation of the kingdom of God on earth* by vigorous and untiring human effort. Also note that the divinity of Jesus was not the result of His incarnation, but was due to "his ethical and religious perfection." This is a critical distinction we must not miss. The traditional view held that Jesus was born the Son of God. The emerging new view claimed He *became* the Son of God through "his ethical and religious perfection" (similar to the heresy of Adoptionism). Again, it must be said that these are very different understandings of the divinity of Jesus and reflect the influence of theological liberalism on the church's Christology.

For liberal theologians and pastors, focus on ethics and the kingdom of God was a natural and socially popular emphasis. First, it avoided the controversial, problematic supernatural themes of the Christian message. Second, it was especially timely in light of the crushing social problems in the nation's urban centers. It was, however, a subtle but highly significant change for the Christian churches when liberal churchmen began to believe that the purpose of the Christian proclamation was to "transform *society* into God's kingdom" rather than to win *men and women* to Christ and His church through the atoning death and resurrection of Christ.

Realization of the Kingdom of God in History

As we have seen, a dominant concept in social gospel thought was the importance of the kingdom of God. Early in his ministry, Walter Rauschenbusch discovered this theme and his interest was deepened and solidified by his study of Ritschlian thought. It became the central concept in his thought and eventually, in the thought of the social gospel. Rauschenbusch saw the kingdom as a collective concept involving the whole social life of man. Hopkins went so far as to say, "The doctrine [of the kingdom in history] is 'itself the social gospel.'"[12]

The theme of the kingdom of God was preached by increasing numbers of ministers and theologians in America and found warm reception among Methodist spokesmen. The editor of the *Western Christian Advocate*, Levi Gilbert, wrote early in the twentieth century:

> Christianity's conception of the Kingdom of God, namely the permeation of all human society with the ethical and spiritual conceptions of religion as held by Jesus—the domination of the rule and will of God in all commercial, social, domestic, and civic life—is distinctly along the line of the efforts being made under the direction of sociological science.[13]

It is important to notice that the "spiritual conceptions" of Jesus that Gilbert mentioned are "along the line of" the efforts seen in the new discipline of "sociological science." The church was beginning to get more of its cues from the new and popular secular disciplines that were emerging in the evolving new era.

Harris Franklin Rall, a Methodist leader who later would become a bishop, noted with great optimism the realization of the kingdom: "We are coming to see more clearly each day that the kingdom of God means not simply new individuals but a new world, a new social order. It is this to which the prophets looked forward."[14]

This sense of optimism and expectancy was found in the discovery of the new social message by churchmen in urban centers, university settings, and in some of Methodism's larger churches. God was working out in history the consummation of human society in the perfect will of God on earth. This conviction was a part of the heartbeat of many churchmen of the day. Harry F. Ward, one of the leaders in Methodist social thought early in the century, exclaimed, "It is doubtful if any period of human history, unless it was that immediately preceding the birth of Jesus, has known such a universal expectancy of the dawn of a new day."[15] He even described the goal of this social message as "frankly a City of God established on the earth."[16] One is amazed at the optimism of such a near-utopian expectation. God would soon set up His kingdom on earth.

To his credit, Rauschenbusch did not buy into the illusory and naive optimism that came to characterize many of his contemporaries who would embrace the social gospel. He insisted, rightly, that the kingdom of God is neither inevitable nor exhausted in history. He knew it always remains a future, transcendent possibility, only partially manifest in the present age. Neither did he forget the problem of human sin. He wrote, "History laughs at the optimistic illusion that nothing can stand in the way of human progress. . . . What guarantee have we, that our modern civilization with its pomp will not be one with Nineveh and Tyre?"[17] But most social gospel advocates were not so cautious. Their enthusiasm and optimism left them confident the kingdom would soon be realized on earth.

Christianizing the Social Order

Closely related to the emphasis on the kingdom and perhaps just another expression of it for many was the emphasis on Christianizing the social order. As liberal theology during this period focused on the social and ethical teaching of Jesus, this part of the Christian message could be affirmed with little difficulty. For some it became nearly the entire substance of the Christian message. For again, one could enthusiastically embrace and proclaim the church's social and ethical teachings without having to deal with the problematic supernatural aspects of the faith. Advocates of the social gospel, influenced by the new theology of liberalism, had a growing confidence that in the teachings of the New Testament, especially those of Jesus, were to be found the ultimate solution for all the problems of the social order. These teachings, they believed, when diffused through society, would cause the social evils of civilization to disappear. Again, such optimistic idealism about Christianizing the social order was a very new and different understanding of the Christian church's mission.

As mentioned earlier, one of the first exponents of a Christianized social order was Washington Gladden, a liberal Congregational pastor and probably the first prominent spokesman for the social gospel. In 1893, in his book *Tools and the Man*, he wrote:

> The Christianization of society involves the Christianization of the prevailing social sentiments . . . so much as this must then be involved in this promised Christianization of society—that the sentiments, theories, customs, institutions, laws, and governments of the people are to be penetrated by Christian law.[18]

One must not miss in this statement the conviction that America's "institutions, laws, and governments of the people" are to be directly influenced or "penetrated" as he said, by "Christian law." Interestingly, there was no reservation whatsoever about a need for the separation of church and state here. The clear goal of the churches was to be the Christianization of American society. The church was to Christianize the state.

Walter Rauschenbusch took up this theme and gave it prominence in his book *Christianizing the Social Order*. He wrote of the difference between a Christian and an unchristian social order, saying, "An unchristian social order can be known by the fact that it makes good men do bad things."[19] By comparison, he claimed that "a Christian social order makes bad men do good things."[20] As we will see later, the sinfulness of man was getting lost amid the naive optimism that humankind was basically good and needed only education and an improved environment in order to flourish. As Rauschenbusch saw it, "Christianizing the social order means bringing it into harmony with the ethical convictions which we identify with Christ."[21]

One of the leading Methodist voices in this new endeavor to Christianize the social order was Frank Mason North. Born in New York City, North learned early of the social and religious needs of the great urban areas. In 1910, he echoed his conviction of this vision for society:

For the conviction is becoming central in the Christian consciousness that Christ died not only for each man nor for all men, but for the race; that humanity is in a sense an organism, and that the rule of God means, not the rescue of a few from the mass, but the permeation of all human life with the spirit of Christ, the application of the principles of heaven to the affairs of earth, the actual demonstration of the meaning of the Sermon on the Mount in terms of the present life of men.[22]

North went on to say that the completeness of this new order comes when "everything contrary to that rule [the spirit of Christ] is driven out and destroyed."[23] Again, what was reflected in such sentiments was a new understanding of the mission of the church, a faulty understanding of the sinful nature of humanity, and a shift toward universalism—the belief that all people will be saved. This, of course, was a very different doctrinal understanding from that which American Methodists believed throughout the nineteenth century.

Another well-known Methodist voice of the period was Francis J. McConnell—author and spokesman for the social gospel, and later a bishop in the Methodist Episcopal Church. He used the Christian doctrine of conversion to describe the change needed in the actual institutions of society. One gets his sense of passion about the new focus on the social order, as he wrote boldly: "Industry, politics, governments need to be converted, born again, baptized by the Holy Spirit into newness of spirit."[24] One hears such words and is inclined to say, "How's that again?" But to his credit, McConnell did affirm that the necessary changes in social systems can best be made by those who, themselves, have been born into newness of spirit. However, such an evangelical doctrine of personal conversion had difficulty surviving amid liberalism's new emphasis on the new social understanding of man.

In addition to a focus on the kingdom of God and the Christianizing of the social order, the social gospel also included in its proclamation the new, social view of man and society as a reaction to the individualism of Protestant thought at the time. As early as 1895, in one of the first formulations of a social theology, William DeWitt Hyde wrote:

> I have called it Social Theology, because the Christianity of Christ and his disciples was pre-eminently a social movement, and because we are looking at everything today from the social rather than the individualistic point of view. In ethics, in economics, in sociology, in politics, we no longer treat man as capable of isolation.[25]

Clearly, the complexity of massive urban areas and gigantic institutions and factories forced a reevaluation of the nature of society amid the new cities and giant industries. Undoubtedly, traditional social thought geared to rural and small-town settings was inadequate in understanding the complex problems of urbanized America. Lloyd J. Averill made this point, writing, "Social gospel liberalism held that society is not simply an aggregate of individuals to be affected only by first affecting its discrete individual members."[26] Others made similar points. Rauschenbusch often drove home the conviction, reacting strongly to the individualistic pieties of traditional religion.

However, while the social gospel spoke to the danger of individualism in the approach to the social problems of the day, it nearly lost sight of the importance of an individual response to the offer of the gospel.

A Focus on Business and Industry

Developing as a movement in response to the problems of industrialization and urbanization, the social gospel naturally focused heavily upon unchristian ethics in business and industry. In 1895, a Methodist layman, John G. Woolley, speaking in New York City to the National Conference of Reforms, made a strong plea for the churches to step in to help the government in matters such as labor, money, taxation, suffrage, transportation, civil service, tariffs, and the liquor traffic.[27] Woolley insisted that though politics should not place a controlling hand upon religion, religion must assimilate politics into itself and this was, indeed, the business of the church in the world. He saw a very definite role for government when guided and influenced by churchmen: "I think that the government ought to control the price of fuel, freight and flour, and keep it as fair and relatively equable as postage."[28] Woolley saw these problems as moral and religious issues, demanding increased knowledge and involvement on the part of the Christian churches.

It was particularly the misuse of wealth and power that brought the strongest rebuke from the prophets of the socialized Christianity. Leaders such as Washington Gladden, Richard T. Ely, and Walter Rauschenbusch were among the first spokesmen against the evils and immoral methods of business. They looked beyond the traditional issues of individual morality to the more sophisticated and complex wrongs, such as "stock manipulation and watering, corners in foodstuffs, speculation, bribery, railway exploitation, fraudulent manufacturing, and adulteration of food."[29]

Rauschenbusch observed in 1912 that of the five areas of American society, four had already been largely Christianized. These were the family, church, school, and politics. These had been changed at least to the degree that the spirit of Christ could work through them. The one area yet to be redeemed was business. He saw this challenge as the greatest facing a Christian America.[30]

An emphasis that appears again and again among social gospel spokesmen is the great harm that was being done to the credibility of the message of the church through lack of ethics in business. This was particularly true in the relationship of the church with the laboring force in America. As the twentieth century progressed, this theme finds more explicit development in Methodist periodicals. Methodist theologian William Balch, writing in 1909, charged that the conventional standards for Christian businessmen were a scandal to the church. Beyond telling the truth, paying one's debts, and keeping contracts, the claim that "business is business" was being allowed to cover a multitude of sins.[31]

An interesting contradiction of this period was the new emphasis on the inherent goodness of man combined at the same time with a sharp focus on the moral failure of those in business and industry— people who were often upstanding citizens in both church and society. Stock manipulation, bribery, exploitation of laborers, and fraud were, of course, expressions of selfishness and human sin.

The challenge of the social gospel was against a type of Christian experience that brought no corresponding change in one's social values and judgments. It was critical of the claim of conversion when no serious reorientation of one's values resulted from the experience. Unfortunately, such a charge can be found in most any generation in the church's history. At this particular time, the church was confronting unprecedented new moral and ethical issues related to industrialization, urbanization, and immigration, and it is little wonder it was open to such criticism.

F. Ernest Johnson expressed the problem pointedly:

> A "new birth" can mean nothing short of a re-orientation of the conditions of one's entire life. . . . No one knows better than the pastor of a church in an industrial community what a travesty on religion the faith and practice of allegedly godly men can be. Here we have church-school superintendents who are also mill superintendents, charged with the execution of harsh labor policies; elders and vestrymen, trustees and deacons, who drive hard competitive bargains; . . . pious men who are exploiters of the labor of children; . . . "good" fathers who are cruel employers or defaulting bankers.[32]

This statement captures the intensity of the feeling that often existed among some unchurched people toward those within the churches. It was to these blind spots and inconsistencies and sins that the social gospel directed much of its energy. It must be said, however, that criticisms about conversion and the new birth were also convenient points to make when a major theological shift was taking place with liberalism's new preference for social transformation and away from more traditional or personal expressions of Christian experience. Without question, though, American Methodism and Protestantism in general were slowly awakening to the new and complex issues brought about by industrialization and urbanization.

An Assessment of the Social Gospel

An evaluation of the social gospel is not a simple matter. As we have seen, it provided a much-needed new awareness about complex social challenges facing newly industrialized America. However, it also had serious weaknesses as well, being influenced strongly by theological liberalism.

As a positive, the social gospel did serve as a catalyst for a much-needed change in the thinking of Protestant Christians in America. As Robert Handy wrote:

> The social gospel contributed to significant changes in American Protestant mentality; it led many churchmen to take seriously crucial issues in American life and to rethink their philosophies of public life. Many Protestants became much more aware of the way social and economic realities operated in modern industrial society. Even where the movement, with its liberal theological and reformist premises, was specifically rejected, as it was in some churches almost completely, still it raised questions which could not again be easily evaded though its particular answers might be rejected.[33]

Also, the social gospel drew attention to the whole question about the role of the individual in society. The charge that most advocates faced was the oft-repeated "You can only change society by changing the individuals in society." This is a classic half-truth and was at the heart of much resistance as the churches struggled to develop a new social conscience on issues they were facing.

In fact, John C. Bennett, in his volume *Social Salvation*, noted three half-truths concerning individual and social salvation. The first is that individuals can rise above any combination of social circumstances.[34] This was an enormously popular theme during this era as numerous rags-to-riches stories were preached as a possibility for everyone. While there is some truth, of course, it is also a theme that can be used conveniently to justify overlooking social problems that cry out to be addressed. The second half-truth was that since individuals control institutions, it is enough to merely change these individuals.[35] Bennett noted rightly that a conversion to the Christian faith does not always bring with it adequate wisdom and understanding about the complexity of the social order, not to mention the true inner motivation to do something about it.[36] The third half-truth was that you can change society without changing individuals. Here Bennett noted that unchanged men can destroy the values and ideals of the best system in the world.[37] These half-truths, so popular early in the 1900s, were a part of the churches' struggle to meet the critical social needs they were facing, especially in the urban areas.

On the negative side, it must be said that with its emphasis on social man and Christianizing the social order, the social gospel overreacted against individualism. And while there is certainly a danger in focusing too strongly on individualism regarding the Christian faith, we must take care not to confuse personal faith with an individualistic faith. Each individual must respond *personally* to Christ's invitation to discipleship. The resulting faith is not, however, *individualistic*. It is always accompanied by social imperatives. Wesley's dictum that "there is no holiness but social holiness" remains timely for every generation.

Interestingly, some social gospel advocates voiced concern that a division was already taking place during the first decade of the 1900s. They realized that many Methodists reared in revivalism and the importance of a personal response to the gospel believed the social gospel was drifting away from traditional Methodist doctrine and experience. Their suspicions, we have seen, were not without justification.

One progressive, liberal-minded churchman who perceived such a division was Herbert Welch, the president of Ohio Wesleyan University and later a bishop of the Methodist Episcopal Church. Though in full sympathy with the emerging social teachings, Welch warned with passion and great foresight:

> The danger which threatens the church here . . . is the danger of division into opposing camps. The peril is not that there may be too earnest an agitation of social needs, but that on one side should be a group of evangelists with a narrow conception of Christ's mission, intense in zeal, but lacking vision, breadth, adaptation to the needs and ways of the day; on the other a group of social workers, alive to the injustice of the present situation, aflame with love to men and the desire to bring in the kingdom of righteousness and peace, but distrusting the method of evangelism and substituting Utopia for heaven. Our need is not evangelism or social service, but evangelism and social service, now and forever, one and inseparable![38]

One senses in this remarkable statement Welch's uneasiness about those who had thrown themselves wholeheartedly into social service while moving away from evangelism, and one would assume, the traditional theology of classic Methodism. Numerous historians of this period spoke of liberalism and the social gospel being mediating efforts between the traditional expressions of the faith along with the new social theology. However, as in most mediating positions, one side will eventually prevail. Sadly, during this period, evangelism and its theme of personal sin, accountability before God, and personal transformation through conversion would get pushed aside and displaced by the new intellectual social theology.

Francis J. McConnell, an advocate of the social gospel, also expressed a fear that something was being lost from the Christian preaching to the individual.

We concede that much preaching of the social gospel today does encourage a false belittling of the function of the individual. Some social leaders sneer at the doctrine of personal salvation as old-fashioned and proclaim that if we get the right group spirit the salvation of the individual will take care of itself.[39]

F. Ernest Johnson, also a Methodist advocate of the social gospel, acknowledged the misleading character of the term itself. He sensed that it was perpetuating a dualism that was false to the "history and the genius of Christianity as well as to the facts of human experience."[40] He argued that while some resisted the social gospel because they did not want to face its moral implications, there was also legitimate substance to the resistance on the part of many:

It is also in no small part due to a conviction that violence is being done to the gospel itself. Those who are close to the biblical sources find it difficult to derive from them any "gospel" that is not quite as individual as it is social. In the last analysis any effort to make the social teachings of Jesus stand independently of those precepts that are related to the culture of the personal life is doomed to failure, just as we who have been known as social gospel advocates insist that the opposite attempt must fail. There are not two gospels, but one.[41]

Johnson attributed part of the problem to liberalism's false theological understanding of the Christian message and kingdom. In a powerful and thoughtful summary, Johnson wrote:

These concepts are themselves as strikingly individual in their reference as they are social. The gate to the Kingdom is a spiritual gate. One may become a citizen of that Kingdom only by the "naturalization" of his own soul. The concern of our prophetic pulpits with the rebuilding of the social order is essentially and inescapably Christian, but it becomes ineffectual if it fails to take account of the qualifications for citizenship in the City of God.[42]

A highly noticeable trend of the Methodist literature of this period was an oft-expressed pride in a newly achieved intellectualism. Liberalism and the social gospel were seen as evidence that reason and intelligence had won in the battle with the superstitions of the former orthodoxy. "An intellectualized Christianity is being born again," claimed one Methodist writer whose mood was representative.[43] Increasingly, sneers toward the doctrine of individual salvation were becoming more evident. Unfortunately, educational differences added to a growing condescension by those embracing the new theology toward the lesser-educated traditionalists.

Again, it must be said that theological liberalism and the accompanying social gospel movement were mediating movements in America. Early spokesmen of the movement were trying to maintain a balance between the authentic to be found in both the traditional as well as the new theologies. Theologian H. Richard Niebuhr noted, however, that no mediating theology in history has ever been able to keep the balance between the opposing elements that it seeks to reconcile. As time went on, liberal theology and most social gospel advocates leaned more toward liberalism than evangelicalism. The result was an increasingly "vacuous theology" characterized by a loss of the sense of the broken relation between God and man.[44] In his classic summary describing the theology that emerged in this period, Niebuhr wrote these stinging words: "A God without wrath brought men without sin into a kingdom without judgment through ministrations of a Christ without a cross."[45]

F. Ernest Johnson wrote this important summary of the weaknesses of the social gospel, a movement he, himself, supported:

The social gospel movement is criticized on the ground that it is theologically shallow; that it has missed the real meaning of the Kingdom of God in relation to history; that it is "humanistic" and lacking in recognition of the supernatural factors in redemption; that it has glorified the immanence of God at the expense of his "otherness"; that it is hopelessly romantic in its conception of human nature; that it has substituted for divine architecture the work of men's hands.[46]

By any measure, this is a devastating critique of the social gospel. What is highly significant in Johnson's assessment is that nearly every point mentioned addressed a tenet of theological liberalism.

In making reference to the lack of emphasis upon the individual, Johnson cited, with great insight, that the social gospel did not realize "the social significance of the penitential attitude which worship fosters and which keeps man under the sense of a divine imperative."[47] Each time I read that sentence, I think of two powerful examples of people who were "under the sense of divine imperative." One is William Wilberforce, who battled against the slave trade in England. The other is Charles (Chuck) Colson, founder of Prison Fellowship International, a Christian ministry to those incarcerated in prisons around the world.[48] The faith of these two Christian giants compelled them. They were not idealistic reformers or utopian dreamers. They were sinners, redeemed by God's grace and "under the sense of a divine imperative."

The Social Gospel Was Never a Popular Movement

One final point needs to be made in a critique of the social gospel. The question must be asked why it never received widespread and popular acceptance among the membership of the Methodist churches, and among the other Protestant churches as well, for that matter.

Walter Mueder wrote about this significant point:

The "social gospel" movement's expression of intense criticism and action was never a popular movement. Only a minority in the denominations identified themselves with it, and many of these were related to theological seminaries, to boards and agencies, or to councils somewhat remote from the power tensions of local churches.[49]

Richard M. Cameron agreed with Muelder, saying about the leaders and spokesmen of the social gospel, "They were always few."[50] But they did move quickly into positions of leadership within the denomination. It is highly significant that the social gospel, with its new social ministry, *failed* to move beyond the seminaries, boards and agencies, and a few selected leaders, on down to the local church level. It was an elitist and intellectual movement that had little vigorous involvement with the large majority of Methodism's local churches.

The same can be said of theological liberalism. It was quickly embraced by Methodism but primarily among the upper echelon of the church's leadership. Riley Case wrote in his important work *Evangelical and Methodist*:

> By 1920, modernism [liberalism] basically controlled Methodism, at least institutional Methodism, in both the north and the south. The colleges, the seminaries, the pastors' schools, the Courses of Study, the Church press, the Sunday school material, the Church agencies, and finally even the Council of Bishops were, or would soon be, in the hands of modernists [liberals].[51]

Theological liberalism was, indeed, resisted by many Methodists because it represented a very different understanding of the Christian message from what most Methodists at the time embraced. Many local church pastors and church members may not have fully understood exactly what this new teaching was that was being preached and taught in Methodism's large pulpits and theological institutions. However, they had growing suspicions that what they were hearing was a different gospel from what they knew and had experienced personally.

Case wrote that while liberalism was soon controlling Methodism at the leadership levels, populist Methodism—evangelical Methodism—was largely untouched by it. The result was tension and alienation, so much so that the liberal Protestant journal *Christian Century* carried an article in 1926 titled "What Is Disturbing the Methodists?" Case added, "The truth was that hundreds, perhaps thousands, of Methodist preachers were in a mood of incipient revolt, and it would tax the ingenuity of denominational leaders to make the organization function and not goad these ministers into open rebellion."[52]

The social gospel, then, was a very significant movement within the American church, including Methodism. It drew attention in a new way to the social imperatives of the faith, especially for the nation's teeming urban problems. Yet, the social gospel enthusiasts, strongly influenced by the new theology as well as movements in Britain and Germany, "went further to the left than most Americans, prompting a great many church members to find their ideas objectionable."[53] Some Christian leaders and many laity refused to compromise. For these folks, Scripture came from the Creator and was to be interpreted faithfully and with great seriousness. "The Bible, in their judgment, was truth, providing all that we needed to know about our origins, proper conduct, and our ultimate destination."[54]

The Methodist Church, then, experienced significant tensions during this period as a result of the new and popular theological liberalism, and the accompanying social gospel. Along with the tensions came alienation, controversies, and even schisms to the Methodist Church, far more than most of us realize.

Chapter 8

Methodist Resistance: Tensions, Alienations, and Schisms

THE RESISTANCE TO theological liberalism and the accompanying social gospel was much more pronounced in American Methodism that most of us realize. Profound differences of belief about the new liberal theology led to problems of communication and trust between both denominational leadership and parish clergy as well as between clergy and laity. Liberalism and the social gospel were, as we indicated earlier, only embraced by a minority within Methodism, albeit a very influential minority. And if many clergy were having serious difficulty with the heady new theology of their denominational leaders and professors, one can only imagine how perplexed laypersons were about it.

Tensions between Methodist Leadership and Clergy

In a candid and perceptive article in the *Methodist Review* in 1923, Methodist pastor Albert Edward Day lifted the lid on a festering sore within Methodism. Day considered himself an advocate of the social gospel and welcomed liberalism's new studies in sociology and biblical criticism. However, in his ten-page article, he expressed grave concern about existing attitudes of some bishops and board chairmen toward Methodist pastors. He was alarmed about frequent reports of impatience on the part of the leadership toward the pastors. He regretted that some Methodist departmental officials, basking in their feelings of personal superiority, strongly resented differences of opinion or criticism from pastors.[1]

One denominational official, hearing of a contrary view from a pastor, angrily responded: "What right have the fellows on the side lines to criticize the men who are straining every nerve to carry the ball down the field?" Day responded: "The painful element in the assumption is that the pastors are on the side lines and that the officials sitting at their desks devising programs and dictating letters are the men who are bucking the line and wearing out their energies in actual scrimmage."[2]

In response to another complaint, a department official wrote: "The brethren should be very careful how they dissent from the judgment of our official leaders."[3] Day also expressed concern about intimidation by bishops of clergy with creative or independent ideas as well as a general sense of scorn from them toward any challenging ideas or differing opinions.[4] He hinted in his article that this attitude of condescension was more widespread than just a few local grievances:

> The opinion of the great body of Methodist preachers cannot be ignored or repressed without creating great unrest. It is wholly un-American to presume that you can make a company of automatons out of a great body of educated, self-respecting men such as compose the Methodist ministry. . . . Autocracy [i.e. unlimited power, dictatorship] in Methodism is the poorest possible method of administration.[5]

The "great body of Methodist preachers" would have been, in this case, the large majority of clergy who had entered the ministry through the Course of Study, not through seminary. From this and other, similar accounts, one senses that serious tensions had developed between a more supposedly enlightened liberal Methodist leadership and a less-enlightened traditional clergy. There was a growing sense of pride among many of the progressive leaders about the new "intelligent" Christianity that had been born. With exhilaration, they saw this as stepping out of the darkness of traditional orthodoxy into the light of the new, liberating, and enlightened thought.

The problem was made more acute by the fact that some Methodist leaders had gone abroad to study or had attended Methodist graduate schools, while most Methodist clergy, as noted earlier, had become pastors through the Conference Course of Study. Along with the new themes of theological liberalism, the educational gap became increasingly significant, evoking scorn toward the less formally educated and generally orthodox clergy. This problem was addressed, interestingly, by no less than Borden Parker Bowne, one of the leading advocates of liberalism at Boston University School of Theology:

> Orthodoxy comes in for many a clever sarcasm; and to call a man orthodox is almost to reflect on his intelligence. Dogma is likewise a word of evil sound, and to speak of a man as dogmatic is to stamp him as strong in assertion, but weak or wanting in argument. Orthodoxy and dogma have kept such bad company in the past, consorting often with unreason, oppression, and violence, that it is quite the fashion to decry and deride them. But this . . . is an error.[6]

Bowne's remark about sarcasm and deriding of the orthodox indicates that as early as 1910, if not earlier, condescending personal attacks had begun against the more traditional Methodists.

Francis McConnell, in his volume *Christian Citizenship*, let a derogatory slur slip out while writing about traditionalists who unwisely attack radical movements with insufficient arguments to back up their charges. He referred to these individuals as "ignoramus conservatives," speaking not necessarily in the theological sense but socially and intellectually.[7] But clearly, the condescending caricatures and name-calling had begun, and the chasm between liberal and more traditional clergy widened rapidly.

In the foreword to his *A Christian Manifesto*, Edwin Lewis wrote about responses he had received to his article "The Fatal Apostasy of the Modern Church," which we noted in an earlier chapter. His *Manifesto* was a follow-up to that article, which had resulted in a large volume of correspondence in response. He noted, sadly, that "a considerable number" of letters he had received were "definitely hostile [the word, he acknowledged, was not too strong]."[8] He was told that he had "sold out to the Fundamentalists," and that he was becoming "senile and conservative," and so on. One colleague asked condescendingly if he had "slipped back into orthodoxy."[9] It is sobering, but insightful, to realize that for one to affirm orthodoxy in the substance of the faith would have been seen as a tragic plight.

Interestingly, by 1934, the terms "fundamentalist" and "orthodox" had clearly taken on a pejorative character. One's embrace of orthodoxy was viewed as a tragic descent into intellectual irrelevance. While orthodox theologians we cited earlier—Faulkner, Wilson, Lewis, Sloan, et al.—all raised their voices in protest against the new theology, none of them identified themselves as a fundamentalist. Sloan was clear that while he affirmed the basic doctrines, such as the virgin birth, the Trinity, the atoning death of Christ, justification by faith, and the full authority of Scripture, he also added that the verbalism and literalism of the fundamentalist movement had no part in his reform efforts.[10]

Nonetheless, the sweeping, pejorative caricature was soon employed against those who refused to embrace the new liberal theology. Attitudes such as these reflected that a major rift was taking place among Methodist clergy during this period. This should come as no surprise, of course, as theological liberalism was in the process of radically changing, or more accurately *displacing*, the essence of the Wesleyan doctrinal tradition among an important segment of Methodist leadership.

This rift did not go unnoticed nationally. As mentioned in the previous chapter, in 1926, the *Christian Century* carried an article entitled "What Is Disturbing the Methodists?"[11] The editors noted Methodism's reputation for doctrinal disinterest and even cited Methodist leaders who ridiculed the idea that Methodism might somehow be disturbed by doctrinal matters.

Interestingly, the editors identified Methodist clergy in three grades. The upper grade was made up of seminary professors, agency heads, bishops, denominational leaders who were progressive and liberal in theology. Most were seminary graduates. The second grade consisted of those clergy who aspired to be part of the upper grade, but who had probably come into the ministry through the Conference Course of Study. The third grade was made up of pastors with limited formal education who served the smaller and more rural churches with the smallest membership and least amount of financial resources.

According to the editors of the *Christian Century*, a rebellion was, indeed, taking place among the second and third grades of Methodist clergy against those in the upper grade. These ministers (in the second and third grades) had not embraced the new liberal theology as had most of the upper grade clergy—those who were likely to have been seminary-trained. The *Christian Century's* analysis was that their protests were "disturbing Methodist tranquility." For the *Century* to describe the turmoil as a "rebellion" spoke to the depth of the conflict taking place within the denomination.

It should be noted that this article was published in 1926, just two years before the 1928 General Conference. That was the Conference before which Harold Paul Sloan and his Methodist League for Faith and Life would bring ten thousand petitions from 522 Methodist churches in forty-one states calling upon the Methodist Church to investigate charges of gross disloyalty to Methodist doctrinal standards. Their concerns were broad, covering Methodist seminaries, pulpits, literature, and the content of Conference Course of Study. By any measure, that was a widespread grassroots protest by Methodists determined to address their concerns through the appropriate channel—the denomination's quadrennial law-making assembly, the General Conference. As we saw earlier, delegates rejected Sloan's call for an investigation. The question must be asked, Why were Methodists so reluctant to take Sloan's protest seriously? We will look at that later in the chapter.

Case also cited another study conducted in 1929, which confirmed the general conclusions of the *Christian Century* article. An extensive study by George Herbert Betts of Northwestern University, titled *The Beliefs of 700 Ministers and Their Meaning for Religious Education*, sought an answer to the question, What do the ministers of our churches believe?[12] He wanted to know that when the minister led his congregation in a confession of faith such as the Apostles' Creed, does the pastor expect the members to believe the doctrinal assertions of the creed and more, does the pastor, himself, believe them?[13]

The very nature of the study revealed that some clergy and theologians were obviously having difficulty with the doctrinal affirmations of the creeds. We noted earlier that Edwin Lewis had lamented this trend in his 1933 "Fatal Apostasy" article. Many Methodists, he charged, were having difficulties affirming the virgin birth and the resurrection of the body. The result was they were setting aside the Apostles' Creed, preferring instead the new Social Creed of the Churches.

Betts sent his survey to some fifteen hundred Protestant clergy in the Chicago area. He received seven hundred responses, two hundred of which were from students in seminary. The largest number of responses came from Methodists, but all of the historic mainline denominations had enough responses to be included. The Congregationalists were the most liberal, Case noted, followed by the Methodists. For example, answers to the question concerning the virgin birth were telling. The study revealed that "ninety percent of Lutherans affirmed the virgin birth, followed by 80 percent of Baptists and Evangelicals, 69 percent of Presbyterians, 54 percent of Methodists, and 25 percent of Congregationalists."[14] Again, Betts asked: "Was Jesus' death on the cross the one act that made remission of sin possible?" The response:

"Ninety-nine percent of Lutherans believed so, followed by 78 percent of Evangelicals, 75 percent of Baptists, 67 percent of Presbyterians and Episcopalians, 60 percent of Methodists, and 20 percent of Congregationalists."[15]

After citing a number of these responses, Betts made a troubling summary observation about this study within the denominations: "No denomination except perhaps the Lutherans has any right to demand that fixed creeds shall be taught the young. For the clergy of those denominations do not subscribe to a common creed beyond belief in the existence of God."[16] Again, this study was done in 1929.

While Betts's study was concentrated more heavily in an urban area, it still reflected that major changes were taking place in the beliefs of Methodist clergy at the time. He also addressed what he believed the church would look like in the next few decades, based on the beliefs of the seminary students. The students, he noted, "reflect a more distinct drift away from the older or orthodox positions and a tendency to be in accord with the scientific thought of the day."[17] For example, while some 71 percent of pastors believed in the virgin birth, only 25 percent of students did; while some 70 percent of pastors believed that Jesus' death on the cross was the one act that made possible the remission of sins, just 29 percent of students did. Some 53 percent of pastors believed that people are born with sinful natures, compared to just 13 percent of students.[18] These comparative statistics revealed that the next generation of Methodist leaders—seminary-trained clergy who would move into positions of denominational leadership—were sure to be far more liberal than those pastoring churches in 1929.

Up until the emergence of theological liberalism, Case observed, there had been critics of certain aspects of American Methodism, such as the emotionalism of its revivals and camp meetings, its Holiness gatherings, and its preaching against worldliness. He noted that suddenly, it was not just the "excesses of Methodism" that were an embarrassment to the liberal Methodist. "It was the core of the faith itself: the Bible as the written revelation of God, original sin, the supernatural intervention of a transcendent God into human affairs, the Atonement, and the Resurrection."[19]

It is little wonder, then, that tensions and alienation arose between liberal Methodist leaders and theologians on the one hand, and the pastors of local Methodist churches on the other, most of whom did not embrace the new theology. They were living in two very different worlds theologically.

Tensions between Liberal Clergy and Laity

Liberalism also brought serious tensions between clergy and laity during this period. Charles C. Morrison, in his *The Social Gospel and the Christian Cultus*, written in 1933, claimed that the social gospel had come to a point of arrested development. One of the reasons he gave was that a widening gap was developing between the clergy and the laity about the purposes of ministry.

> A gulf between the clergy and the laity is beginning to yawn, a gulf of which both clergy and laity are increasingly conscious. The modern minister is not so close to his laymen as ministers used to be. There is a lack of frank understanding, mutually conscious tension, inhibited candor, suspicion by the laity that the minister entertains ulterior purposes which he does not dare fully to avow.[20]

One senses in such a statement the beginning of a serious and very sad problem of trust on the part of laity toward their clergy. Morrison admitted that there was a larger awareness of social need than ever before, but acknowledged that this new social conviction had not made an appreciable impression on the various Christian churches as a whole. The reason it had not, he believed, was that the new theology of the social gospel had not yet been preached. Concerning this theology, he wrote:

> The laity of the churches have only the vaguest idea of its existence. It is held by the clergy as a kind of esoteric body of

doctrine, but they are unable to give it public expression as an integral part of religious truth. The high hopes of Walter Rauschenbusch have not been fulfilled. And the reason for it, I think, is clear. The Social Gospel has been altogether a prophet's gospel. It has produced no priesthood.[21]

Perhaps we should not be surprised at such a remark about the social gospel. The churches were awakening to the need to address the critical social needs found in America's urban centers. But at the same time, an embracing of the new theology brought a diminishing of the gospel's focus on the personal spiritual needs of persons. As the social gospel centered on meeting the social needs of the individual, it neglected and even discounted the priestly function of the church. That is, it failed to effectively invite people to personal faith in Christ. This new theology, of course, was the seedbed from which people would then grow as Christian disciples and become involved in ministries that met all kinds of human needs. So, it is no surprise they were unable to give "public expression" to this new message. The substance of the message had changed. Nor is it a surprise that Morrison would write that the social gospel had come to a point of "arrested development."

Albert Day also saw the clergy-versus-laity divide as a critical problem within Methodism. He acknowledged that many pastors had been studying science, historical criticism, and philosophy, and as a result, many had undergone a literal revolution in their thinking on basic Christian doctrines and issues. But while all of this was taking place, the ministers were remaining very uncommunicative about it. He described it this way:

The result has been that while they themselves have accomplished a long intellectual and spiritual pilgrimage, their congregations have remained in the old traditional strongholds. One day some of the laymen became suspicious and began to ask questions, and before long the whole situation stood revealed. Between preachers and people there was discovered a gulf almost as great as that between Dives and Lazarus. Which was in Abraham's bosom and which was in hell is still a matter of debate.[22]

Day described the new teachings of liberalism as a "great break with tradition," though he welcomed them heartily. What alarmed him most was how far removed the laymen were from it all and the need for new frankness and increased communication with them.[23] For the laity, they were hearing a very different theology than they had known. They sensed a lack of candor from their pastors and became suspicious that something else was going on that their pastors would rather not discuss. And they were right in their suspicions.

Theological liberalism was rightly and accurately described as a "great break with tradition." In significant ways, it was directly contradicting the church's doctrinal tradition. I will say again, we are not speaking about mere nuances and subtle emphases here. We are talking about a substantive discontinuity with doctrines the American church had believed, preached, and taught for more than a hundred years. As we saw earlier, it was a *negation* of doctrines central to Methodism's Wesleyan tradition.

It is no wonder that many ministers at the time were inclined to remain "very uncommunicative" about their new theological views. Many in positions of leadership and pastors in the larger urban congregations had, indeed, undergone a literal revolution in their thinking on basic Christian doctrines. So drastic was the change that many were reluctant to be forthright with their laity about what they no longer believed concerning those essential doctrines. They knew the laity would find it devastating, thus many of them opted to remain quiet and uncommunicative.

Harold Paul Sloan once reported on a conversation he had had with a young liberal Methodist pastor. He asked the minister whether the people in his congregation were aware of his liberal beliefs. When the young pastor said no, Sloan asked him why not. The pastor replied that he avoided preaching on subjects that would expose his liberal views and that he "only revealed his positions at these points a little bit at a time." Needless to say, Sloan was distressed at such dishonesty, which he believed would result in "undermining" the church and its doctrines.[24]

Tensions and Divisions from the Holiness Controversy

One other major source of tension during this period came from the decades-long controversy centered around the Holiness Movement. This controversy, in fact, led to a serious division within Methodism between 1894 and on into the 1920s, during which time tens of thousands of Methodists left to start new Holiness and Pentecostal organizations and associations.[25] Understanding the breadth and emotion of this division helps us understand why many Methodists may have been reluctant to join in protest about allegations of doctrinal disloyalty among Methodist professors and leaders. They still remembered the painful divisions Methodism experienced in 1894 and the years immediately following.

The Holiness Movement was focused around the Wesleyan doctrine of "perfect love" or "entire sanctification," and its adherents were convinced they were being true to Wesley's crucial doctrine that had brought such vitality to the people called Methodists. These were orthodox, grassroots Methodists, often, but not always, from smaller communities and more rural settings.[26] These devout and dedicated Methodists believed that through conversion and the second subsequent experience of entire sanctification, in addition to living a full and victorious Christian life free from bondage to sinful practices, the major social ills of society also could be cured.[27]

This emphasis existed from the middle of the nineteenth century but was greatly revitalized by the organization of the National Association for the Promotion of Holiness in 1867. John L. Peters reported that by 1887, the association could report that it had held "sixty-seven national camp meetings and eleven Tabernacle meetings . . . distributed through sixteen states of the Union, extending to both shores of the Continent, and to the far-off East."[28]

In addition to having some 350 Holiness evangelists, the movement was prolific with numerous publishing ventures:

> In 1888 it was reported that not less than four publishing houses were engaged in the exclusive publication of holiness materials. Twenty-seven holiness journals were being periodically issued, most of them on a monthly basis. By 1892, there were forty-one such periodicals. Holiness literature was abundant.[29]

As the movement grew, the response of institutional Methodism moved from being supportive, to a guarded caution, and then in 1894, to opposition. Some of the Holiness advocates, it must be said, brought problems on themselves with an overemphasis on Christian perfection as an instantaneous "second work of grace," to the neglect of any gradual dimension that Wesley also acknowledged. Riley Case referred to these adherents as "Methodism's populist wing," and noted that without adequate supervision, some in the movement slipped into unhealthy extremism. Some evangelists were preaching a "sinless perfection" and unrealistic expectations, while others were adding additional subsequent works of grace. Beyond a second work of grace, some preached a third, fourth, and fifth blessing.[30]

For several decades the controversy raged within both the northern and southern branches of the Methodist Church. Animosity and accusation, charges and countercharges, and debate over instantaneous versus gradual understandings of sanctification continued in Methodist publications. Many Holiness advocates sincerely believed they were holding firmly to Wesley's doctrine of Christian perfection at a time when Methodism seemed in danger of losing it. And there was justification for that concern.

While most of the Holiness folks came from the smaller towns and more rural areas of the church, they also felt concerns about the new teachings of theology that seemed far removed from traditional Methodist doctrine. An estrangement was happening that left Holiness folks feeling more ill at ease in their denomination as they heard Methodism's institutional leaders making disparaging remarks about Methodism's Holiness advocates as well as about traditionalist, orthodox believers.

In 1894, the bishops' message to the 1894 General Conference addressed the issue by first affirming that perfect love, or Christian perfection, was a well-known teaching of Methodism. Then, however, the bishops went on to complain, "There has sprung up among us a party with holiness as a watch-word; they have holiness associations, holiness meetings, holiness preachers, holiness evangelists, and holiness property." They charged that the movement was too exclusive and also simplistic in its understanding of the experience of entire sanctification. While not questioning the sincerity and zeal of the Holiness advocates, the bishops nonetheless made this critical charge: "But we deplore their teaching and methods in so far as they claim a monopoly on the experience, practice, and advocacy of holiness, and separate themselves from the body of ministers and disciples."[31]

Many of the Holiness advocates felt their only option was to leave the Methodist Church to form new religious bodies, organizations, institutes, and denominations. A major movement out of the denomination began soon after the bishops' critical address and within just the next six years, no fewer than ten separate religious bodies came into existence with entire sanctification as their central doctrine. All were primarily Methodist in their former church affiliation.[32]

William Warren Sweet noted that from this period up until about 1926, "at least twenty-five holiness and Pentecostal bodies came into existence, most numerously in the Central West where their chief feeders, the Methodist bodies, were the most numerous."[33] Two of the larger groups spawned by the departure of the Holiness groups were the Church of the Nazarene and the Church of God (Anderson, Indiana). The sad reality is that Methodism lost tens of thousands of sincere, dedicated, and Wesleyan-oriented members during a period of about thirty years.

However, it needs to be said that historians of this period perhaps have not captured the full story of how many Methodist Holiness advocates resisted being "come-outers" and chose to remain in their church. Vinson Synan estimated that a third to a half of the four million Methodists in the 1890s were believers in Holiness and estimates that the "come-outers" probably numbered no more than one hundred thousand.[34] This would mean that a little fewer than two million Methodists sympathetic to the Holiness message were *still* in the denomination early in the 1900s. Joseph H. Smith, a leader of the Holiness Movement from the 1880s on into the 1940s said in 1912 that a "large majority" of those who identified themselves with the Holiness Movement still were a part of the Methodist denominations.[35]

Many Holiness loyalists loved their church and were loath to leave it. However, many of them also realized that something more than just Holiness teaching was at stake in the controversy. A laywoman who wrote in 1904 expressed sentiments that probably represented thousands of Methodists at the time:

> No, I do not believe that there should be a new church organized for the holiness people. . . . Yes, the old Methodism is what we holiness people hold to, and shall we withdraw from a church whose doctrines and polity are what we believe, because some New Methodists are trying to inject some new doctrine?[36]

Not only was the Holiness message a point of conflict, but the faithful Methodists who were a part of the Holiness Movement were also troubled at the realization that "some new doctrine" indeed, was being taught in their church. That realization was no doubt part of what made many Holiness advocates feel they had to leave the Methodist churches. But again, the overwhelming number of this group chose not to leave, though the controversy was bitter in many parts of the church.

Now, the point that I want to make here is that this bitter controversy and the resulting departure of members out of both the northern and southern Methodist churches had another, less obvious, but long-term impact on American Methodism. It influenced for years to come how Methodists viewed theological conversation.

Several decades of controversy and debate about the Holiness experience had taken its toll in the church. Many had grown tired of the debate. John Peters wrote that no matter how well phrased it might have been, "doctrinal polemic was finding a diminishing welcome."[37] The church had grown weary of it.

He illustrated his point with an incident from 1896. Methodist Bishop J. F. Berry received a letter and book from a James Mudge, who requested the bishop review his controversial work about the Holiness issue. Berry's reply is quite telling:

> I read your book with very great interest and thoroughly admired its clear, strong chapters. The fact is, however, I do not believe in controversies over the "Holiness" question. To me it looks like rather an unholy business. We have had in the Methodist Episcopal Church within the last twenty-five years so much debate on the subject that a good many people have in that way grown tired of and prejudiced against the doctrine. Don't you think we ought to stop debating about it now and begin to be holy?[38]

Indeed, the ongoing debate about the Holiness issue, which had carried on from the last quarter of the 1800s through the early 1900s, had gotten old. "There was a genuine weariness of controversy," wrote Peters. He added that pleas were made for conciliation and unity with even a call for a moratorium on "traditional doctrinal terms, especially since such terms were so often used with differing meanings by those who represented opposing points of view."[39]

Another Methodist leader exhorted the church: "Let us have done with theorizing, moralizing, philosophizing, and Wesleyizing on a teaching that shines in the New Testament with the clearness of the sun in the heavens."[40] This leader seemed to be saying that the theme of holiness is presented with "clearness" in the New Testament, so let's not worry about trying to understand it or find the biblical basis for the teaching. Let's just affirm it and live it. One wonders if this sentiment might reflect a church beginning to move from being biblically centered to being more experience centered. "Just affirm it and live it." The danger of such a view, of course, is that the church is always in need of Scripture to help it critique, inform, and interpret religious experience.

Peters's summary statement about what was happening within Methodism as a result of the Holiness controversy is simply this: "Theology was in bad odor."[41] One feels a profound sadness at such a statement. The cry was for an end to the controversies that had become such a distraction to the church. Methodist leaders were determined to bring about "a cessation of doctrinal hostilities."[42] The words of John J. Tigert reflected perfectly the church's mood as it sought conciliation and peace: "If the spirit of come-outism anywhere exists, let it be put away at once and forever. If the spirit of crush-outism has anywhere found expression, let it not be so as mentioned among brethren. . . . 'let us have peace.'"[43]

Tigert's plea was for peace. He wanted an end both to talk about leaving the church as well as talk about stamping out (crushing) those in the Holiness Movement. Indeed, theological fatigue had set in.

It is my conviction that for Methodism at the turn of the century, this weariness with theological dispute and a growing aspiration for peace, conciliation, and an end to controversy about doctrine had enormous implications for Methodism's theological future.

The Methodist Church was about to encounter the perfect storm. At the turn of the century, as we have seen, Methodism was facing sweeping intellectual and theological challenges. Theologians were returning from doing graduate studies in Germany under philosophers such as Ritschl, Harnack, and others. The philosophy of religion was replacing studies in historic Christian doctrine. Evolution and the New Science were presenting the church with intellectual challenges unlike anything it had experienced previously. Theological liberalism, the controversial "new theology," was emerging as an effort to save the Christian faith by supposedly making it relevant and intellectually respectable to those schooled in the new thought, as we have seen earlier. If ever there were a time when the church needed to be ready for a responsible theological engagement with the intellectual views of the culture of the day, this was a time.

Unfortunately, though, the mood within Methodism was for something altogether different. The ringing cry "let us have peace" was reverberating across the church and echoed by many. While some traditional Methodists expressed alarm about the new teachings finding their way into the seminaries and the Course of Study, others were reluctant to join in the protests. After all, these Methodists, both clergy and laity, still had fresh memories of the emotionally charged division and departure from Methodism of thousands of their colleagues over the bitter debate about holiness. To enter into theological controversy could well be the prelude to more ugly division. Many wanted to avoid such a thing at all costs.

At a time when the churches in the urban centers were faced with heart-wrenching social need and suffering, many pastors dismissed the theological concerns about liberalism, saying in so many words, "With all of the tragic suffering and human need we see around us, how can we waste time arguing about matters of theology?" It is a bit easier to understand, in this context, why journals carried articles decrying creeds and doctrinal formulation, which were referred to as mere "child's play," fit now only for the "museums." But what a tragic and devastating sentiment this was.

Looking back now, it is no surprise to see that when doctrinal issues arose, many found ways to avoid the controversy by constructing a narrative claiming that Wesley was much more interested in *experience* than in *doctrine*. Or that what was most important at the time, even as the church faced questionable doctrinal views, was that the church be faithful to the moral and ethical teachings of Jesus as it ministers to the poor, sick, marginalized, and suffering. The crushing human need manifest so painfully in the cities, many argued, demanded social action, not doctrinal debate.

This context helps us understand, I believe, why the General Conference of 1928—when presented with Harold Paul Sloan's ten thousand petitions from forty-one states charging doctrinal disloyalty in the church—chose *not* to take action in response to his enormous, grassroots initiative. The memory of the departure of thousands that had taken place from 1896 until the mid-1920s was still fresh in the minds of Methodists. Many believed that more doctrinal controversy in the church would once again lead to division and further loss of members for the Methodist Church. There was simply no time for that.

So at a time when Methodism desperately needed to challenge, question, and refute the new theology that was emerging, with its modifications and denials of historic tenets of the faith, it had forces at work internally that hindered a united response to the challenge. Instead, the mood of the period drove the church to *minimize* the importance of doctrine and creedal formulation and *maximize* the importance of the church's social and ethical teachings.

The claim made by many of Methodism's intellectual leaders was this: Methodists, and even Wesley himself, were not primarily interested in doctrine but in experience; and furthermore, Methodism was never a doctrinal or creedal denomination. These claims served a highly useful purpose. They were repeated increasingly and readily welcomed by many at the time and were useful in cloaking the enormous doctrinal transition taking place within Methodism during this period. They were also timely and convenient new sentiments that would help relegate doctrine to a secondary, even remote, place in the life of the Methodist Church for years to come.

Certainly, and most unfortunately for Methodism's future theological health, as Peters graphically noted, "theology was in bad odor."

A denomination that desired a moratorium on doctrinal debate and wanted to be done with "theorizing, moralizing, philosophizing, and Wesleyizing" about the Holiness issue would likely have a similar disdain about theological debate on other doctrinal questions as well. With these strong and widely spread sentiments among much of its leadership, Methodism was left in a highly vulnerable situation.

We have seen in this chapter, then, that there was serious resistance to the new teaching of theological liberalism and the accompanying social gospel—far more than most United Methodists are aware today. There were tensions between those clergy and theologians who embraced liberalism and many Methodist pastors, and some theologians as well, who did not. Terms such as "orthodox," "traditionalist," and even "fundamentalist" were used pejoratively against those who would not affirm the new doctrine. To describe broadly what happened, there were two major tributaries that emerged in Methodism from this era: one representing those who had studied abroad or been influenced by theological liberalism in their seminary training, and the other representing those who were more likely to have entered the ministry through the Conference Course of Study. The latter would likely not have embraced the new theology. They would have considered themselves more in the classic Methodist tradition, doctrinally.

There were also tensions and a widening gap between Methodist clergy and laity as the latter sensed something was changing in the life of their church, but they were not aware of what it was. However, laity sensed that some Methodist clergy had changed the substance of their preaching but obviously did not want to discuss it, preferring to be uncommunicative about it.

And there were alienations that led to schism on the part of many dedicated Methodists who believed that the church was both leaving its classic doctrines and also abandoning its distinctive Wesleyan message of holiness. Fortunately, an overwhelming majority who affirmed Methodism's Holiness message remained, choosing not to be "come-outers," but rather to remain and stay loyal to the Methodism they had known all of their lives. In the next chapter, we will look briefly at the significant body that remained within Methodism and one of that group's most beloved preachers and educators.

Chapter 9

A Remaining Evangelical Presence

TO UNDERSTAND THE impact of theological liberalism, we must visit again the matter of how widely accepted the new doctrine was within American Methodism in the early decades of the twentieth century. We saw in the last chapter that clergy had sharp differences among themselves and that laity found themselves bewildered at the changes they perceived in their pastors, though they did not always understand the nature of those changes.

Certainly, many theologians, seminary professors, bishops, urban clergy, denominational staff, and editors of publications embraced theological liberalism with enthusiasm. But what about Methodism as a whole? There is reason to believe that most non-seminary-trained clergy and most local church laity did not embrace the new theology. In fact, there remained within Methodism a much greater evangelical presence than is normally thought.

In his unpublished doctoral dissertation, cited earlier, Howard Glen Spann observed that Methodist history before 1900 is usually focused primarily on revivalism, personal morality, and the rapid growth of the denomination. However, he said that "after 1900, the historical accent has fallen on the church's involvement in social ministry, liberal theology, and ecumenical impulses."[1] He cited historian Charles W. Ferguson, who said, with some condescension, about this transition from revivalism to social ministry, that "Methodism had returned from the West."[2] In other words, the revivalism that led to Methodist growth in the Western frontier of America had been replaced by a more mature, sophisticated, and intellectual approach believed to be more suited to take on the social ills of the urban, industrialized communities in the East. Methodists were becoming better educated and more cultured.

Having looked carefully at the historians who have covered this period in American Methodist history, Spann claimed that most of them have little to say of "any remaining evangelical presence within Methodism in the twentieth century."[3] He believed this was a serious oversight.

An example Spann cited is Frederick Norwood's *Sourcebook of American Methodism*, which was a collection of "documents through which Methodism is to be understood historically."[4] While the editor of the *Sourcebook* claimed the documents included are "comprehensive," an examination of the documents from the twentieth century reveals that only one selection "representing evangelicalism found its way into the *Sourcebook*," and it was from the 1920s.[5] While the *Sourcebook*, published in 1982, claimed to take into account the historical trends that had come into focus as recently as the "last decade," which would have included the 1970s, there were scarcely any references to evangelicalism, which Spann said is a "glaring example of a more general neglect of evangelical themes within twentieth-century American Methodist historiography."[6] He added that "few and far between are the historical accounts, either in popular histories or scholarly works, of the continued strong evangelical presence in the Methodist Church since 1900."[7] It is a curious omission about a church that was characterized from its very beginning as evangelical and revivalistic.

The "Great Deep" of Methodism

How would such an oversight of Methodist evangelicalism happen? Spann cited a fascinating, and plausible, explanation in an "oceanic analogy" from Ronald E. Osborn's *The Spirit of American Christianity*.[8] Osborn compared a church's theologians and professors of religion to the surface waves in the ocean. These waves are "constantly in movement," while "the winds and occasional storms" that drive them are the "contemporary schools and trends, the controversies of the day." This "superficial portion of the ocean presents itself to the eye of the casual observer," but below this fairly shallow surface, Osborn noted a second level of religious life, the "currents and crosscurrents" like the Gulf Stream and other ocean currents. These "represent the major movements of Christian theology which affect the life of the churches and the preaching of the gospel for generations" or longer. And, says Osborn, "it is these two 'upper levels' of our sea of faith which generally attract the attention of scholars and writers."[9]

However, underneath these upper currents is what Osborn called the "great deep," which corresponds to the "faith of the people." This deep has "pulsations of its own movement," but it is largely "untroubled by the waves of surface storms and relatively undisturbed by the currents."[10] Osborn's point was that the vast depth of the popular faith of the people is something that both theologians, with their intellectual sophistication, and church historians tend to overlook. It is Osborn's contention that in spite of the theological developments and emergence of liberalism within twentieth-century American Protestantism, the "average American Christian" has retained a largely evangelical, traditional faith.[11]

Spann believed that Osborn's analysis was applicable to the recent history of the Methodist Church. Certainly, during the last hundred years, the theological surface of Methodism took on a pronounced liberal character, as seen in our seminaries, theologians, and institutions of higher education. And on the "second level" following Osborn's analogy, many of the shapers of theological opinion within Methodism—editors, writers, bishops, board and agency staff, and some clergy—have generally reflected the liberalism of the professors and theologians from our denominational seminaries. But Spann was convinced that "a reservoir of evangelical faith has persisted within the Methodist 'deep,' faith that in its broad outlines—and even in some specifics—is largely unchanged from the faith of traditional Methodism."[12] The echoes of this faith have not always been articulated clearly in the official positions of the denomination, but he believed, nonetheless, that "traditional Christian orthodoxy has retained the loyalty of millions of Methodists in the modern era."[13]

If the analogy of the "great deep" was accurate for twentieth-century Methodism, and there is reason to believe it is, then it helps explain a number of realities. It helps explain why there had been continued voices of protest throughout most of the twentieth century by those in the church who found themselves differing strongly with the denomination's liberal direction. (We will look briefly at some of those voices later as well as in the final chapter.) It also helps us understand why Methodism (and, since 1968, United Methodism) seemed to be a conservative and traditionalist denomination at the local church level, led by a more liberal leadership at the conference and national level.

The "great deep" analogy, in fact, seemed to find confirmation in a major survey done by the United Methodist General Council on Ministries (GCOM) in 1988. Researchers polled both lay and clergy delegates to the 1988 General Conference and then surveyed non-delegate lay and clergy members on the same issues. The results of the survey were highly significant. "While theological liberalism continues to dominate the seminaries, boards, agencies, and many influential pulpits of United Methodism, United Methodists at the grassroots clearly are marching to a more conservative tune," wrote R. Michael Sigler in a major article about the study.[14] A remarkable 69 percent of United Methodist laity (non-delegates to General Conference) defined themselves as *conservative* on both theological and moral issues.

Sigler summarized that even after years of liberalism in our denominational seminaries and pulpits, and after many thousands have left the church because of its liberal leanings, "still roughly 70 percent of the people in our pews hold to a conservative set of beliefs!"[15] Equally surprising, some 52 percent of non-delegate clergy defined themselves as conservative, in spite of the liberalism of the denominational seminaries.[16]

One could readily conclude that these nearly 70 percent of our laity and 52 percent of our clergy, following Osborn's oceanic analogy, were representative of the "great deep" of United Methodism. These numbers represent a substantial majority of United Methodists who just twenty-five years ago considered themselves orthodox in their beliefs, though their denominational and institutional leaders were generally considered to be liberal, theologically. If this reality has changed any since then, it is more likely the denomination has become yet more orthodox. But it is a reality that helps us understand how consultants found in their research a pervasive distrust within United Methodism.

The Early Twentieth Century: A Period of Resistance

One would conclude from a careful look at these early decades of the twentieth century that the resistance to theological liberalism was real and multifaceted. Unfortunately, however, it still remains a part of Methodism's "forgotten history," as we mentioned earlier. While the new theology was enthusiastically embraced by key Methodist theologians, seminary-trained pastors, editors, and some denominational leaders, it was not embraced by many other clergy or by most laity in local Methodist churches. While Methodism did not experience the upheaval of a fundamentalist/modernist controversy during the decade of the 1920s, it did experience a time of steady and prolonged protests and challenges to the doctrinal changes taking place.

William R. Hutchison claimed that some Protestants chose to associate with the term "liberal" because it was popular and in vogue, but many of them were likely not opting for all of the substance of theological liberalism. He stated that "all the evidence indicates that 'liberal' was rarely a preferred term outside the theological seminaries and the more sophisticated periodicals."[17] Referring more specifically to Methodism, John G. McEllhenney argued that while by 1930 Methodist theologians and professors may have embraced liberalism, generally, the "older patterns of evangelical theology inherited from the previous century were still dominant."[18] Thus, the stage was set for ongoing doctrinal controversies and disputes within twentieth-century Methodism.

Henry Clay Morrison: A Voice for Holiness and against Liberalism

We looked earlier at voices of protest raised in the early part of the twentieth century against theological liberalism. Those included George Wilson, John Alfred Faulkner, Edwin Lewis, Harold Paul Sloan, and others.

Another significant voice on behalf of the Wesleyan Holiness message and *against* the popular new theology of theological liberalism was Henry Clay Morrison. Born in Bedford, Kentucky, in 1857, he was converted at a Methodist revival at the age of thirteen. A few years later he sensed God's call to preach and soon entered the Methodist ministry. After a year of study at Vanderbilt University, Morrison returned to the pastorate and quickly moved into positions of leadership in the Kentucky Conference of the Methodist Episcopal Church, South. He soon became pastor of a Methodist church in Frankfort, the capital of Kentucky, and was chaplain for the state legislature. In 1890, he left local church ministry to become a traveling evangelist.

Morrison was a strong advocate of the Holiness message of entire sanctification and launched a paper in 1888 called the *Old Methodist* to spread Holiness teaching. In 1893 Morrison reported some fifteen thousand subscribers to his paper, and by 1920, the publication, renamed the *Pentecostal Herald*, had doubled to thirty thousand subscribers.[19] One might say that Morrison was a voice for the "great deep" of Methodism during this period. He was connecting with a vast reservoir of traditional Wesleyan and Holiness Methodists across America.

It would be difficult to overstate the impact of H. C. Morrison's preaching and ministry, as well as the sheer breadth of his influence on the people called Methodists. He served as president of Asbury College (now University) in Wilmore, Kentucky, and took the lead in launching Asbury Theological Seminary (also in Wilmore) in 1923 as a graduate school to train ministers and preachers in the Wesleyan Holiness tradition.

Morrison, a gifted and anointed preacher of the Word, was enormously popular across both northern and southern Methodism. Methodist bishops Mallalieu, Joyce, and McCabe invited Morrison and Joseph H. Smith to hold Holiness meetings at the General Conference of 1904 in Los Angeles, California. The meetings were so well received that Bishop Mallalieu, the chairman of the denomination's General Commission on Evangelism, asked them to preach again at the 1908 General Conference in Baltimore.[20] Glen Spann wrote that "beginning in 1913, Morrison preached in fifty-two sessions of twenty-six different annual conferences of Southern Methodism." Beyond that, he preached before eight annual conferences of the northern church and three annual conferences of the united church after the union of 1939.[21]

Morrison was elected twice—in 1902 and 1906—as a delegate to the General Conference of the Methodist Episcopal Church, South. In 1909 he was awarded an honorary doctor of divinity degree from Ohio Northern University, an institution related to the Methodist Episcopal Church, North. Morrison's wide popularity within both the northern and southern branches of Methodism is indicative of the strong Holiness presence still remaining in the Methodist Church—the tens of thousands who chose not to be "come-outers."

Morrison was an extraordinarily gifted person. He was powerful in the pulpit, constantly in demand at camp meetings, an effective writer and editor, an able fund-raiser, an insightful apologist for orthodox Christianity, and a soon-to-be educator and administrator. During the first decade of his presidency of Asbury College

(1910–1920), he received numerous letters from graduates of Asbury as well as from seminary students who had attended other Christian colleges, telling of seminary professors who did not believe major Christian doctrines such as the inspiration of Scripture, original sin, the atonement of Jesus Christ, and Christ's promised return one day.[22] He began to address these concerns through editorials and articles in the *Pentecostal Herald*. These reports led him to begin envisioning a seminary where young pastors could be trained in the evangelical and Wesleyan doctrinal tradition.

In 1920, Morrison published an article in the *Pentecostal Herald* addressing the problem of pastors who had been influenced by theological liberalism:

> We have many pastors today who have practically given up the orthodox faith; they do not hesitate to deny the inspiration of a very large portion of the Holy Scripture. They deny . . . the fall of man, the existence of original sin, the depravity of the race, the need of regeneration, [and] the future punishment of the wicked.[23]

Just two years later, he wrote about the importance of the right kind of seminary training: "There is nothing more important than a theological seminary absolutely true to the teaching of the Holy Scriptures, sending out a body of young men well trained with a gracious experience of . . . the Holy Spirit and genuinely true to the Scriptures as interpreted and preached by John Wesley."[24]

The next year, 1923, under his leadership, Asbury Theological Seminary was launched on the campus of Asbury College.

Morrison and his colleagues often expressed their disappointment that "many Methodist leaders who personally believed the doctrines of historical Christianity remained silent about Methodism's theological drift."[25] It was the same complaint made by Harold Paul Sloan and others that we noted earlier. G. W. Ridout, a friend of Morrison's, asked a bishop, "Why do you not take a stand with others holding as you do to Methodist doctrine?" The bishop replied, "Because I am afraid of splitting the church in two."[26]

Unfortunately, early in the 1920s, Methodist bishops who knew the church was not abiding by its doctrinal standards were opting to stand for institutional *unity* rather than for doctrinal *truth*. This strong sentiment among the bishops was likely to have been the reason for Bishop Adna Leonard's sudden withdrawal of his support and involvement in Harold Paul Sloan's Methodist League for Faith and Life, as discussed in chapter 4.

Though Morrison spoke candidly about the doctrinal drift in Methodism, he also spoke graciously as a Christian gentleman. But he did so without fear, addressing the problem head-on. He also was not willing to let his disappointment at the silence of many orthodox clergy go unaddressed:

> It is not worth while for any class of men, however devout or sincere they may be, to seek to justify their silence at this critical period in the history of the Christian Church, by insisting that religious controversy is sinful. Is it sinful to condemn error, to guard the people against the wolves of skepticism? A popular skepticism is making startling headway in the Church, and we should have the candor to look . . . facts in the face, and then use all legitimate means to save the people from the fearful blight of infidelity.[27]

These words were obviously in response to the popular sentiment among some Methodist leaders at the time that for them to give serious attention to doctrinal matters could well spawn division once again among the Methodist Churches (both north and south). Here, then, was the curious charge by some that to call attention to doctrinal neglect and infidelity would result in controversy and thus, would, itself, be "sinful."

Morrison's ministry of preaching, writing, educating, and speaking out on behalf of the evangelical Wesleyan message and against theological liberalism covered more than six decades. The publication he began in 1888 was still being published at his death in 1942—an amazing span of fifty-four years. He had wide support and was highly respected by many leaders in both the northern and southern churches. His writings in the *Pentecostal Herald* drew support from many prominent leaders who agreed with him on the critical importance of providing a sound, biblical theological education for future ministers. Those supporters included Harold Paul Sloan, E. Stanley Jones, James M. Buckley, numerous Methodist bishops, and thousands of pastors and laypeople across the country.[28]

Morrison died in 1942 during a preaching campaign in the First Methodist Church in Elizabethton, Tennessee.[29] The last sermon he preached was on the evening of March 23 on "How to Win a Sinner to Christ." The next day, he fell ill and died quietly while resting in a chair.

Henry Clay Morrison was a strong and much-loved leader in his day, a man who used his many gifts to proclaim the Christian faith in the Wesleyan tradition. He also did all he could to oppose the emergence of the new doctrine, the theological liberalism that he believed was having such a devastating impact on the church. To his credit, while he faithfully defended the essentials of the orthodox Christian faith, his writings consistently "displayed a respectful and courteous tone toward those with whom he disagreed theologically."[30]

At his funeral, Methodist bishop Urban Valentine Darlington said, "I doubt if the death of any one man in Methodism brings so much sorrow as this. I doubt if there is a man in the world who has meant more to so many people."[31] Methodist bishop Arthur J. Moore, a friend and admirer of Morrison, wrote: "To him, more than any other one man, we are indebted for keeping this original standard of Methodism alive in the modern church."[32] Moore is generally considered to have been one of Methodism's great bishops during that period.

Roy Smith, editor of the *New York Christian Advocate*, wrote this moving tribute:

A tall tree has fallen in the forest, but it went down with a great shout of victory. He died as he lived . . . in the midst of a campaign for souls. . . . And in the midst of the sorrow occasioned by his going, tens of thousands will breathe a prayer of gratitude for the fact that his shadow fell upon their lives to heal them.[33]

Just a few weeks after Morrison's memorial service, E. Stanley Jones preached in Asbury College's Hughes Auditorium, where Morrison's service had been held. He spoke of how Morrison had meant so much to him. The great missionary to India and Christian statesman said:

I stood beside his grave this afternoon [and] prayed that the mantle of his life might fall upon some of the rest of us . . . that single-minded fervor, that one pointedness of mind, that one holding to a goal through thick and thin, where [we] could say, "this one thing I do," that passion to lead men to Christ, can fall upon us.[34]

These words of tribute came from people who were well-known in the world of Methodism during this period, several almost legendary in Methodism at the time. One senses their deep admiration and high regard for Morrison's preaching, writing, and educational leadership.

Morrison's voice was an authentic voice on behalf of the gospel in the Wesleyan and Holiness tradition. His was also a voice speaking prophetically *against* theological liberalism, which he saw as destructive and dangerous for the well-being and future of the Methodist Church. Morrison was not an irresponsible church critic. Nor was he a separatist from Methodism. He was a lover of his church. While he disagreed vehemently with many of its theologians and professors, he chose to stay and lift his voice on behalf of Wesleyan Christianity in the Holiness tradition. He did so lovingly and graciously, and was admired by Methodist leaders—at all levels of the church.

In addition, he founded a theological seminary, which today has some sixteen hundred students on three campuses (Wilmore, Kentucky;

Orlando, Florida; and Memphis, Tennessee), where some 60 percent of the students are consistently United Methodist and most of the others represent smaller denominations in the Wesleyan tradition.

Morrison's voice and influence spanned more than five decades as he spoke on behalf of a large, remaining evangelical Methodist presence that could well be referred to as Methodism's "great deep."

Now, in these final chapters, we will look at what I believe has been the enduring legacy of theological liberalism. The question we must ask is what impact this era of upheaval and doctrinal change has had on Methodism throughout the twentieth and into the twenty-first century. Clearly, the tensions and doctrinal transitions that resulted as theological liberalism emerged to accommodate the Christian faith to the new secular and scientific worldview during the early 1900s have had a deep and lasting influence on Methodism right up to the present time.

Chapter 10

A History of Protests and Calls for Reform

AS ONE LOOKS at Methodism in the twentieth century, one realizes it has been, indeed, a period of prolonged protests, challenges, and attempts at reform, as mentioned earlier. The voices raised in protest early in the century were responding to the troubling new doctrine. They believed something destructive was happening to the great doctrines of the church. We noted prominent theologians and pastors, including George Wilson, John Alfred Faulkner, Edwin Lewis, Harold Paul Sloan, and others who addressed this concern.

During this era, as noted in the previous chapter, Henry Clay Morrison also emerged as a prominent voice of protest about the new theology and its harmful effects on the church. His popular magazine reached more than thirty thousand subscriptions during his years of active ministry and was the rallying cry for hundreds of thousands of Methodists. He felt so passionately about what was happening to Methodism's historic doctrine that he founded a new theological seminary to train Methodist clergy faithfully in the teachings of the historic faith and Wesleyan doctrinal tradition

Another major voice of doctrinal protest for Methodism was Robert Pierce Shuler, who became pastor of Trinity Methodist Church

in Los Angeles in 1920, an appointment he held until his death in
1965. Shuler took a struggling church and saw it grow to some five
thousand members throughout the 1930s. During the 1940s and
'50s, he edited and published the *Methodist Challenge*, which was
among other things a strong voice in *opposition* to theological liberalism. Shuler published the *Methodist Challenge* until 1960, when at
eighty years of age, health issues forced him to retire. Reading some
back issues of the '40s and '50s, I discovered Shuler's concerns about
liberalism in the Methodist churches during his day sounded remarkably familiar to concerns still being raised today.[1]

The Good News Movement

Protests and attempts at reform continued. In 1967, the Good News
movement was launched when Charles W. Keysor, a Methodist pastor
in Elgin, Illinois, published a small digest-sized magazine that he called
Good News. The impetus for the magazine came when Keysor penned
an article titled "Methodism's Silent Minority" for the July 14, 1966,
issue of the *New Christian Advocate* (Methodism's denominational
clergy journal).[2] Keysor wrote on behalf of those he claimed were not
represented in the "higher councils" or leadership of the denomination, those who would be called "evangelicals" or "conservatives" or,
as he believed was a more accurate description, "orthodox." These
were Methodists who believed that the Christian faith "is compre-
hensively declared in Holy Scripture and is succinctly summarized
in the Apostles' Creed."[3] Keysor noted five foundational doctrines
that constitute a common ground for those who are truly orthodox
Christians. Those doctrines included, he believed: (1) the inspiration
of Scripture; (2) the virgin birth of Christ; (3) the substitutionary
atonement of Christ; (4) the physical resurrection of Christ; and (5)
the return of Christ. Beyond these foundational doctrines, Keysor
acknowledged there was "an enormous area of Christian truth where
orthodox Christians disagree vigorously." However, he also noted that

in many a Methodist mind, there was "a deep intolerance toward the silent minority who are orthodox."[4]

The response to Keysor's "Silent Minority" article was amazing, as more than two hundred letters and phone calls came in, most from Methodist pastors. Two themes surfaced in those responses. Many said, "I thought I was the only one left in the church who believes these things," and others said "I feel so alone—so cut off from the leadership of my church." As he prayed about the letters and phone calls, Keysor, a trained journalist before entering the Methodist ministry, decided he must do something. He would launch a magazine that would affirm the evangelical message of the Wesleys and Francis Asbury. He did just that and *Good News* magazine was born, the first issue coming out in March 1967.[5]

Just two months after the publication of the first issue of *Good News*, Keysor chose a board of twelve people, and the movement was incorporated as a Forum for Scriptural Christianity, Inc. At the movement's first national convocation in 1970 in Dallas, Texas, some sixteen hundred United Methodists registered, and evening crowds of some three thousand packed the Adolphus Hotel ballroom. They came from all across the United States and felt the emotion and excitement as might a family, long separated, finally coming together again. (Methodism's "great deep"?) Discouraged United Methodists, both clergy and laity, found hope that they weren't alone in their evangelical concerns and convictions.

The ministry of Good News, which continues today, has been focused on doctrinal issues from the start. While the denomination has continued to affirm in its *Book of Discipline* the historic doctrines of Methodism, Good News has always expressed concerns that these doctrines are being neglected, ignored, or reconstructed. Most of the early initiatives of Good News were efforts to address problems it saw with doctrinal and theological matters.

One of Good News's first concerns was with the widespread dissatisfaction with the denomination's Sunday school literature. This was where weak, if not unacceptable, church school curricula intersected with local churches who were irate about the poor quality of the materials. There was also dissatisfaction with the official confirmation materials from the United Methodist Publishing House. In 1975, Good News published its first edition of *We Believe*, a confirmation series for junior high youth that was enthusiastically received and still has broad usage in United Methodist churches today, having been revised, updated, and marketed by Bristol House, Ltd. in Fort Valley, Georgia. In the spring of 2015, Bristol House closed its doors after nearly twenty-five years of ministry. *We Believe* is now marketed by the Seedbed publishing group at Asbury Theological Seminary.

In 1972, the United Methodist General Conference adopted a new doctrinal statement, "Our Theological Task," to be included in the *Book of Discipline*. The new statement affirmed the principle of theological pluralism, which was undefined and confusing, as we saw earlier. Though perhaps not the original intent, the statement allowed many of our pastors and theologians to embrace doctrines far beyond the orbit of scriptural Christianity, believing this was allowed because of our new principle of theological pluralism. Good News continued to question, critique, and criticize the ambiguous concept of theological pluralism, which we believe played a major role in the decision of the 1984 General Conference to authorize a new doctrinal statement for the denomination. The theological commission, chaired by Bishop Earl G. Hunt Jr., brought a new and stronger statement, which was adopted overwhelmingly at the 1988 General Conference. The term "theological pluralism" had been removed and in its place was the new guiding principle for doing theology—"the primacy of Scripture."

In 1974, two years after General Conference passed the statement affirming theological pluralism, the Good News board of directors authorized a "Theology and Doctrine Task Force" to prepare a fresh new statement of "scriptural Christianity," which was to remain faithful to both the Methodist and Evangelical United Brethren traditions. In 1975, the task force presented its statement to the Good News board, and it was adopted at its summer meeting at Lake Junaluska, thus becoming known as the Junaluska Affirmation. (For the full text of the Junaluska Affirmation, see appendix A.) Interestingly, Albert Outler at Perkins School of Theology and primary author of "Our Theological Task" praised Good News for being the only group within the church to respond to his challenge for United Methodists to "do theology."

In 1976, Good News began publishing a newsletter, *Catalyst*, which was, and is yet today, sent free to all United Methodist seminarians, with the goal of making them aware of evangelical scholarly resources. In 1977, Good News sent teams to most all of our official United Methodist seminaries, engaging them in dialogue and encouraging them toward greater openness to evangelical faculty, course materials, and library resources.

In 1974, a group of evangelical United Methodists from twenty-three states gathered in Dallas, Texas, to address their concerns about the denomination's world missions program. Major concerns included the mission board's preoccupation with social and political issues, the declining number of overseas missionaries, and the board's lack of concern for matters of faith—such as assisting the national church in evangelism, the fulfillment of the Great Commission, and helping with the planting of new churches. Out of this gathering came the Evangelical Missions Council (EMC), which became an official part of Good News's ministry in 1976. In the fall of 1983, the EMC leadership was a part of a larger gathering of United Methodists in St. Louis at which time the Mission Society was planned. It was then launched in February 1984.[6] The Mission Society was founded as a supplemental sending agency, committed to helping United Methodists who felt called by God get to the mission field. Its purpose was not to compete with the official United Methodist Mission board, but to help folks serve in places where the gospel had not yet been heard or heeded.

Now let's return to church school literature for a moment. Longtime Good News board member Riley Case made the point that while Methodism's grassroots (the "great deep"?) may not have understood all the finer doctrinal issues in the seminaries and among boards and agencies, they did have great frustration about the denomination's church school curriculum. It was here that United Methodists "were confronted almost weekly by Sunday school literature that seemed at odds with their own understanding of the Christian faith."[7]

Case cited a classic example of how during this period there were still those in official positions or represented in official publications who did not affirm the supernatural elements of the Christian faith. Consider, as just one example, an audacious statement from the spring 1969 issue of *United Methodist Teacher I and II:* "The drama of Jesus would be far stronger and make a far greater appeal to this post-Christian age without all this supernatural claptrap brought in at the end with a dead man suddenly brought back to life again." Such a sentiment sounds like a refrain from the 1920s, when theological liberalism was questioning, even putting aside, the supernatural elements of the faith, including the Apostles' Creed. The unbelievable curriculum article went on to say, "Wouldn't the story of Jesus of Nazareth be more powerful and truer to itself in being less self-centered, if his life had ended in death?"[8] For orthodox United Methodists, such sentiments were infuriating and simply inexplicable. The resurrection of our Lord being described as "supernatural claptrap"! One nearly gasps at such language!

Case wrote that "otherwise loyal Sunday school teachers and parents were convinced something was wrong, although they weren't always sure what it was." But he added, rightly, "From the Good News perspective the problem was not just weak theology, but weak theology (or worse) forced upon churches." This was because the United Methodist General Conference had recently mandated that only "official" curriculum could be used in Methodist churches. This would be, of course, materials "planned, written, and edited by theological liberals, and there were no evangelical alternatives."[9]

More could be said about Good News, which continues as a ministry of renewal and reform to the present day. But the point being made here is that for more than forty-nine years, this ministry representing orthodox United Methodists has continued its witness on behalf of scriptural Christianity, while also challenging theological liberalism and its more recent manifestations within the denomination.

Additional Grassroots Protests and Declarations

Numerous other expressions of disagreement, protest, and concern could be cited during recent decades.

The Houston Declaration. In 1987, forty-eight leading United Methodist ministers from forty-two churches in eighteen states gathered in Houston to draft what would be known the Houston Declaration. (For the full text of the Houston Declaration, see appendix B.) It was a statement warning the denomination about moving away from traditional Christian doctrine. It affirmed strong support for three central United Methodist positions: (1) the primacy of Scripture; (2) the traditional language of the Holy Trinity as "Father, Son and Holy Spirit"; and (3) the ban against the ordination of individuals practicing homosexuality (the integrity of ordained ministry). The organizing ministers of the Houston gathering included James B. Buskirk, Maxie D. Dunnam, Ira Gallaway, William H. Hinson, J. Ellsworth Kalas, John Ed Mathison, and O. Gerald Trigg. They called both clergy and laity "to join with us as persons who have been called to follow Christ and give our lives to advancing the gospel and the historic Christian Faith." Then, just a few months later, a group of forty-seven prominent United Methodist laypersons met in Chicago in February 1988 and issued "A Call to Action," a laity statement in support of the Houston Declaration. (For the full text of "A Call to Action," see appendix C.)

The Louisville Declaration. In July 1990, nearly one thousand United Methodists gathered in Louisville, Kentucky, for a "Convocation on World Mission and Evangelism." The event was jointly sponsored by Good News, the Mission Society for United Methodists, a Foundation for Theological Education, and the National Association of United Methodist Evangelists. On the final morning, participants were invited to join in expressing support for a statement that had been prepared and distributed the previous evening for reflection and prayerful feedback. The statement, "The Louisville Declaration: A Call to Faithfulness in Mission," called United Methodists to "reaffirm that Jesus Christ is the only Savior of people everywhere," and for renewed dedication to evangelization at home and around the world, and urged the denomination "to recognize that at the heart of our church's crisis is a defection from her essential Wesleyan doctrine." The statement was affirmed by near unanimous consensus and circulated across the church. (For the full text of the Louisville Declaration, see appendix D.)

The Memphis Declaration. Then, in January of 1992, more than one hundred United Methodist clergy and laity gathered in Memphis, Tennessee, again to express concerns about the theological direction of the denomination. The gathering issued a statement that would "challenge United Methodists to live more faithfully as the body of Jesus Christ, under his lordship. This involves confessing, proclaiming and living the Apostolic faith." The first statement in what would become known as the Memphis Declaration was the affirmation that "God revealed himself in Jesus Christ, the only way of divine salvation." Dr. Maxie Dunnam, then senior minister at Christ United Methodist Church in Memphis, served as host pastor and chairman of the Coordinating Committee for the gathering. At a press conference at the 1992 General Conference, just three months after the Memphis gathering, Dunnam and other prominent evangelical clergy and laity were present with bags filled with petitions containing some 212,000 signatures *affirming* the Memphis Declaration—an unprecedented grassroots expression by United Methodists from every state and every annual conference in the denomination. Dunnam believed these were tangible expressions of hope for a much-needed renewal of the church. (For the full text of the Memphis Declaration, see appendix E.)

The Confessing Movement within the United Methodist Church. Then, in April 1994, ninety-two United Methodists gathered in Atlanta, Georgia, to consult about the future of the United Methodist Church. Those attending came out of concern for the crisis presented by the church's liberal theology and doctrinal trends they feared could split the denomination. Three prominent United Methodist leaders convened the gathering: Bishop William R. Cannon (then retired); Maxie Dunnam, then pastor of Christ United Methodist Church in Memphis and president-elect of Asbury Theological Seminary; and Thomas C. Oden, then professor of theology at the School of Theology at Drew University.

Leadership of the group said they expected to go beyond just issuing written documents. In a statement representing the consensus of the gathering, "An Invitation to the Church," they said: "In order to enact the *Discipline*'s call to 'doctrinal reinvigoration,' and to avoid schism and prevent mass exodus, we intend to form a Confessing Movement within the United Methodist Church." It was clear that the heart of the group's concern was the church's doctrinal failing and neglect. (For the full text of "An Invitation to the Church," see appendix F.)

The document said in the opening paragraph: "The United Methodist Church is at the crossroads. We face the peril of abandoning the Christian faith, thereby becoming unfaithful disciples of Jesus Christ." It went on to say, "The causes of the crisis are complex and multiple. However, we believe that the central cause is our abandonment of the truth of the gospel of Jesus Christ as revealed in Scripture and asserted in the classic Christian tradition and historic ecumenical creeds." It became even more specific, noting: "Specifically, we have equivocated regarding the person of Jesus Christ and his atoning work as the unique Savior of the world." These were doctrinal matters that went right to the core of classic Christian belief.

Just a year later, in April 1995, as a follow-up to the 1994 Atlanta meeting, more than nine hundred United Methodists gathered in Atlanta for the first national meeting of the Confessing Movement within the United Methodist Church. In the Confessional Statement issued by the new movement at this gathering, it declared that "the United Methodist Church is now incapable of confessing with one voice the orthodox Trinitarian faith, particularly Jesus Christ as the Son of God, the Savior of the world, and the Lord of history and the Church." The Confessing Movement within the United Methodist Church was launched with strong grassroots support from across the denomination. (For the full text of the Confessional Statement see appendix G.)

At its second national gathering, held in Cincinnati in 1996, the Confessing Movement moved ahead to employ a full-time executive director[10] and establish a central office (in Indianapolis, Indiana) with several full-time staff, and a national board of directors to give guidance to the movement. The Confessing Movement continues today as a vibrant ministry on behalf of doctrinal renewal and reform within the denomination.

One cannot miss the clear, unmistakable theme running through these various renewal organizations and national gatherings. What was their concern? It was and is a deep, abiding concern about matters of doctrine within the United Methodist Church. The perception among those involved is that the church is in a serious doctrinal crisis. Consider the phrases being used, such as, "the peril of abandoning the Christian faith," "our abandonment of the truth of the gospel of Jesus Christ," "equivocated regarding the person of Jesus Christ and his atoning work," "compromised in our mission to declare the true gospel to all people," and "incapable of confessing with one voice the orthodox Trinitarian faith." These are not concerns about minor differences or opinions, subtle programmatic weaknesses, or structural deficiencies. These are heartfelt concerns that the denomination had lost its way theologically. When a teachers' manual for denominational curriculum questions "all this supernatural claptrap brought in at the end with a dead man suddenly brought back to life again," it is not difficult to conclude that the denomination had, indeed, lost its way theologically.

One could also conclude that the pattern of denial of the supernatural elements of biblical faith that flourished among liberal Methodist leadership in the early decades of the twentieth century continued on through the rest of that century and into the twenty-first century. And it is remarkable to trace the presence of groups and movements of Methodists who have constantly lifted voices in protest and called for renewed fidelity to the apostolic faith and Wesleyan doctrinal standards.

This also helps us better understand why there has been, and continues to be, a pervasive and recurring lack of trust within the denomination, as reported in the Congregational Vitality research project led by the Towers Watson consulting firm cited earlier. There have been, and remain, serious theological disagreements within United Methodism that have not been acknowledged or addressed, but usually ignored or seen as being of little importance.

Chapter 11

Doctrinal Problems in Our Denominational Seminaries

AN APPROPRIATE QUESTION to be asked here is whether those who have raised voices of protest about doctrinal concerns in United Methodism are justified in doing so, or are they merely overreacting to a few isolated situations.

In 1993, Bishop Louis Schowengerdt (now deceased) said to an audience at a national Council on Evangelism meeting that false ideas and wrong teachings have diluted the church's zeal to save the lost. These defective teachings, he charged, totally denied the saving power of Christ.[1] It was the first time many could recall hearing a bishop make such a statement publicly. Many felt at the time, "That's a disturbing claim! If it's true, the whole church should be alerted! In fact, the Council of Bishops should put aside lesser issues and appoint a blue-ribbon panel of our best theologians and biblical scholars to examine the charge and deal with the crisis of these destructive 'false ideas' if they, in fact, exist." Nothing more was said about it, however.

Unfortunately, questions about theology have been, and remain, relegated to a secondary, almost tangential role in the denomination. This seems to be a real part of the legacy of theological liberalism. As noted earlier, the denomination engaged in a major self-study during the 2009–2012 quadrennium, employing a New York consulting firm to help the church find its way out of membership loss, demoralization, and decline. However, in its study, the church inexplicably chose not to consider matters of doctrine and theology as possible factors in recovering the church's vitality. Such a remarkable omission reflects an unmistakable value judgment about how the denomination views the role and importance of doctrine in the life of the church. And the reasons for the diminution of the role of doctrine have changed little from the era when liberalism emerged. The litany is familiar and has been repeated often, as we noted earlier: we are not a creedal church; Wesley was more concerned about experience than doctrine; and we must give our attention to the pressing social issues that are facing our nation today.

Clearly, a compelling case can be made that there remains a pattern of doctrinal denial and revisionism within United Methodism today, and one would have to conclude that our denominational seminaries have been complicit in the problem. The word *pattern* is appropriate here because that is what we have seen—a pattern, not just anecdotal situations or occasional wrong teaching.

Early in my ministry, just a few years after being ordained elder, I learned about this pattern of denial and revisionism. It came from a small but important book by John Lawson, a British Methodist who was a professor of church history at United Methodism's Candler School of Theology. His book addressed specifically the plight of mainline theological education.[2] He stated in the very first sentence of his opening chapter that there is a "very widespread grass-roots discontent with much of the theological leadership of the mainline . . . Christian denominations." (He included Candler in his concern, but stated his seminary was probably no worse than others.) He noted the emergence of popular evangelical movements taking the official leadership of the churches "seriously to task for selling out on the gospel."[3] He went on to say that it is common knowledge that "some teaching which is regularly, and indeed customarily, given in seminaries *is*

contrary to scripture, and to the chief planks of the historic Christian faith,
and to the doctrinal standards of the responsible Christian denominations
(emphasis mine)."[4] This was like a professor at a medical school admitting that his graduate institution was not being faithful in training future doctors to do surgery or prescribe medications.

Lawson clearly was writing this book with a heavy heart. For in his personal experience of counseling seminary students at Candler, he said "they often find it a devastating experience to be faced in a seminary with new and ingenious arguments on behalf of unbelief, fortified with an array of scholarship."[5] The most painful thing, Lawson lamented, was that "seminarians often receive teaching that is diametrically opposed in important particulars to the articles of faith to which they have to subscribe at ordination."[6] That leaves them with the difficult choice of (1) disbelieving some of their respected and learned professors; (2) perjuring themselves on the very sacred day of their ordination by saying they believe certain things they no longer actually believe; or (3) deciding against going on to ordination at all.

For those who go on to ordination, many were what Lawson called "reduced believers." They cannot bring themselves to break entirely with the "sentiment of the Christian tradition" that brought them to seminary. He said, "A nostalgia for 'God-talk' clings to them, the use of which also makes it more comfortable to continue in the church. So they go on speaking about God, but meaning by the word something entirely different from what the Bible means."[7] His words have a haunting relevance. He wrote (remember: this was in 1972), "They sing hymns because it makes them feel good, but they do not seriously believe what they are singing. Their worship is a wave of sentiment, not a confession of faith."[8]

He went on to write words that have been etched deeply upon my heart since first reading them: "Someday there will have to be a great awakening, a far-reaching repentance, and a painful reappraisal."[9] Why? Because young clergy are going out from seminaries into Christian ministry confused about the substance of Christian doctrine and uncertain about their own personal faith. Lawson wrote of the "dangerous influence" upon the church of both professors and pastors, who speak of God and profess to love the ideals of Christ, but have so much they cannot affirm of historic Christian teaching. He lamented the liberal teacher who

> shows himself totally unsure about the actual existence of a personal God, . . . doubts whether we know much . . . about Jesus as a divine incarnation, does not believe in the resurrection, does not like the word "atonement" (in fact, assumes that man must save himself by the educational process), does not believe in intercessory prayer, and has no real confidence in any human destiny beyond this present life.[10]

One is both saddened and angered to read those words. The liberal teacher's list, by the way, is reminiscent of the list of negations that characterized theological liberalism as noted in chapter 6. These liberal views (again, note they are all *denials*) have always been difficult for laity to comprehend. Most churchgoers scratch their heads when they hear such sentiments. One usually has to attend a liberal theological seminary to end up believing such things. It does, however, help us understand why someone would describe the mainline theological seminary in America as that remarkable institution that has the unique capacity "to make Christian postulants [ministerial candidates] into agnostic social workers."[11] Seeing this happen to idealistic young ministerial candidates gives one deep sadness, even anger, at such a breach of trust in the life of the church. Again, these patterns do not necessarily reflect all of our seminaries, but there is truth here that must be faced.

Interestingly, Lawson had written an earlier work on Christian theology in which he critiqued a "non-miraculous" view of Christianity (his description of theological liberalism) that attempts to increase (supposedly) one's chance of winning to the Christian faith those of a scientific background. He described it as an accommodation of the gospel to "secular intellectual presuppositions" by toning down the supernatural elements. He wrote this in his chapter dealing with the doctrine of the resurrection and concluded, "It is not possible permanently and convincingly to preserve the resurrection faith apart from acceptance of the actual . . . resurrection fact."[12]

He was challenging the liberal interpretation of the resurrection, which viewed it not as an actual bodily resurrection but rather as myth made up by the early church. It claimed that after Jesus' crucifixion, the church developed the concept of "resurrection faith" as it tried to find some meaning in His tragic death. According to this view, Jesus was not actually raised bodily from the tomb, but believers could still take heart and find comfort through the myth of "resurrection faith," which emerged among the early church in an attempt to make sense of the tragic turn of events. The myth was, according to liberal reconstructionists, an attempt to affirm that good will eventually overcome evil, that hope can emerge from tragedy, that the sun will eventually break through our darkest clouds, and so forth. These are all nice sentiments, but they don't begin to capture the explosive truth that Christ had been raised from the dead and was seen by many witnesses. Professor Lawson got it right: you really can't have resurrection *faith* without accepting resurrection *fact*.

Interestingly, Lutheran theologian Carl Braaten made the same point in an essay honoring United Methodist theologian Thomas C. Oden. Braaten was critical of those seeking a "historical Jesus," a Jesus fashioned to suit "modern sensibilities and not the real living Jesus Christ of apostolic preaching."[13] He cautioned against using the New Testament writings as source documents from which a "scientifically reconstructed life of Jesus can be written," noting they are written from the "standpoint of faith and for the sake of proclaiming and passing on the faith." He went on to say that whenever that framework is deconstructed and another is superimposed from the outside, "we lose the gospel in the Gospels, for the preaching of Jesus as the incarnate Word, as the crucified Messiah, as the risen Lord and as the coming

Judge is an essential part of the framework."[14] He concluded, in agreement with Lawson: "The real Jesus of history is the risen Christ; we cannot have one without the other."[15]

This sounds so familiar. One is struck that both Lawson and Braaten were engaging the view embraced, taught, and written about in the early 1900s when liberalism became dominant in many Methodist (and Protestant) institutions of higher education. During that period, as we saw in earlier chapters, the supernatural elements of the Christian faith created serious problems for a modern, scientific generation and thus, some church leaders believed that somehow the Christian faith had to be recast with new secular presuppositions to prevent the new generation of modern churchgoers at the time from abandoning the faith altogether. There is ample reason to believe, today, that the denomination has brought these secular intellectual presuppositions and liberal denials on through the twentieth century and into the twenty-first.

One might ask if Professor Lawson had been unfair in the concerns he raised about what was happening in theological education. For instance, some may say that was true for a few professors at the time (in 1972), but certainly was not a widespread pattern in our United Methodist seminaries. One senses, however, that Lawson's concerns were more than isolated incidents but reflected a problem far more pervasive within United Methodism than we might think.

It is significant that another professor at the time, Claude Thompson, an esteemed professor of systematic theology at Candler School of Theology, made a highly critical charge about the harm being done by mainline seminaries. Again, he would not exclude Candler as he made his case about seminary education, speaking at the first national Good News Convocation in Dallas, Texas, in 1970. Professor Thompson said:

> We should take a new look at theological seminaries. They may be doing more harm than good. What can we expect from our pulpits when men are trained under teachers who

profess no faith in God; who doubt His existence; who regard Jesus as only a good man—not a Savior; who have no place for prayer; who minimize the authority of the Bible; who have dismissed any idea of spiritually transformed lives under the Holy Spirit; who do not believe in life after death; and who have long since come to regard our Wesleyan heritage—both theologically and evangelically—as out of date?[16]

While both John Lawson and Claude Thompson were professors at Candler School of Theology, Lawson was speaking in the context of being a British Methodist while Thompson was speaking as a United Methodist. But both were orthodox Wesleyan believers whose hearts were deeply troubled by what they were seeing in mainline theological education in America.

But the question could be asked, What were students from our seminaries saying about their seminary experience? Were they unhappy about their experience in theological education? In the feedback section of our United Methodist pastors' journal *Circuit Rider*, several letters were printed in the April 1991 issue that raised serious questions about what students were encountering in our United Methodist seminaries. In one letter, a graduate from one of our denominational seminaries, living at the time in California, described his seminary experience as a disgrace. He said he had been taught that there was no actual resurrection of our Lord, or a Holy Spirit. He was told our bodies will rot, helping the future growth of trees and flowers, and this constitutes resurrection. He was told, further, that Jesus was dead and the Bible was an outdated book. God was not the God of Scripture, but an evolving principle of the universe.

In a second letter in the same issue, another graduate from one of our seminaries, living in Michigan, described his ministerial training with a blistering eleven-point critique. He wrote about faculty who sang the virtues of lesbian marriage, proclaimed the Scriptures to be an untrustworthy witness, and announced Jesus to be only one limited expression of a cosmic Christ.

The letters struck a familiar chord because just a few weeks earlier, I had spoken at length with a recent graduate from one of our denominational seminaries. Bill (not his real name) was serving a church in the Midwest and recalled painfully from his seminary experience an unrestrained advocacy for radical feminism as well as a "wild" openness to homosexuality, including active recruiting of gays and lesbians. He spoke of a professor who told him, "There is no resurrection of Jesus—it's a myth; it doesn't matter." The professor told him his evangelical/conservative sources were wrong and gave him a C for the course, the worst grade of his seminary career. Bill reported that students at his seminary learned right away never to say "God our *Father*." That, too, would lower your grade. Then he added wistfully, "We learned that you don't challenge professors. You learn to be a writer of fiction." Bill admitted that at least, he survived. A close friend of his didn't and dropped out of seminary.

In another conversation at about the same time, a bright young man serving as youth pastor shared with me that he had to discreetly stand up to his pastor in a Bible study about the reliability of Scripture. He discovered that his pastor had entered a United Methodist seminary as an evangelical. But while there he suffered an emotional breakdown and emerged from seminary as a liberal, having come to embrace the seminary's liberal theological commitments. One wonders how often this has happened.

Across the years, scores of seminarians have shared their own experiences, speaking of a similar adversarial environment they had encountered at a United Methodist seminary, enough for one to conclude these were not just rare, isolated experiences. Many students chose to transfer to Asbury Seminary or another more conservative seminary after a very difficult and disturbing first year at one of our denominational seminaries. Most admitted that at Asbury they were being challenged to think and face difficult theological issues. However, they acknowledged that it was being done in the context of a prayerful and supportive community of faith, not in an environment sometimes hostile or that would sometimes ridicule orthodox beliefs.

This is not to say that all the students at our denominational seminaries with whom I spoke had such negative experiences. Nor that there were no godly professors who were endeavoring to be biblical in their teaching and fair in their approach. It is simply to say that many students did report such experiences. And when idealistic young seminarians encounter such skepticism and hostility about their deeply held biblical convictions—that led them to consider ministry in the first place—it can be a devastating experience, both emotionally and spiritually.

Professor Lawson saw seminarians at Candler experience the painful anguish of such encounters and felt compelled from a troubled heart to write a book about it. Unfortunately, one senses there has been more of this than we might know. The troubling experiences of seminarians are, I believe, a part of the legacy of theological liberalism and by any measure, it is a troubling legacy. One is deeply grateful for the courage of Professor Lawson and would agree with him about the need of a "far-reaching repentance and a painful reappraisal" of our denominational seminaries.

Just a few years after the *Circuit Rider* ran the letters from the seminary graduates, I read a journal article by a longtime professor at one of our Midwestern denominational seminaries. While himself liberal in his theology, he wrote candidly and somewhat sadly about the impact of our seminaries on fledgling pastors. He said these students experienced in seminary a loss of innocence theologically, and must then struggle with the question, If others knew what I now know, would they still believe? (Think about that. What they "now know" sounds as though they have at seminary somehow become privy to an insider, secret body of information that laity don't know. It's like a modern-day Gnosticism, a secret wisdom that only seminary-trained clergy can know.)

The professor went on to note that in the first year, the students may lose confidence in and even surrender many of their core doctrinal convictions. The result, said the professor, is that from then on the student is left with the challenge of bypassing: that is, the student has three years to learn how to say one thing and be heard to say something quite different. Or, simply, to learn the art of stating liberal convictions while making them sound orthodox and scriptural so the laity in the pews won't get alarmed, angry, and perhaps seek another church. The tragedy in such a situation is that a pattern of dishonesty has begun. In such cases, language is being used not to communicate and clarify, but rather to obfuscate and mislead.

Insights from Thomas Oden's Theological Reversal

As we reflect upon United Methodist theological education, we can learn much from the remarkable theological journey of the late Professor Thomas C. Oden, who taught for more than thirty years as a professor of theology and ethics at the theology school at Drew University. Dr. Oden, a longtime colleague in denominational renewal, was a courageous, loyal United Methodist who loved the church. He was a theologian without peer within United Methodism. He was also highly respected in Protestant, Catholic, and orthodox communions as well as numerous evangelical denominations. He authored more than twenty books, including a three-volume *Systematic Theology*.[17] He was also the general editor of the acclaimed Ancient Christian Commentary on Scripture series, a twenty-seven-volume work published by InterVarsity Press. His story and work are profoundly significant for United Methodism today, as well as for the larger Christian church. The importance of his contribution cannot be overstated.

The story of Oden's personal journey is timely because he left seminary having been influenced by the secular and humanistic premises of his liberal seminary instruction. He wrote, "I left seminary having learned to treat scripture selectively, according to how well it might serve my political idealism. I adapted the Bible to my ideology—an ideology of social and political change largely shaped by soft Marxist premises about history and a romanticized vision of the emerging power and virtue of the underclass."[18] This ideology led him to involvement in numerous trendy movements, such as the United World Federalists promoting world government, liberalized abortion, the demythologizing movement (about which he did his PhD dissertation), transactional analysis, parapsychology, biorhythm charts, tarot cards, and the list goes on. Oden looked back on those years with some amusement at his obsession with such trends, and admitted that he felt he was doing Christian teaching a marvelous favor by it and even considered this accommodation the very substance of the Christian teaching office.

He wrote, "For years I tried to read the New Testament entirely without the premises of incarnation and resurrection—something that is very hard to do."[19] He assumed that truth in religion "would be finally reducible to economics (with Marx), or psychosexual factors (with Freud), or power dynamics (with Nietzsche)." He confessed "I was uncritically accommodating to the very modernity that pretended to be prophetic, yet I did not recognize modernity's captivity to secular humanistic assumptions."[20] During those years, Oden acknowledged, "I never dreamed that I would someday grant to scripture its own distinctive premises: divine sovereignty, revelation, incarnation, resurrection, and final judgment."[21] Reading those words, one is struck that they described, as we have seen earlier, the very premises that were essentially put aside during the heyday of theological liberalism. They were rejected, as we have seen, because they assume the reality of the supernatural and the miraculous.

Oden went on to say, "I had been taught that these premises were precisely what had to be transcended, reworded, circumvented, and danced around in order to communicate with the modern mind."[22] Frankly, this is the kind of theological ballet many evangelicals have watched for decades as liberal pastors and theologians have often "wrongly handled the word of truth" (to paraphrase Saint Paul), dancing and circumventing and rewording the intended meaning of the biblical text. The phrase Oden used is haunting as one reflects upon it. He wrote, "I had been taught." But taught what, exactly? Well, in his words, taught that the premises of divine sovereignty, revelation, incarnation, resurrection, and final judgment had to be "transcended, reworded, circumvented, and danced around." He was taught that these premises or theological convictions could no longer be valid in a new era of enlightenment. These were premises we must somehow *improve* upon. Yes, Oden *had been taught,* by sincere and no doubt well-meaning professors. One wonders how many seminarians have had such theological instruction in their preparation for ministry but *never came back home* to reaffirm the integrity and intellectual credibility of apostolic Christianity.

Thankfully, Thomas Oden came back home. He had a major theological reversal, as he described it. He celebrated the grace of God at work in his bizarre journey. He wrote, "Now I revel in the very premises I once carefully learned to set aside: the triune mystery, the preexistent Logos, the radical depth of sin passing through the generations, the risen Lord, the grace of baptism."[23] Let's admit the obvious here: when you set aside these major themes of Christian doctrine, what remains of the historic Christian faith? There was a commendable honesty in Oden's admission. He didn't claim that he was simply *reinterpreting* those themes. He admitted these were themes he had learned "to set aside."

What was it, then, that brought about this remarkable reversal in Oden's life and theology? It's a beautiful, powerful story and worth reading in its entirety.[24] But hear this brief portion in his own words: "What changed the course of my life? A simple reversal that hung on a single pivot: attentiveness to the text of scripture, especially as viewed by its early consensual interpreters."[25] Most laity would be perplexed that a theologian might not give great attentiveness to the text of Scripture. That seems so basic to the ministerial vocation. But again, it reflects how Scripture was, and is, perceived in the liberal/modern perspective. Oden wrote, "Before my reversal, all of my questions about theology and the modern world had been premised on key value assumptions of modern [liberal] consciousness—assumptions such as absolute moral relativism. After meeting new friends in the writings of antiquity, I had a new grounding for those questions."[26]

Reflecting on the difference the reversal has made, Oden wrote:

> Then [before his reversal] I distrusted even the faint smell of Orthodoxy. I was in love with heresy—the wilder, the more seductive. Now I have come to trust the very consensus I once dismissed and distrusted. Generations of double-checking confirm it as a reliable body of scriptural interpretation. I now relish studying the diverse rainbow of orthodox voices from varied cultures spanning all continents over two thousand years.[27]

One smiles, but with thanksgiving, at this former movement theologian writing of his newly found commitment to "unoriginality." He insisted, "That is not a joke but a solemn pledge. I am trying to curb any pretense at 'improving' upon the apostles and fathers."[28] Acknowledging the "deceptiveness of originality," he went on to write, "I can now listen intently to those who attest a well-grounded tradition of general consent rather than a narrow contemporary bias. I listen to voices that echo what has been affirmed by the community of saints of all times and places."[29]

In his new autobiography, he described it as a "cycle of learning, unlearning and relearning."[30] This was reflected in "my joyful reception, then in my sophisticated rejection, then later in my embracing the hymns of my childhood."[31] At first he believed naively that God had come in the flesh. Then he learned that God had not really come in the flesh "but rather in some symbolic sense acceptable to modern assumptions."[32] Then, "At last I learned to recover the uncomplicated truth that God precisely becomes human in the flesh, dies for me, rises again and saves me from my sins. All these are viewed by consensual Christianity as historical events."[33]

It should come as no surprise that a theologian who spent his professional life in the world of theological education would, like John Lawson, decide to write a book that addressed the problems of modern-day seminary education.[34] Oden did so, though regretfully he admitted, as he loves the United Methodist Church and he loved the School of Theology at Drew, where he spent so much of his professional teaching career.

In *Requiem*, he critiqued the failure of contemporary theological education and called for a return to classical Christian theology. He could have chosen to just gloss over the current ailment in the seminary world, he admitted, but "not with a healthy conscience."[35] While confessing that he is a "conflict-avoiding peace lover," he wrote these troubling words: "So after a lifetime of teaching . . . I am very nearly convinced that the present system is practically irreformable. This I say sadly, not irately."[36] He lamented the seminaries being "tradition-deprived," and wrote about an academic tenure system that is "fixed in stone."[37] He also noted the academic distrust of the parish. In fact, "brilliant academics with no experience whatever in the actual practice of the ministry of Word, Sacrament, and pastoral care are often those who compete best in the race to become teachers of ministers in the trendy, fad-impaired seminary."[38] He noted sadly that having parish experience is more likely to be a negative factor than a positive one when seeking a teaching position in the seminary today.

Oden also cited the triumph of latitudinarianism, that is, a complete tolerance of all doctrinal views. The result is the complete absence of heresy. He wrote frankly that "heresy simply does not exist."[39] This is something never before achieved in Christian history, he observed. But the "liberated seminary" has finally "found a way of overcoming heterodoxy [departure from traditional doctrine] altogether, by banishing it as a concept legitimately teachable within the hallowed walls of the inclusive multicultural, doctrinally experimental institution."[40] The only heresy one might possibly encounter, said

Oden, is an offense against inclusivism. One might add another—the failure to use politically correct language for God. (This, perhaps, would be considered a part of inclusivism.)

In the late 1970s, studies reported the sobering news that United Methodism's seminaries were failing. There was a high dropout rate among young clergy, both male and female. In addition, there was an increasing struggle for student registration and tuition. Oden suggested at the time that if his seminary would only appoint a few new faculty who could connect with evangelical students, it would help solve that problem. Unfortunately, the new faculty appointments were "all in the opposite direction," Oden wrote,[41] adding, "Most new appointments were made to left-leaning scholars who were dedicated to their ideologies and who either ignored, loathed or demeaned evangelicals."[42]

The day of ignoring what is happening in our denominational seminaries is over, according to Professor Oden. In a word of warning, he wrote, "Christian worshipers can no longer afford to neglect what is happening to the young people they guilelessly send off to seminary, entrusting that they will be taught all that is requisite for Christian ministry."[43] He concluded with a timely warning to the church about seminaries that have clearly lost their way theologically: "When the liberated have virtually no immune system against heresy, no defense whatever against perfidious [treacherous, breaking of trust] teaching, no criteria for testing the legitimacy of counterfeit theological currency, it is time for laity to learn about theological education."[44]

Professors often justify teaching anything they want to teach by appealing to academic freedom, but Oden was not so ready to let them off the hook on that. He wrote, "If the liberated have the freedom to teach apostasy, the believing church has the freedom to withhold its consent." He made the case even stronger: "If they teach counter-canonical doctrines and conjectures inimical to the health of the church, the church has no indelible moral obligation to give them support or to bless their follies."[45]

Oden affirmed that as a former sixties radical and now an out-of-the-closet orthodox evangelical, he shared concerns with a new generation of young classic Christian men and women who affirmed the faith of the apostles and martyrs. He found himself "ironically entering into a kind of resistance movement in relation to my own generation of relativists, who have botched things up pretty absolutely."[46] We must not miss the sobering implications of what he said—that he as an "orthodox evangelical" saw himself as being part of "a kind of resistance movement" in today's church. He would assure us that this was not fantasy or hyperbole or some messianic obsession. He engaged the church theologically for more than four decades and his words are a sobering critique, perhaps an indictment, of the theological setting in contemporary United Methodism: to be an "orthodox evangelical" is to be part of a "resistance movement." Many evangelical seminarians would understand that sentiment from their own personal seminary experience.

Edmund W. Robb Jr., Albert C. Outler, and AFTE

From what has been written previously, it is clear that United Methodist evangelicals have had their problems with the denomination's theological seminaries. But there is a story here that must be told, as it represents a source of hope and encouragement for potential renewal within the United Methodist Church. And interestingly, this story began with a message of protest.

In July 1975, Dr. Edmund W. Robb Jr. gave a powerful address to some two thousand people gathered at Lake Junaluska, North Carolina, for the sixth annual Good News Convocation. Robb spoke on the crisis of theological education in the United Methodist Church. At the time Robb was pastor of St. Luke's United Methodist Church in Lubbock, Texas, and was second vice-chairman of the Good News board of directors. It was a muggy July evening, with the Lake Junaluska auditorium jammed with United Methodist laity and clergy from all across the United States. Robb had prepared vigorously and prayerfully for what he hoped would be a major address as he called for renewal and reform in United Methodist theological education.[47]

Robb began by affirming his long Methodist ancestry, claiming family members who entertained Francis Asbury in their home in "this very state" (North Carolina). He noted Methodist ministers in every generation since then. He cited his church in Texas as one that was paying its apportionments in full and giving generously to second-mile missions giving in the denomination. His point was that he was a loyal United Methodist.

He then went on to say, "If we have a sick church it is largely because we have sick seminaries." He asked for a new openness to evangelical education in United Methodism. He then asked a series of rhetorical questions that focused on many of the themes of theological liberalism. He asked: "Where are the professors in our seminaries who affirm, without mental reservation, the deity of Jesus Christ—he is God—he is man?" Again, "Where are the professors who affirm that our Lord was born of a virgin, not just symbolically, but miraculously—biologically?" And again, "Where are the professors who affirm the bodily resurrection—not just a continued spiritual presence, but who proclaim the empty tomb and glorified body?" And again, "Is there an acceptance and advocacy of supernatural Christianity in our seminaries today? Is there a question mark placed on the miracles of the New Testament?" He then made a sweeping claim that would get the attention of theologian Albert C. Outler, at Perkins School of Theology. He thundered, "I know of no UM seminary where the historic Wesleyan Biblical perspective is presented seriously, even as an option."

When Dr. Outler heard of Robb's charge about no seminary presenting the "historic Wesleyan Biblical perspective" he was deeply offended. He penned a strong letter critical of Robb and sent it to the *United Methodist Reporter*, a widely circulated weekly independent paper in the denomination. The result was that soon Robb, along with fellow Good News board member Paul Morell, pastor at Tyler Street

United Methodist Church in Dallas, went to sit down and talk to Dr. Outler personally to try to correct possible misunderstandings. Robb believed that in doing so, he was being sensitive to the Spirit's leading. The results of that tense and uncomfortable initial visit with Professor Outler would prove, indeed, that was the case.

From that first, strained conversation came an unlikely friendship between Outler, the highly esteemed Wesleyan scholar and ecumenist, and Robb, a hard-preaching Texas pastor and evangelist. From that friendship would come a strong mutual respect between the two United Methodists and a joint endeavor that would result in a Fund for Theological Education, which would later be renamed a Foundation for Theological Education (AFTE).

The stated goal of the foundation was "to help revitalize a supremely important area of the church—theological education." And it has been successful in doing so. Since 1977, AFTE has awarded grants of more than $3 million to help promising evangelical scholars receive their PhD degrees from graduate schools such as Princeton, Harvard, Yale, Oxford, Duke, Emory, Notre Dame, Durham University, and Drew, to name just a few.

As of this writing, there have been 141 John Wesley Fellows (the name of scholars receiving AFTE grants) accepted into the program, with one hundred having received their PhD degrees, and at least another thirty-six in process. Some fifty-three scholars now serve as professors and/or administrators in theological schools, and another twenty-six as professors or administrators in colleges and universities. Fifteen are serving as pastors of some of our largest churches. Four of the John Wesley Fellows have served as seminary presidents or deans, and one, Scott Jones, has been elected as a bishop.[48] Many view the AFTE program, which began with Robb's address of protest about the crisis of theological education, as one of the most encouraging programs for future, lasting renewal within the United Methodist Church.

We long to see renewal and revitalization in our denominational seminaries. It can happen. Many have been encouraged by the turnaround at United Theological Seminary in Dayton, Ohio, one of our denominational institutions. A decade ago the seminary was struggling to survive, both financially and in student enrollment. In what some call a "re-branding" of the institution, United has committed to focusing on basic Christian orthodoxy, holiness, and church renewal. It has become a seminary community saturated in prayer and the enrollment has gone from some 150 students to more than 600 today. The president during this time of growth was Dr. Wendy Deichmann, who happens to be an AFTE scholar. But she attributes the turnaround at United Seminary as more a sovereign work of God than anyone's smart plan.[49] Not to be overlooked in the turnaround is the seminary's renewed focus on orthodox Christian doctrine.

The AFTE scholars are making a difference. We hope they might help bring a renewed, lasting interest in the role and place of our orthodox and Wesleyan doctrinal standards in the life of our church. However, one of the ongoing legacies of theological liberalism has been what I call the trivialization of doctrine in the life of the denomination.

Chapter 12

The Trivialization of Christian Doctrine

AS WE HAVE focused on the ongoing legacy of theological liberalism, we have noted that matters of doctrine and theology have been, and remain today, relegated to a secondary, almost tangential role in the life of the United Methodist Church. We have, in fact, seen the *trivialization* of the role of doctrine and theology in the church. Justification for this downplaying of doctrine gets expressed in various phrases heard often in church conversations: we have many differing theologies; we are not a creedal denomination; no one person or group has all the truth; we only "see through a glass dimly"; our differences are only matters of interpretation; we are a diverse people, so let's celebrate our diversity; experience unites but doctrine divides; and on it goes.

The sense one gets is that doctrine—what we believe as a Christian people—is simply not all that important. We just need to get on with being the church, meeting human need, and transforming the world. Such sentiments, however, remind me of the remark noted earlier by Oxford professor Alister McGrath, who wrote, "Inattention to doctrine robs a church of her reason for existence, and opens the way to enslavement and oppression by the world."[1] One only wonders whether "inattention" is a strong enough word.

The Re-Imagining Controversy

One of the classic examples of this attitude of trivialization was the church's response to the Re-Imagining Conference held in Minneapolis on November 4–7, 1993. Billed as "A Global Theological Conference by Women, for Men and Women," Re-Imagining was an ecumenical gathering associated with the World Council of Churches for those of the feminist, womanist, or lesbian perspective. With some 2,200 registrants from many mainline denominations, 391 were United Methodist. The Women's Division (of the General Board of Global Ministries) staff and directors were urged to attend the conference as the quadrennium's theological workshop with Women's Division staff and directors' expenses paid for by the division.[2] In fact, at its spring meeting, the Women's Division took action to cancel its own staff and directors' theology workshop and approved in its place involvement of staff and directors in the Re-Imagining event. The Women's Division acknowledged its full financial support of thirty-six directors, nine staff members, and eleven conference vice-presidents, plus a grant of $2,500 for scholarship support. The Women's Division's involvement clearly amounted to official support of the event.

The Good News staff read carefully the transcripts from most all of the more than thirty-four presentations, and we were convinced that this was without doubt the most bizarre, theologically aberrant event we had ever read about, far removed from Christian teaching and tradition. Consider just a few examples:[3]

- Womanist theologian Delores S. Williams said, "I don't think we need a theory of atonement at all . . . I don't think we need folks hanging on crosses and blood dripping and weird stuff." The statement drew enthusiastic applause.
- A United Methodist clergywoman told a workshop, "The Church has always been blessed by gays and lesbians . . . witches . . . shamans . . . artists."

- Theologian Mary Hunt said, "I have far more hope in substituting 'friendship' as a metaphor for family. . . . Imagine sex among friends as the norm, young people learning to make friends rather than to date. Imagine valuing genital sexual interaction in terms of whether and how it fosters friendship and pleasure."

- Melanie Morrison, cofounder of Christian Lesbians Out Together (CLOUT), was given time to celebrate "the miracles of being lesbian, out, and Christian," and invited all other lesbian, bisexual, and transsexual women to come forward, join hands, and encircle the stage. More than one hundred women responded and Morrison said, "I'm pleased and honored to lead you in prayer and to talk to earth maker Mauna, our creator."

- Nadean Bishop, the first "out" lesbian minister called to an American Baptist church, said that Mary and Martha in the Bible were not actual sisters but lesbian lovers.

- Chung Hyun Kyung, one of the speakers, explained that Asian theology totally rejects the idea of sinful man, propagating the understanding that humans are good and become better from the god within.

- Chinese feminist Kwok Pui Lan told the group "We cannot have one savior—just like the Big Mac in McDonalds, prepackaged, shipped all over the world. It won't do. It's imperialistic." She offered China's 722 gods and goddesses as an example of "radical inclusivity."

- Aruna Gnanadason, staff member of the World Council of Churches, said that the church "centered its faith around the cruel and violent death of Christ on the cross, sanctioning violence against the powerless in society."

- Virginia Mollenkott said, "We would understand Jesus to be our elder brother, the trailblazer and constant companion for us who are here in time and space, but ultimately one among many brothers and sisters in an eternally, equally worthy siblinghood."

These excerpts reflect the tone and substance of the Re-Imagining Conference. At least ten presenters were self-identified lesbians. Prayers were offered repeatedly to the goddess Sophia, including the offensive prayer in the communion-like "Service of milk and honey," which said, "Our sweet Sophia, we are women in your image; with nectar between our thighs we invite a lover, we birth a child." This blending of sexuality and spirituality seemed more Canaanite than Christian. Not one of more than thirty-four major speakers represented the orthodox Christian faith as expressed in the classical creeds of the church. The gathering, rather than being *ecumenical* in terms of focusing on the classic Christian faith, was actually *inter-religious*, with its major emphasis being on non-Christian and other religious traditions.[4]

These excerpts help one understand why the Re-Imagining Conference caused such an ongoing controversy that continued throughout most of 1994. It was a very public conference officially supported by a major United Methodist program agency. It included prayers to and worship focused on the goddess Sophia, as well as the denial of essential Christian doctrinal tenets such as the deity of Christ, his atoning death, the sinfulness of humanity, creation, the authority of Scripture, the church, and the biblical understanding of human sexuality. These doctrines were not only denied, but often done so derisively.

Why, then, is the Re-Imagining Conference an example of a trivialization of doctrine within United Methodism? For this reason: the Good News board took action at its January 1994 meeting, about a month after the conference, asking the Council of Bishops to address this troubling event, believing the conference represented a theological crisis in the church. Our bishops, of course, are charged with the task of guarding the church's doctrine and teaching. In fact, three retired bishops did speak out. Two invited by Good News (William R. Cannon and Earl G. Hunt), wrote articles for *Good News* magazine. A third, Mack Stokes, penned a lengthy letter to the editor in *Good News*. All were deeply distressed about the substance of the conference and its introduction of the goddess Sophia in the worship liturgy.[5] They were retired at the time, but all three went on record publicly, expressing their deep concerns about the conference and Sophia worship.

Unfortunately, the Council of Bishops released no statement about Re-Imagining at its May (1994) meeting but rather created a task force to address the continuing Re-Imagining controversy. The task force produced a statement entitled "Biblical Wisdom," which was adopted unanimously by the Council of Bishops at its November (1994) meeting. The statement noted the existence of considerable theological and doctrinal ferment within the United Methodist Church. Concerning the matter of Sophia, it did state that "Woman Wisdom was never an object of cultic reverence for the Israelites and there are no Biblical warrants for goddess worship." It went on to affirm that "the worship of Sophia as a goddess is contrary both to the Biblical revelation and our doctrinal standards."[6] This was a welcomed word for evangelicals to hear. Unfortunately, however, there was no reference to any of the egregious attacks on and denials of the historic doctrines of the church.[7]

Then at the November meeting, where the council approved the "Biblical Wisdom" statement, the new president of the council said in his opening address that the bishops needed to help church members get past the "gnat-camel" syndrome (citing Jesus' rebuke of the scribes and Pharisees for "strain[ing] out a gnat but swallow[ing] a camel" in Matthew 23:24).

He reported receiving hundreds of letters protesting United Methodist involvement in the controversial Re-Imagining Conference—letters expressing concern than some United Methodists had given up devotion to Jesus to worship the goddess Sophia. He went on to say dismissively that he had looked around and did not find one person who had left their devotion to Jesus to worship Sophia. The implication was that the entire matter was of little seriousness, more of a "gnat-camel" kind of issue. His point was that those of us who were upset about Re-Imagining were like the teachers of the law and Pharisees, focusing on minor and insignificant matters while neglecting the more important matters of the law. He said what he did see were drug sales on the streets and children at risk in their schools, concluding: "These are some of the things God is calling us to deal with, but we spend a lot of time fussing within our family. God is calling us to quit that."[8]

Here, then, was a clear example of the *trivialization* of the role of doctrine in the church: very serious matters, such as goddess worship, the atonement, the incarnation, the sinfulness of humanity, and the deity of Jesus Christ, that resulted in a year-long controversy were viewed merely as "gnat-camel" concerns. According to the president of the United Methodist Council of Bishops, these doctrinal concerns were things we really shouldn't be "fussing" about within our church family. We should not focus unduly on the president of the council about his statement, because the address of the council's president generally reflects the consensus of the entire council. But to say we shouldn't be "fussing" about these kinds of doctrinal issues reflects a serious diminution of the importance and place of doctrine in the church's life and ministry.

Again, the statement by the council's task force avoided any comment or criticism about the numerous non-Christian teachings at Re-Imagining, including the derision and denial of major Christian doctrines, the advocacy of pantheism, and the public approval—even celebration—of homosexuality. Many wondered at the time, *If our bishops will not address the many egregious denials of Christian doctrine expressed at the Re-Imagining event, is there any aberration or doctrinal denial they would speak out against in defense of our United Methodist doctrinal standards?* This was all the more disappointing when we reflect that our bishops are charged with being the guardians of the church's doctrine.

This national conference and our leaders' reaction to it left many of us even more convinced that matters of doctrine have, indeed, been relegated to a secondary, tangential place in the life of our church. This seems, without question, to be a major part of the legacy of theological liberalism.

A Candid Admission from a Liberal Pastor

Another event that stands out as an example of the *trivialization* of the church's teaching came at about the same time as the Re-Imagining controversy. In the Winter 1995 issue of *Open Hands*, the pro-gay/lesbian journal of the Reconciling Congregations program at the time, Tom Griffith, then pastor of Crescent Heights United Methodist Church in West Hollywood, California, wrote a remarkably candid article entitled "Three Cheers for Our Evangelical Brothers and Sisters." Why the praise? Because with our evangelical concerns for "belief in Scriptures and the normative creeds and confessions of faith of the church," they are calling us to be honest, wrote Reverend Griffith.

Reverend Griffith went on to write, "Now it is our turn to get honest. Although the creeds of our denomination pay lip service to the idea that Scripture is 'authoritative' and 'sufficient both for faith and for practice,' many of us have moved far beyond that notion in our theological thinking." Griffith's words reflected a degree of candor that most evangelicals had never heard before. He wrote, "*We are truly deceiving ourselves—and lying to our evangelical brothers and sisters— when we deny the shift we have made*" (emphasis mine).[9]

What Griffith wrote helps us better understand why the Towers Watson Congregational Vitality research study found a persistent lack of trust within the denomination. Griffith got even more specific:

> We [liberals] have moved far beyond the idea that the Bible is exclusively normative and literally authoritative for our faith . . . Furthermore, few of us retain belief in Christ as the sole way to salvation. We trust that God can work under many other names and in many other forms to save people. Our

views have changed over the years and evangelicals know it. At least they have the honesty to call us to honesty.[10]

His candor is commendable. He put his finger on what many of us evangelicals have suspected, and witnessed, for many years—that a number of United Methodist clergy who were trained in the liberal theological tradition may not affirm much of the substance of classic Christianity. Actually, it was not a risky thing for Griffith to write so candidly, because he serves in the California-Pacific Annual Conference, which is one of United Methodism's most liberal annual conferences. But what it makes clear is that for many liberals, the substance of their preaching is not the great doctrinal themes of the faith: redemption, justification, atonement, sanctification, the Great Commission, and the promised return of Christ. It is not "the faith that was once for all entrusted to the saints" (Jude 3 NRSV).

Again, it is a *trivialization* of the church's doctrine when it can be so casually put aside for something newer, more supposedly relevant and in touch with the times. The claim to have "moved far beyond" Scripture leaves clergy and theologians who do so at liberty to refashion and create a new message free from normative biblical standards. Thus, other things are being preached, much of which would no doubt include good advice, helpful counsel, and words of encouragement and warm religious sentiment. The problem is—these *other things* are not the faith proclaimed by the church for nearly two millennia. They are not the great doctrinal themes of the great tradition of the church.

Nor are these liberal pastors being faithful to the ordination covenant in which they personally affirmed the church's doctrines to be in harmony with the Scriptures and thus pledged publicly to preach and maintain those doctrines. Griffith knew this, admitting that for many/most liberals, Scripture is no longer "normative" or "sufficient" for faith and practice. That is a notion they have "moved far beyond," and Griffith was saying it is time for "us liberals" to get honest with evangelicals and admit it.

A Bishop Dissents from the Faith of the Church

One last example of the trivialization of the role and place of doctrine can be seen in the dissenting theological views of Bishop C. Joseph Sprague (now retired).[11] Sprague was elected as bishop from the West Ohio Conference of the United Methodist Church. He was known to be a kind and compassionate person, especially concerned about the poor and marginalized. His theological views first became more widely known when the *Kane County Chronicle*[12] carried an article about a review that Bishop Sprague gave of theologian Marcus Borg's new book at the time, *Meeting Jesus Again for the First Time*.[13] In his book, Borg reflected on his first New Testament seminary course. There he learned that the image of Jesus from his childhood, as the divine Savior who knew Himself to be the Son of God and who offered up His life for the sins of the world, *was not historically true*. His journey in seminary led him to a new state of "post-critical naivete—a state in which one can hear these stories as 'true stories' even while knowing that they are not literally true."[14]

Borg's words help explain the great gulf that exists between the seminary classroom and the church pew. Laity in the pews hear about "true stories" that are "not literally true." To most laity, that sounds like double-talk. It also helps explain the gulf between some liberal clergy and other, more orthodox, traditional pastors. Borg expressed his personal difficulty accepting the crucifixion. This story, he wrote, is hard to believe. "The notion that God's only son came to this planet to offer his life as a sacrifice for the sins of the world, and that God could not forgive us without that having happened, and that we are saved by believing this story, is simply incredible."[15] Borg is certainly right in saying that. The story is exactly that. Incredible! And it has been for countless numbers of believers across the centuries. Charles Wesley expressed that very sense of wonder: "Amazing love! How can it be that thou, my God, shouldst die for me?"[16]

For Borg, this story when taken metaphorically can be very powerful. But "when taken literally, it is a profound obstacle to accepting the Christian message. To many people, it simply makes no sense."[17]

For many of us, however, the biblical story of the crucifixion is not an *obstacle* to accepting the Christian message; it *is* the Christian message. In one of his early letters, Paul wrote, "But God forbid that I should boast except in the cross of our Lord Jesus Christ" (Gal. 6:14 NKJV).

Now, what got the attention of many of us was that Bishop Sprague, at the conclusion of his review of Borg's controversial book, acknowledged that the book is "a very provocative and, I think, *very much on target* piece of work" (emphasis mine).[18]

The bishop also made a remarkable admission at the conclusion of his review: "We who are clergy have done a disservice to the laity for about 100 years. We've feared that if we told the truth about what we learned in seminary, [you laity] couldn't take it."[19] Think carefully about those words. His reference to one hundred years, of course, goes back to the early 1900s, the time of the emergence of theological liberalism and the period when the central supernatural elements of the Christian faith were being denied or simply set aside.

Bishop Sprague's words remain troubling, even though written more than twenty years ago. For here was a United Methodist pastor, having been elected to the episcopacy, who acknowledged that he and numerous other clergy have not been able to be honest with laity in the church about what they learned—or unlearned or set aside—in their seminary training. He believed laity couldn't take it if they found out. This admission, we should remember, came from one of our bishops, those who have the responsibility to "guard the faith, order, liturgy, doctrine, and discipline of the Church."[20]

In his work *Affirmations of a Dissenter*, Bishop Sprague expanded on some of these controversial views he learned in seminary. He began by sharing his personal appreciation for a faculty member who influenced him during his seminary days. He wrote warmly of his New Testament professor, Fred D. Gealy, who he said was a giant among the faculty at the Methodist Theological School of Ohio, where Sprague did his seminary work. Gealy was, in Sprague's words, "steeped in the demythologizing methodology of Rudolf Bultmann."[21]

Bultmann is a name many clergy will recognize. He was a German New Testament scholar who taught at Marburg from 1921 to 1951. He had an enormous influence on American biblical scholars after World War II. He had a radical skepticism about the historicity of the New Testament records. He believed the gospels contain almost no authentic historical information about Jesus. Thomas Reeves says of Bultmann that he claimed "virtually nothing reliable could be known about Jesus. He rejected the Virgin Birth and the Resurrection, among other things, as primitive nonsense. The early church, in his view, invented most of the sayings ascribed to Jesus."[22] Sprague made clear that Professor Gealy, who was "steeped" in Bultmann's theological methodology, had a major influence on him during his seminary experience.

In his work, Sprague stated openly his intent "to be candid and vulnerable" in addressing basic theological issues. He was, indeed, both candid and vulnerable, the latter word meaning "open to criticism." And he received much of that.

Concerning the "theological myth of the Virgin Birth," he wrote that to treat the myth "as a historical fact is to do an injustice to its intended purpose and to run the risk of idolatry, namely, treating a means as an end itself."[23] He wrote, "If Jesus were born of human parents, as I affirm he was, and if Jesus did not possess trans-human supernatural powers, as I do not believe he did, what sense can we make of the miraculous stories about him in the Gospel accounts?"[24] What we have here is an admission that to make sense of Jesus, there must be the removal of the supernatural from these biblical narratives. This, of course, is nothing new. It is a continuation of what was done by adherents of theological liberalism in the early 1900s. So, for Sprague, there was no miraculous virginal conception, no supernatural powers, no bodily resurrection of Jesus, and thus, no miracles.

This, of course, will require a major reconstruction of any number of New Testament stories.

Concerning the deity of Jesus Christ, Sprague wrote that Jesus (simply born of human parents) was a man who could have said no to God, but "the confluence of God's grace with the human response of faith, as trust and obedience, found perfection in Jesus and the Christ was made manifest." In a remarkable departure from the church's historic understanding of Christ's incarnation, he went on to write that "Jesus was not born the Christ. Rather, by the confluence of grace with faith *he became the Christ*, God's beloved in whom God was well pleased" (emphasis mine).[25] This notion of Jesus reaching such a level of devotion and commitment to God that he "became" the Christ is a reappearance of the ancient heresy of Adoptionism, which was rejected by the church in the third century. Such a view also precludes Jesus being the eternal Logos, the preexistent second person of the Trinitarian Godhead.

The bishop said he affirms his belief in the resurrection of Jesus, but with qualifications. He said he "cannot affirm that his resurrection involved the resuscitation of his physical body. The inconsistent reports in the New Testament of his several and initially unrecognized resurrection appearances add support to this point of view."[26] He spoke of God working through the boundaries that He has established. "And while I do not pretend to know the limits of these boundaries and realize that we all see but through a glass darkly, I am certain that the miracle of resurrection, preeminently that of Jesus, is not tied to bodily resuscitation." To link the resurrection of Jesus with bodily resuscitation "is to make a literal religious proposition of a metaphorical, symbolic expression of truth itself. This is the kind of idolatry from which I dissent,"[27] said Sprague.

Most traditionalists, it should be said, reject the term *resuscitation* when thinking of our Lord's resurrection. What the church has affirmed across the centuries is that Jesus was raised "bodily," that the tomb was empty, and that the great Easter affirmation that "He is risen!" was not merely metaphorical or symbolic. When believers of every age have affirmed the Apostles' Creed, saying that "the third day he rose from the dead," they have not understood that to be something figurative or symbolic. In this historic creedal affirmation across the centuries, the church has been affirming that Christ had indeed been raised from the dead and had been seen by the disciples and others. A part of that affirmation was an empty tomb.

This was not some kind of a scheme carried out by the Lord's disciples. They were themselves surprised by it and could scarcely believe it. This pivotal truth was at the heart of all early church preaching. Paul wrote, "For what I received I passed on to you as of first importance: that Christ died for our sins according to the Scriptures, that he was buried, that he was raised on the third day according to the Scriptures, and that he appeared to [Peter], and then to the Twelve" (1 Cor. 15:3–5). Paul went on to mention further appearances, including to more than five hundred at one time. The biblical text is clear that these were not mythical or metaphorical appearances. They saw and experienced the risen Lord personally. He was alive and had been seen by many of the disciples. This has been the faith of the church for nearly two millennia. About this foundational truth, Bishop Sprague said simply that he dissented. He was "certain" it did not happen.

One final doctrine needs mention. The bishop affirmed his view of Jesus as the fully human one whose faithful trust and radical obedience provided for the church "the preeminent manifestation of at-one-ment with God." He went on to say that this view leaves "no room for me to affirm the substitutionary atonement theory." This is the view, he said, "that portrays Jesus' blood on the cross as satisfying an angry deity through one majestic sacrificial human death, much as sacrifices of unblemished sheep and goats in ancient Israel were understood to appease God and atone for the sins of all."[28] One could say much about the objectionable caricature of Jesus' blood satisfying an "angry deity," but it is enough to point out that he believed the substitutionary theory of the atonement, which is one of several valid Christian theories of atonement, to be "at odds with other images of God reflected by the witness of Jesus and experienced by this writer [Sprague]."[29] He went on to say, "The concept of blood sacrifice to appease God is superstition at best and an idolatrous allegiance to a non-Jesus methodology of God-human relationship at worst."[30]

These examples are sufficient to illustrate that the bishop did make himself "vulnerable" in his book. He was dissenting from major themes of classic Christian doctrine. One thinks of the United Methodist Articles of Religion, a part of the official Doctrinal Standards of the denomination. Consider article 2, "Of the Word, or Son of God, Who Was Made Very Man." It states:

> The Son, who is the Word of the Father, the very and eternal God, of one substance with the Father, took man's nature in the womb of the blessed Virgin; so that two whole and perfect natures, that is to say, the Godhead and Manhood, were joined together in one person, never to be divided, whereof is one Christ, very God and very Man, who truly suffered, was crucified, dead, and buried, to reconcile his Father to us, and to be a sacrifice, not only for original guilt, but also for actual sins of men.[31]

Or consider article 3, "Of the Resurrection of Christ." It states: "Christ did truly rise again from the dead, and took again his body, with all things appertaining to the perfection of man's nature, wherewith he ascended into heaven, and there sitteth until he return to judge all men at the last day."[32]

The Articles of Religion, we would say again, are a part of the official Doctrinal Standards of the United Methodist Church. They are considered foundational and are thus protected by the first Restrictive Rule. Unfortunately, they are truths that the bishop appeared unable to affirm. The passages from his book noted earlier seem to confirm that. Indeed, he was aware, and said so, that in being candid, he was opening himself for criticism. Why? Because he was dissenting—to use his word—from the teachings of his church. That was the purpose of his book. To *dissent* means "to disagree, to think differently, to refuse to accept the doctrines and forms of an established church."[33] One has, of course, the right to dissent from the doctrines of the church. But it becomes problematic when clergy do so, having promised publicly that they believe the church's doctrines and will faithfully preach and teach them. It becomes even more problematic when one who dissents from the church's teaching accepts election as bishop, as our bishops have the primary responsibility of guarding the faith, doctrine, and discipline of the church. They are to be the defenders of our church's doctrine and teaching.

Bishop Sprague expected criticism for his views and did, in fact, receive exactly that from a number of pastors and laity across the church. More specifically, in December 2002, twenty-eight clergy and laypersons from eleven annual conferences brought a complaint against Bishop Sprague for several offenses, one being "dissemination of doctrines contrary to the established standards of doctrine of the United Methodist Church."[34] This is one of eleven offenses in the *Discipline* for which United Methodist clergy and bishops might be formally charged.

It was in the handling of the complaint that the church's doctrine, once again, seems to have been trivialized. A four-person Supervisory Response Team (SRT) met to handle the complaint according to the *Book of Discipline*, with the purpose of trying to find a satisfactory resolution to the complaint or to decide whether the matter should be passed along to a Committee on Investigation to determine if the complaint merited a church trial. Unfortunately, after several meetings of the SRT, the bishop who chaired the team announced surprisingly that the complaints filed against the bishop had been dismissed. There had been no "just resolution," which is the goal of the supervisory process. (A resolution would have to be agreed to by both parties.) The complaints were simply dismissed.

The SRT asked Bishop Sprague to release a public statement clarifying and reaffirming his adherence to the Doctrinal Standards of the United Methodist Church. This, of course, was the very matter about which there were serious questions in the first place. The team also suggested Bishop Sprague and the complainants participate in a third-party dialogue, and that the Council of Bishops enter into serious theological reflection on issues of Christology, biblical authority, and the mission of the church. Finally, the SRT asked that the complainants offer a public apology for disregarding the spirit of confidentiality intended in the supervisory process. The complainants noted, however, that the *Discipline* says nothing about confidentiality about the *fact* that a complaint has been filed.

The complainants were very dissatisfied with the SRT response for several reasons. First, they were disappointed that the SRT's response to them seemed hostile, as if they and their complaint were the point of focus, not Bishop Sprague's problematic theology. They also objected to the charge that by bringing their complaint, they were attempting to "drive" the church "toward becoming a doctrinal or creedal church, rather than a church rooted primarily in Wesley's "heart religion."[35] In this charge against the complainants by the SRT, we see the ongoing liberal notion cited earlier, that United Methodism is not a doctrinal or creedal church. However, we must remember that "dissemination of doctrines contrary to the established standards of doctrine of the United Methodist Church" is listed in the *Discipline* as a "chargeable offense," as we saw earlier. Unfortunately, it seems that most of our denominational leaders believe that a complaint should *never* be brought against another United Methodist over *any* matter of doctrine. Matters of doctrine and theology seem to remain relegated to a secondary, tangential place in the life of the denomination.

Rather than seriously considering the substance of the complaints brought against the bishop, the SRT responded condescendingly to those bringing the complaints, raising issues about their "spiritual maturity," of their trying to "pressure church leaders and agencies to reflect their positions," and finally and unbelievably, asking that they "desist from exploiting this and other serious matters facing the church to gain financial support or incite division in the body of Christ." The complainants responded, with some exasperation, that they were not seeking to divide the body of Christ, but rather to unify it around the stated doctrinal identity of the denomination. They insisted, "It was not we who precipitated this crisis by publishing a book dissenting from the established doctrine of the church. We are only responding in an attempt to be faithful to our calling as United Methodist laity and clergy."[36]

Those who are ordained elders in the United Methodist Church are asked publicly during the service of ordination, "Will you faithfully proclaim the Word of God and defend the church against all doctrine contrary to God's Word?" The ordinands are expected to answer affirmatively. All United Methodist elders have a covenantal responsibility to defend the doctrines of our church. This disappointing episode left many of us feeling that for a number of our United Methodist leaders, matters of Christian doctrine have, indeed, been trivialized.

I have cited examples of serious doctrinal error. Let me note one more. Bishop John Shelby Spong is a retired bishop of the Episcopal Church in America and is known, amazingly, for his many books *denying* major core doctrines of the Christian faith.

On his website a few years ago, in his "A Call for Reformation," he listed his twelve theses of Christianity, about which as bishop he obviously would be considered a major spokesman. Surprisingly, Spong denied traditional God-talk today as meaningless, and thus dismisses any idea of Jesus as an incarnate deity. He denied the virgin birth and Christ's miracles, and said the view of Christ dying on the cross for the sins of the world is a barbarian idea based on primitive concepts of God. His views were so radical that ten Episcopalian theologians (including two bishops) joined in writing a book *Can a Bishop Be Wrong?*[37] The ten charged that Bishop Spong had essentially placed himself outside the Christian tradition and was actually using his very privileged church position as a bishop to attack that tradition.

The same year the book was published, some fifty bishops of the Episcopal Church USA made a public declaration that Spong's views had become so radical that they were disassociating themselves from him. Clearly, Spong's theological views, even within the liberal Episcopal Church, have been considered utterly unorthodox, even heretical. So well-known were his unorthodox views that he was forbidden to preach or officiate in the Sydney diocese during his 2007 Australian book tour by Sydney archbishop Peter Jensen.[38] Yet, Spong is popular, smooth, and winsome, and his books have sold in the hundreds of thousands.

Now, why mention an Episcopalian bishop? Because unfortunately, he has had considerable entree into the United Methodist Church. In the spring of 2002, Spong was a featured speaker at the Kairos CoMotion Conference in Madison, Wisconsin, a gathering of United Methodists that also included two United Methodist bishops. A month later, on Palm Sunday weekend, Spong gave four addresses at the Dilworth United Methodist Church in Charlotte, North Carolina. On Friday evening alone, some five hundred people paid fifteen dollars each to hear his revisionisms! At the conclusion, the bishop received a standing ovation. Then, a few years later, he was invited to give five lectures to pastors at United Methodist-related McKendree College in southern Illinois. He spoke on the theme of the resurrection, the central doctrine of the Christian church, which he totally rejects.

The reason for introducing Bishop Spong here is that obviously we have United Methodists who share his unorthodox, heretical theological views. He was not invited to these United Methodist gatherings to illustrate to our members just how errant a church leader might become. No, he was invited to preach, teach, and enlighten. No doubt, his sponsors would say he had come to challenge the church to think more deeply, to cause listeners to think outside the box, and to be a catalyst for dialogue.

Unfortunately, Spong has clearly taken up his theological residence outside the box of the church's great doctrinal tradition. He is a popular, outwardly impressive Episcopal leader who has made a huge amount of money—traveling, speaking, and writing (some twenty-four books)—telling of his nonbelief of the major doctrines of the Christian faith, i.e., the Trinity and incarnation, the virgin birth, the miracles, the bodily resurrection of Jesus, the ascension of our Lord, and His promised return. All of these doctrines crumble under his supposed superior new insights. What is obvious here is that Spong clearly embraces all of the major denials we identified as being at the heart of theological liberalism. Any expression of the supernatural is summarily dismissed. While he occasionally bristles with hostility toward the traditional Christian gospel, he generally seems able to present his unbelief in a disarming and winsome way, helped along by his personal charm, Episcopal title, and clerical collar.

This kind of doctrinal denial and revisionism is nothing new. Actually, it is part of a long shadow cast from the decades of the early 1900s, as we have documented in this work. One of C. S. Lewis's more memorable essays reminds us how long the church has struggled with these issues. His address titled "Christian Apologetics" was given in 1945 to a group of Anglican priests and youth leaders of the Church in Wales.

Lewis began the address with what he called some "unpleasant business." He needed to address a problem. He said that it seemed to the layman that in the Church of England, "we often hear from our priests doctrine which is not Anglican Christianity."[39] And just how does it depart from Anglican Christianity? He stated, "It may be so 'broad' or 'liberal' or 'modern' that it in fact *excludes any real Supernaturalism and thus ceases to be Christian at all*" (emphasis mine).[40] How familiar that sounds. The priests had trimmed their doctrine of anything supernatural, and Lewis believed that in doing so, it was no longer Christian. He continued with his great penetrating paragraph that is vintage Lewis:

It is not, of course, for me to define to you what Anglican Christianity is—I am your pupil, not your teacher. But I insist that wherever you draw the lines, bounding lines must exist, beyond which your doctrine will cease either to be Anglican or to be Christian; and I suggest also that the lines come a great deal sooner than many modern priests think. I think it is your duty to fix the lines clearly in your own minds: and if you wish to go beyond them you must change your profession. This is your duty not specially as Christians or as priests but as honest men.[41]

Lewis went on to make sure the priests understood exactly what he was saying. He anticipated that some who had passed beyond those boundary lines would certainly defend themselves by saying they had come to their unorthodox doctrines honestly. But he would have none of that. He replied, "But this simply misses the point which so gravely scandalizes the layman. We never doubted that the unorthodox opinions were honestly held: what we complain of is your continuing your ministry after you have come to hold them."[42]

After addressing the matter of teaching doctrine that is in direct contradiction to Anglican Christianity, Lewis then turned to the task of the Christian apologist—that of defending the Christian faith. He wrote memorably that our task is "to defend Christianity itself—the faith preached by the Apostles, attested by the Martyrs, embodied in the Creeds, expounded by the Fathers. This must be clearly distinguished from the whole of what any one of us may think about God and Man."[43] Certainly, he admitted, we all have our emphases, views, and opinions, but "as apologists it is not our business to defend *them*. We are defending Christianity; not 'my religion.'"[44]

In Lewis's view, for the Anglican priest, fidelity to the doctrines of the Church of England was clearly a matter of personal integrity. To continue in the church's employ when one no longer believed its doctrines would be a shameful breach of trust. Covenants of ordination were sacred and meant to be kept. One's promise to believe and faithfully teach the doctrines of the church was not a trivial matter. It was a matter of sacred honor and personal integrity.

I have suggested in this chapter that a part of the legacy of theological liberalism was the trivialization of doctrine in the United Methodist Church. Clearly, Lewis believed this was happening in the Church of England in the mid-1940s. Further, he understood that to make something trivial is to view it as unimportant or insignificant. When that happens, then something else will inevitably be introduced to take its place. Lewis would have none of it. He knew that when it comes to the foundational doctrines of the Christian church, fidelity is an absolute necessity. One senses he would bring the identical message today were he alive and addressing a gathering of United Methodists.

As we have seen, the evidence is compelling that doctrine and theology have been trivialized and relegated to a secondary role in the life of the United Methodist Church. Many have trimmed the church's doctrine of all things supernatural. When this is done, one must acknowledge that it ceases to be Christian. Some might smile and describe it as Christianity lite, but that does not change the reality.

As one looks at the history of Methodism over the last century, one is impressed of the critical importance of being sure we are being faithful to the doctrinal truths of the gospel, of which we are stewards. If we are to be faithful to our calling, we must be sure that we are getting the gospel right.

Chapter 13

Getting the Gospel Right

IN THIS FINAL chapter on the legacy of theological liberalism, several general impressions come immediately to mind. The first is that one should easily realize the impact these trends have had on United Methodism today, especially in its attitudes toward the role and place of doctrine. One might more readily understand why only five thousand of our more than thirty thousand congregations would be considered "highly vital." One might also more easily understand how the Towers Watson Congregational Vitality research project found a "lack of trust" to be a pervasive and recurring theme in the majority of their interviews. It has helped me, an ordained pastor in the United Methodist Church for more than forty-five years, understand better how the denomination has relegated doctrine to a very secondary role and felt it was being quite Wesleyan in doing so.

An illustration of this diminution of doctrine is seen in the *Call to Action Steering Team Report*, the quadrennial project noted in the introduction of this work. A task force of twenty church leaders published the report based on the findings of the Towers Watson consulting team survey. It identified five drivers behind the vitality of the most vital local churches, but amazingly said nothing about the importance or place of theology. In an analysis of the report, George G. Hunter III, former distinguished professor of evangelism and church growth at Asbury Theological Seminary, wrote of several "great omissions" he noted in the report, the very first being: "You would never know, from the *Call to Action*, that revitalization could have anything to do with theology, or that there could possibly be anything sub-Christian, dysfunctional, heretical, or eccentric about anyone's theology." He went on to note the obvious, saying, "But there *is* a very strong connection between theology and vitality."[1] Indeed, only a church that has relegated theology to a subordinate role would omit it from serious considerations when seeking denominational revitalization.

A second general impression is that the implications of how early Methodist leadership and institutions were influenced by theological liberalism are so very far-reaching as to be difficult to fully grasp. My hope would be that others might continue the study about the many ways Methodism has been negatively influenced by the new theology in the early twentieth century. In numerous conversations with many United Methodist pastors and clergy, I have found it is a period about which many know very little. Some are aware of a fundamentalist versus modernist controversy long ago or they have heard about the Scopes trial, but beyond that they know little of our Methodist history during that era.

The Danger of Accommodation

Interestingly, there is a brief, almost passing reference to this historical period in the present *Book of Discipline*.[2] Under the section "Our Doctrinal History," it refers to "the waning force of doctrinal discipline and the decreasing influence of the Wesleyan theological heritage among the American Methodists"[3] at the beginning of the twentieth century. Of this period, it states that "theologians and church leaders began to explore ways of expressing the gospel that were *in keeping with developing intellectual currents*" (emphasis mine). It goes on to say "These years were times of theological and ethical controversy within Methodism as new patterns of thought clashed with the more familiar themes and styles of the previous two centuries."[4] Read that last sentence again carefully. This is a major understatement. As we have seen, there was indeed a "clash." And it was highly significant and about far more than "patterns of thought" clashing with "themes and styles" from an earlier era. It was a major clash over *substance*, as the central doctrines of the historic faith were being accommodated to the new intellectual milieu of secularism and rationalism—accommodated, if not set aside entirely.

During this era, Methodism was indeed accommodating itself to the new secular thought sweeping across the intellectual landscape. In every age, of course, the church is always in danger of accommodation, and especially as it attempts to present the gospel in ways that are "in keeping with developing intellectual currents." This phrase should always trigger our internal alarms. Accommodation, in simpler terms, means to adapt, adjust, or reconcile differences. That was exactly what was happening during that period. The gospel was being adapted or changed with the hope of making it more palatable to the modern, scientific outlook that was emerging.

German theologian Wolfhart Pannenberg warned about accommodation as the church seeks ways to confront and respond to the challenge of secularism. He said, "The absolutely worse way to respond to the challenge of secularism is to adapt to secular standards in language, thought, and way of life."[5] He said people who turn to religion are looking for something other than what that culture already provides. He added, "It is counterproductive to offer them religion in a secular mode that is carefully trimmed in order not to offend their secular sensibilities."[6] When the church's message and ritual are accommodated and the offending edges removed, the result is "people are invited to suspect that the clergy do not really believe anything so very distinctive."[7] This was largely what happened within Methodism in the early twentieth century. The offending edges of the church's message were, indeed, being trimmed, if not removed. It is mentioned only briefly in the *Discipline's* paragraph "Our Doctrinal History," but the historical reality was much larger, more far-reaching, and longer-lasting than is implied in the few sentences in the *Discipline*.

With the hope that others will investigate further this era and how it has affected Methodism, I will present here briefly what I believe to be a major part of the ongoing legacy of theological liberalism.

Seeds of Distrust and Decline Sown in the Early 1900s

We have seen in this work that the seeds for Methodism's decline were sown more than a hundred years ago—in the period of the early 1900s. This was an era in which theological liberalism brought sweeping change to the substance of Methodist thought and teaching. While not embraced widely by local church pastors and most laity, it was affirmed by much of Methodism's leadership during that period— including many bishops, theologians, editors of publications, board and agency staff, and pastors of large urban churches.

In the previous chapters, we looked briefly at the deep intellectual ferment that took place in America at the beginning of the 1900s. With the emerging of the new science and social Darwinism as well as the influence of German rationalism, the churches encountered massive social and intellectual challenges they had not faced before.

This is a part of our forgotten past. It was an era in which Methodism and the other mainline denominations experienced major doctrinal transition and revision. For a number of Methodist pastors and leaders (and most all of the mainline Protestant churches in America, for that matter), there was a move away from the super-natural elements of the faith. Doctrines such as the virgin birth, the resurrection of Christ, the miracles, the ascension, and the prom-ised return of Christ were difficult to affirm amid the exhilarating and supposedly liberating views of the new science and emerging rationalism.

During this period, the great creeds of the church (i.e., Apostles' and Nicene) were deemphasized and in their place came the new, more relevant "Social Creed of the Churches." The crushing social needs emerging in the major urban areas of America made it easy for many larger churches to justify their change in focus to center more on the social and ethical teachings of Jesus while downplaying the controversial and divisive doctrines (which assume supernaturalism) at the heart of the Christian faith.

It was this intellectual and social milieu that gave rise to theological liberalism, the movement that accommodated the Christian faith to the new, anti-supernatural axioms that had quickly become widely accepted in American Protestant churches, including Methodism. With its diminution of the historic creeds of the faith, liberalism also helped give birth to the social gospel, the movement that focused on the social and ethical teachings of Jesus, with an emphasis on establishing the kingdom of God on earth by vigorous and untiring human effort. For many who had embraced theological liberalism at the time, this primary focus on ethics and building the kingdom of God was a natural and very popular new theme. Adding to its popularity was its convenient avoidance of the problematic supernatural doctrines of the traditional Christian message.

During this time of intellectual ferment, American Methodism was loath to enter into serious theological controversy. After more than a quarter of a century of debate, controversy, and eventually schism over the Holiness Movement, the church was left weary and apprehensive of doctrinal polemic. At a time in which it was desperately needed, doctrinal controversy and debate within Methodism were in "bad odor," noted John Peters.[8] Also, Methodist bishops were concerned that renewed doctrinal controversy might lead to further division across Methodism. They were determined to avoid controversy at all costs and thus chose to emphasize unity and collegiality rather than engage the serious doctrinal questions that were challenging and changing the historic doctrines of their church. Sadly, this happened even though a number of the bishops knew full well that doctrinal revision and neglect were taking place.

During this period, doctrine was relegated to a secondary role in the life of the church. As noted earlier, this highly significant change was justified by claims that had become widely accepted at the time: (a) Methodism is not a creedal church; (b) Wesley was more concerned about experience than about doctrine; and (c) the church must give its major attention to the critical social needs facing American society, not be distracted by divisive doctrinal questions and controversies. This diminution of the role of doctrine in the church served a useful purpose—it provided convenient cover for the substantive doctrinal changes that were taking place at the time. Interestingly, the three sentiments just noted have had a long shelf life in the denomination. They are cited by some United Methodists yet today, having become firmly embedded as part of our church's oral tradition.

Also coming out of the first decades of the 1900s was the loss of integrity in the church's language about doctrine. To avoid alienating their parishioners and support base in local churches, some clergy and church leaders began using doctrinal terms and phrases that *sounded* consistent with the church's traditional doctrinal understandings, but were often infused with different meanings. These linguistic subtleties were not always perceived by laypersons. On the other hand, many laity did sense that their pastors were saying less and less about what they really believed personally. The result was a widening chasm between laity and clergy, as well as between seminary-trained clergy and those who entered the ministry through the Course of Study. There was a growing lack of unity about the foundational doctrines of the church and a growing sense of distrust and alienation, as we have seen. In many ways, Methodism was becoming a house divided doctrinally, but all the while determined not to talk about it.

I have tried to show in this work that theological liberalism has had a detrimental influence on the Methodist Church across the last century and into the present. In fact, it has also had an impact upon every mainline denomination in America, all of which have struggled with doctrinal malaise, membership loss, and diminished vitality. I have also shown that a significant number of contemporary theologians and clergy no longer affirm the major doctrines of the historic Christian faith. Some have acknowledged as much candidly, while others have claimed they are just reinterpreting these doctrines for the present day. The reinterpretations can be subtle, using the familiar language of traditional Christianity, but often infusing it with non-traditional meanings. This is always done with the best of motives, we are told, to make these doctrines more palatable to modern sensitivities.

Our Responsibility to Get the Gospel Right

This study has left me more convinced than ever of the importance of the church seeking renewed faithfulness in its understanding and proclamation of the message of the gospel. *It is imperative that the church gets the substance of the gospel right.* Our survey of the proliferation of movements to protest, reform, and renew the Methodist Church (and, since 1968, the United Methodist Church) would indicate that the church has, in fact, often gotten the gospel wrong.

In 1999, the evangelical journal *Christianity Today* published a statement titled "The Gospel of Jesus Christ: An Evangelical Celebration," which was a part of the journal's Evangelical Doctrinal Renewal project, supported in part by the Lilly Endowment.[9] It arose from an awareness that evangelicals were working in collaboration with Catholic and Orthodox leaders in endeavors such as the pro-life movement and were developing new friendships in doing so. As a result, it reminded these evangelicals that as Protestants, they needed to know their Protestantism more deeply.

David Neff, then executive editor of *Christianity Today*, wrote an introduction to the statement on behalf of the drafting committee stating that "in evangelicals' ongoing contact and collaboration with the historic churches, it is time for us to revisit, reaffirm and recapture the gospel." The nine-member drafting committee included well-known and widely respected evangelical leaders such as Maxie Dunnam, Timothy George, Thomas Oden, and J. I. Packer.

Neff went on to write that as religious communities and Christian individuals gather to enrich one another and work together, "the biblical understanding of the good news is, first, the most important thing that we can offer friends in these churches and, second, the only thing in which we can find true unity."[10] That is a remarkable statement! He went on to say that we humans "seem to have an infinite capacity for getting things wrong, and unfortunately, we have often gotten the gospel wrong."[11] When I read those words, I can't help but reflect on our more than four decades of decline in United Methodist membership. I do not remember any time during my ministry that United Methodism has taken the time to ask the hard question: Could our struggles and loss of membership and morale be happening because we aren't getting the gospel right?

"An Evangelical Celebration" had a boldness and clarity about it. The preamble stated unapologetically, "This gospel is the only gospel, there is no other; and to change its substance is to pervert and indeed destroy it."[12] This is refreshingly straightforward and reminds us that we must not take liberties with the message of redemption, making of it something other than what it was meant to be. It reminds us why Jude would write and refer to "the faith that was once for all entrusted to the saints" (Jude 3 NRSV). We are not at liberty to rewrite the script.

The evangelical statement is commendable for its richness and clarity. For example, it made this candid affirmation: "The moment we truly believe in Christ, the Father declares us righteous in him and begins conforming us to his likeness. Genuine faith acknowledges and depends upon Jesus as Lord and shows itself in growing obedience to the divine commands, though this contributes nothing to the ground of our justification."[13] Again, it reminds us that "salvation in its full sense is from the guilt of sin in the past, the power of sin in the present, and the presence of sin in the future."[14] And again, "Salvation is a Trinitarian reality, initiated by the Father, implemented by the Son, and applied by the Holy Spirit."[15]

Following in the tradition of the Barmen Declaration[16] of more than seventy years ago, "An Evangelical Celebration" concludes with a list of eighteen affirmations and denials. Not only does the statement celebrate the things God has done to bring redemption to the world, but also takes the time and space "to name and deny the ways the church and her members have misconstrued or even perverted the good news."[17] For instance, under "Affirmations and Denials," number 3 states: "We affirm that the Gospel diagnoses the universal human condition as one of sinful rebellion against God. We deny any rejection of the fallenness of human nature or any assertion of the natural goodness, or divinity, of the human race."[18]

This statement focuses on one of the major tenets of theological liberalism—the denial or rejection of the fallenness of humanity, replacing it with an affirmation of the essential goodness of mankind. This was one of the significant doctrinal changes that took place during the period of the early 1900s, as we noted in chapter 6.

A classic illustration of this change was seen when Edwin Lewis referred to a lost world, and to fallen and sin-doomed humanity in his *A Christian Manifesto,* published in 1934 and cited earlier. A strong critic of Lewis's book and especially his description of a fallen humanity was Jonathan B. Hawk, the associate editor of *Adult Home Publications,* Department of Church School Publications, of the Methodist Episcopal Church. He wrote to Lewis, "If I had to admit that man's nature was essentially sinful, I could certainly not accept any redemption that might be offered." He went on to say, "I could not bring myself to trust a Creator who had made me essentially wicked and then found it necessary to redeem me from that wickedness before he could count me worthy of his grace."[19] One finds here a shocking misunderstanding and denial of the doctrine of original sin.

Another key statement under "Affirmations and Denials" and one that is especially relevant for this work, is number 10. It states: "We affirm that the bodily resurrection of Christ from the dead is essential to the biblical Gospel (1 Cor. 15:14). We deny the validity of any so-called gospel that denies the historical reality of the bodily resurrection of Christ."[20] As we saw in previous chapters, the denial of the bodily resurrection of Christ was a major theme of theological liberalism and has continued on to the present day.

The use of affirmations and denials is a device that, unfortunately, becomes necessary when specific misstatements and wrong doctrine are cloaked in ambiguous language and purposeful obfuscations. It should not be this way, but sadly, it is the nature of our theological reality.

"An Evangelical Celebration" was a timely reminder that a true, biblical understanding of the good news of the gospel is, indeed, the most important thing that we can offer those in our churches. It reminds us that (a) this gospel is the only gospel; (b) we have often gotten it wrong; (c) we must make sure we get it right; (d) we dare not change or pervert it; and (e) it remains the only thing in which we can find true unity.

The Gospel and Authentic Unity

"An Evangelical Celebration" reminds us that a true, biblical understanding of the gospel is the only thing in which we can find true unity. We remember our Lord praying for his followers that "they may be one as we are one" (John 17:11). Paul urged the Ephesians, "Make every effort to keep the unity of the Spirit through the bond of peace" (Eph. 4:3). Most of us would agree that divisions in the body of Christ have sometimes been a scandal. In fact, "An Evangelical Celebration" was an endeavor among Catholics, Protestants, and Orthodox to bridge historic divisions and come to a deeper understanding of the faith. It emerged out of new experiences as people in those communions developed new friendships while working together on behalf of pro-life and other issues.

Unfortunately, most conversation about unity that I recall throughout my years of ministry was a call for unity-at-any-price. This ultimately means, of course, unity at the cost of biblical truth. On scores of occasions an appeal to unity was the card being played to trump matters of questionable doctrine. It was a familiar process. The insistence on unity was always deemed urgent, and even the most questionable doctrinal claims were to be allowed under the mandate of unity.

But unity may not always have the final say in our disputations in the church. Robert George, a professor at Princeton University, cautioned us that there is something even worse than the scandal of division in the church. It is what he referred to as the scandal of the "affectation of unity between those who do and those who do not affirm the core doctrines of Christian faith—particularly its most fundamental moral teachings."[21]

What is an "affectation of unity"? An affectation is a pretending, a pretense, an artificial behavior meant to impress others. So, an affectation of unity is a pretending to be united or a claim to unity that is really artificial, made simply for the sake of others watching. What is it that makes an affectation of unity scandalous? George explained, "It tends to damage and weaken the faith of those who are exposed to it. It sends a message to them that the core doctrines and moral teachings of Christianity need not be taken too seriously."[22] This, as I mentioned earlier, trivializes Christian doctrine and teaching.

George went on to say about this affectation of unity, "It implies that one can be a 'good Christian' while disbelieving the doctrines of the Trinity and Incarnation, the Virgin Birth and bodily Resurrection of Jesus, and while accepting secularist liberal ideas about abortion, euthanasia, pre-marital sex, homosexuality, and so forth."[23] It is on these matters, George said, that "we encounter divisions that must be sustained." He concluded by saying again, "The true scandal is to pretend to a unity that does not exist and cannot exist because there is nothing to base it on."[24] Indeed, the only thing in which we will find an authentic unity is a faithful, biblical understanding of the good news of the gospel.

It is at this point that United Methodism is a house divided. Unfortunately, there are "divisions that must be sustained." We pray for the day when that will not be so. But sharp doctrinal differences are a reality with which we live today. This is the major reason the church struggles with a pervasive lack of trust.

Again, it is critical for the future of the United Methodist Church that we get the gospel right. This will take prayerful discernment. Why? Because often, the changes and revisions that have found their way into the church's preaching and teaching are subtle and not easily discerned.

Philip Turner, an Episcopalian theologian, wrote a very penetrating and timely essay a few years ago about when he made his personal discovery that the substance of the gospel had changed within the Episcopal Church. What he discovered, he suggested, is applicable not just to the Episcopal Church but to all of the mainline denominations in America.[25] That was exactly how I felt when I read his essay. It is profoundly relevant for our United Methodist experience.

Turner is the former dean of the Berkeley Divinity School at Yale. He served ten years as a missionary in Uganda and returned to do graduate work in Christian ethics with Paul Ramsey at Princeton University. Upon completion of his graduate work, he taught at the Episcopal Theological Seminary of the Southwest.

In his essay, he wrote of his excitement as he listened to his first student sermon, "only to be taken aback by its vacuity." The student asked the right question: What is the Christian gospel? But his answer repeated throughout the sermon was simply "God is love. God loves us. We, therefore, ought to love one another."[26]

Turner said he was stunned by the shallowness of it all:

> I waited in vain for some word about the saving power of Christ's cross or the declaration of God's victory in Christ's resurrection. I waited in vain for a promise of the Holy Spirit.

I waited in vain also for an admonition to wait patiently and faithfully for the Lord's return. I waited in vain for a call to repentance and amendment of life . . .[27]

The rich, substantive content of biblical preaching he had heard for a decade in Anglican pulpits in Uganda was simply not there. Nor was this just an isolated incident from a poor and struggling seminary student. He insisted that over the years he had heard "the same sermon preached from pulpit after pulpit by experienced priests."[28] Many United Methodists have also heard it as well.

His conclusion was that the actual or "working theology" of the Episcopal Church, as he called it, begins with the claim that "God is love, pure and simple. Thus, one is to see in Christ's death no judgment upon the human condition. Rather, one is to see an affirmation of creation and the persons we are. The life and death of Jesus reveal the fact that God accepts and affirms us."[29]

From this very simplistic understanding of God, Turner described further this "working theology." Since God is love and wants us to love one another, "such love requires of us both acceptance and affirmation of the other . . . Accepting love requires a form of justice that is inclusive of all people, particularly those who in some way have been marginalized by oppressive social practice."[30] Therefore, the mission of the church is to see that "those who have been rejected are included—for justice as inclusion defines public policy." The result of all this, Turner claimed, is "a practical equivalence between the gospel of the Kingdom of God and a particular form of social justice." For many in the Episcopal Church, he said, the gospel has been equated solely with the social justice concept of "radical inclusion."[31] This equation of the gospel and social justice has become for that denominational body the primary expression of Christian truth.

Turner was convinced that this view represents a huge divide for the Episcopal Church: "This isn't an ethical divide about the rightness or wrongness of homosexuality and same-sex marriage. It's a theological chasm—one that separates those who hold a theology of divine *acceptance* from those who hold a theology of divine *redemption*."[32] A major difference, indeed.

This new "working theology" of the Episcopal Church has had a subtle but real impact on that denomination, said Turner. "In respect to God, it produces a quasi-deist theology that posits a benevolent God who favors love and justice as inclusion but acts neither to save us from our sins nor to raise us to new life after the pattern of Christ." And in respect to human beings, "it produces an ethic of tolerant affirmation that carries with it no call to conversion and radical holiness."[33] For Turner, this is a stunning development. In his church's new theology dominated by radical inclusion, he said that "terms such as 'faith,' 'justification,' 'repentance,' and 'holiness of life' seem to belong to an antique vocabulary that must be outgrown or reinterpreted."[34] He tells how it struck him one day just how far apart the American Episcopal Church was theologically from the rich, basic content of Nicene Christianity.

What Turner has described in his thought-provoking article is the emergence of a new or different gospel within the Episcopal Church. In fact, he went on to make the sobering claim that this "working theology" of the Episcopal Church in America is something that most Anglicans in the rest of the world "no longer recognize as Christian."[35] There is a world of difference between a message of divine *acceptance* and a message of divine *redemption*. One could think that Turner was describing the subtle changes and revisions that have found their way into our Methodist world across the years. There is a breathtaking shallowness in such theology.

A Warning about Other Gospels

The apostle Paul wrote to the church in Galatia about these issues. He was, in fact, astonished that the Galatians were "so quickly deserting the one who called you to live in the grace of Christ and are turning to a different gospel—which is really no gospel at all" (Gal. 1:6–7).

The church in Galatia had been thrown into controversy by false teachers, most likely Judaizers, who were distorting the message of the gospel by adding the necessity of circumcision according to the law of Moses. To the gospel of grace through the finished work of Christ they were adding the requirement of circumcision and works of the law. This was something Paul would not tolerate. Notice his passion about the matter. He wrote, "Evidently some people are throwing you into confusion and are trying to pervert the gospel of Christ. But even if we or an angel from heaven should preach a gospel other than the one we preached to you, let them be under God's curse!" (Gal. 1:7–8). Note, he even included himself in the warning: "If we . . ." Then, he repeated the statement for emphasis.

His charge against them was that they were "turning to a different gospel—which is really no gospel at all" (vv. 6–7). Paul was insisting the gospel was being changed, altered, or perverted, and he simply insisted that there must be no "different" or "other gospel." Elsewhere, he gave a charge to Timothy to "guard the good deposit that was entrusted to you" (2 Tim. 1:14). He was alerting him to the danger of those who would try to alter and distort the message he had entrusted to Timothy.

The late Anglican evangelical John R. W. Stott observed that the false teachers in Galatia were *changing* the gospel and *troubling* the church. He added insightfully that the two always go together:

> To tamper with the gospel is always to trouble the church. You cannot touch the gospel and leave the church untouched, because the church is created and lives by the gospel. Indeed, the church's greatest troublemakers (now as then) are not those outside who oppose, ridicule and persecute it, but those inside who try to change the gospel. It is they who trouble the church.[36]

Paul's words are still timely and instructive for us. We should also note that the Judaizers were not *denying* major tenets of the Christian message. They were not refuting the resurrection of Christ or His virgin birth. They were not denying the miracles Christ had performed. They were simply adding something more to the message of justification by faith. But for the apostle Paul, that was simply not to be allowed. For Paul, to *change* the gospel would be to *distort* the gospel. It is critical that the church get the gospel right.

In Conclusion

In looking at the emergence of theological liberalism in the early twentieth century, one can conclude from the historical data that the new theology that appeared on the scene during that era was a very different understanding of the gospel for the Christian church. Professor Edwin Lewis knew what most of us should realize today. That is, when the supernatural doctrinal elements of Christianity are removed or replaced or radically reinterpreted, you have a new and different religion from historic Christianity.[37]

J. Gresham Machen expressed virtually the same thought when he wrote, "We shall be interested in showing that despite the liberal use of traditional phraseology modern liberalism not only is a different religion from Christianity but belongs in a totally different class of religions."[38]

These theologians, living in the midst of the effusive excitement of the new theology, were witnessing liberal theologians abandoning one doctrine after another and knew that what remained was something quite different from historic Christianity. There is ample historical evidence that the influence of early twentieth-century theological liberalism has had a lasting influence on American Methodism up to the present day—and for that matter, on the other mainline denominations in America as well.

Admittedly, the liberal theological consensus that has dominated United Methodism and mainline Protestantism for many decades is fading away. However, its legacy continues in the denial of all things supernatural, as we have seen. But increasingly, serious Christians are seeing it for what it is—a this-world-only religious system that denies the revealed nature of historic Christianity. It offers a host of moral and ethical platitudes but without transcendent roots.

In rereading the text of the Louisville Declaration recently, part 5 seemed especially timely for what I have been trying to say in this work:

> We deplore our church's defection from its essential Wesleyan Doctrine. The crisis of the United Methodist Church today is a lack of biblical authority and a flawed theology. We must resist imposing upon the church any agenda as a substitute for the central themes of the gospel. The church's preoccupation with the socio-political arena has diminished its credibility and influence in the world. Our faith has come to us at the cost of the lives of saints and martyrs. We must not pass to succeeding generations a gospel which is distorted or defective.

(For the full text of the Louisville Declaration, see appendix D.)

We must pray for and seek a new generation of faithful and courageous leaders who will help the United Methodist Church recover and return to the *sensus fidelium*, the consensus of the faithful, in terms of the historic Christian faith and our rich Wesleyan doctrinal heritage. As we have seen, this magnificent message, about a Savior whose finished work is now offered freely to all of humankind, is the most important thing we have to offer to those in our churches and in the world. And it is the only thing in which our struggling, divided, and demoralized church will find real unity and renewed vitality.

Appendices

One of the impressive realities of this generation is how United Methodist evangelicals and traditionalists have gathered out of concern about the doctrinal and moral issues facing their churches. Many concerned United Methodists, both clergy and laity, have joined in issuing statements or declarations on behalf of the evangelical and traditional constituencies of their churches. In the appendices are historical accounts and complete texts of seven of those statements or declarations (see titles above). Together, they represent an important historical record of calls to the church and its leaders to be faithful to the doctrines and moral standards of our church.

Appendix A

The Junaluska Affirmation

The Junaluska Affirmation of Scriptural Christianity for United Methodists

ON JULY 20, 1975, the statement, "An Affirmation of Scriptural Christianity for United Methodists" was adopted by the Board of Directors of Good News during the 1975 Convocation of United Methodists for Evangelical Christianity meeting at Lake Junaluska, North Carolina.

Preamble

In a time of theological pluralism, Good News and other evangelicals within United Methodism have thought it necessary to reaffirm the historic faith of the Church. Our theological understanding of this faith has been expressed in the Apostles' Creed, Nicene Creed, and in John Wesley's *Standard Sermons* and the *Explanatory Notes* upon the New Testament. We affirm in their entirety the validity and integrity of these expressions of Scriptural truth, and recognize them as the doctrinal standards of our denomination.

We also recognize that our situation calls for a contemporary restatement of these truths. The merging of two great traditions, the Evangelical United Brethren and the Methodist, with their two authentic witnesses to the historic faith, The Confession of Faith and The Articles of Religion, gives further occasion for such a statement. Moreover, we recognize the mandate which the doctrinal statement of the 1972 General Conference has placed upon "all its members to accept the challenge of responsible theological reflection."

Consequently, we offer to the United Methodist Church this theological affirmation of Scriptural Christianity.

The Holy Trinity

Scriptural Christianity affirms the existence of the one Eternal God who has revealed Himself as Father, Son and Holy Spirit, three equal but distinct Persons, mysteriously united in the Godhead which the Church historically has described as the Holy Trinity.

God the Father

Scriptural Christianity affirms that the first Person of the Holy Trinity, God the Father, is the Eternal One and reigns supremely. He has provided a covenant through which His creatures can be redeemed and through which His creation will be liberated from all evil and brought to final righteousness at the end of the age.

God the Son

Scriptural Christianity affirms that the second Person of the Holy Trinity, the Eternal Son, became incarnate as Mary's virgin/born Child, Jesus of Nazareth, the Christ. In His unique Person, He revealed to us both the fullness of deity and the fullness of humanity. By His life, suffering, death, resurrection and ascension He provided the only way of salvation. His sacrifice on the cross once and for all was to reconcile the Holy God and sinners, thus providing the only way of access to the Father. Now He intercedes as High Priest before the Father, awaiting the day when He will return to judge every person, living and dead, and to consummate His Kingdom.

God the Holy Spirit

Scriptural Christianity affirms that the third Person of the Holy Trinity, the Holy Spirit, was active from the beginning in creation, revelation and redemption. It was through His anointing that prophets received the Word of God, priests became intermediaries between God and His people, and kings were given ruling authority. The Spirit's presence and power, measured in the Old Testament, were found without measure in Jesus of Nazareth, the Anointed. The Spirit convicts and woos the lost, gives new birth to the penitent, and abides in the believer, perfecting holiness and empowering the Church to carry out Christ's mission in the world. He came to indwell His Church at Pentecost, enabling believers to yield fruit and endowing them with spiritual gifts according to His will. He bears witness to Christ and guides God's people into His truth. He inspired the Holy Scriptures, God's written Word, and continues to illuminate His people concerning His will and truth. His guidance is always in harmony with Christ and the truth as given in the Holy Scriptures.

Humanity

Scriptural Christianity affirms that man and woman are fashioned in the image of God and are different from all of God's other creatures. God intends that we should glorify Him and enjoy Him forever. Since the Fall of Adam the corruption of sin has pervaded every person and extended into social relationships, societal systems, and all creation. This corruption is so pervasive that we are not capable of positive responses to God's offer of Redemption, except by the prevenient, or preparing, grace of God. Only through the justifying, regenerating and sanctifying work of the Triune God can we be saved from the corruption of sin, become increasingly conformed to the image of Christ, and restored to the relationships which God has intended for us.

The Holy Scriptures

Scriptural Christianity affirms as the only written Word of God the Old and New Testaments. These Holy Scriptures contain all that is necessary for our knowledge of God's holy and sovereign will, of Jesus Christ the only Redeemer, of our salvation, and of our growth in grace. They are to be received through the Holy Spirit as the guide and final authority for the faith and conduct of individuals and the doctrines and life of the church. Whatever is not clearly revealed in, or plainly established as truth by, the Holy Scriptures cannot be required as an article of faith nor be taught as essential to salvation. Anything contrary to the teachings of the Holy Scriptures is contrary to the purposes of God and must, therefore, be opposed. The authority of Scripture derives from the fact that God, through His Spirit, inspired the authors, causing them to perceive God's truth and record it with accuracy. It is evident that the Holy Scriptures have been preserved during the long process of transmission through copyists and translators, and we attribute such accurate preservation to the work of the Holy Spirit. These Scriptures are supremely authoritative for the Church's teaching, preaching, witness, identifying error, collecting the erring, and training believers for ministry in and through the Church.

Salvation

Scriptural Christianity affirms that God offers salvation to a sinful humanity and a lost world through Jesus Christ. By His death on the cross the sinless Son propitiated the holy wrath of the Father, a righteous anger occasioned by sin. By His resurrection from the dead, the glorified Son raises us to newness of life. When we appropriate by faith God's atoning work in Jesus Christ we are forgiven, justified, regenerated by His Holy Spirit, and adopted into the family of God. By His grace He sanctifies His children, purifying their hearts by faith, renewing them in the image of God, and enabling them to love God and neighbor with whole heart. The fullness of God's great salvation will come with the return of Christ. This cosmic event will signal the resurrection of the saved to eternal life and the lost to eternal damnation, the liberation of creation from the Adamic curse, God's final victory over every power and dominion, and the establishment of the new heaven and the new earth.

The Church

Scriptural Christianity affirms that the Church of Jesus Christ is the community of all true believers under His sovereign Lordship. This Church, the Body of Christ, is one because it shares one Lord, one faith, one baptism. It is holy because it belongs to God and is set apart for His purposes in the world. It is apostolic because it partakes of the authority granted to the apostles by Christ Himself. It is universal because it includes all believers, both living and dead, in every nation, regardless of denominational affiliation. Its authenticity is to be found wherever the pure Word of God is preached and taught; wherever the Sacrament of Baptism and Holy Communion are celebrated in obedience to Christ's command; wherever the gifts of the Holy Spirit upbuild the body and bring spiritual growth; wherever the Spirit of God creates a loving, caring fellowship, and a faithfulness in witness and service to the world; and wherever discipline is administered with love under the guidance of the Word of God. The Church, as the Bride of Christ, will ultimately be joined with her Lord in triumphant glory.

Ethics

Scriptural Christianity affirms that we are God's workmanship, created in Christ Jesus for good works. These works are the loving expressions of gratitude by the believer for the new life received in Christ. They do not earn one's salvation nor are they a substitute for God's work of redemption. Rather, they are the result of regeneration and are manifest in the believer as evidence of a living faith.

God has called us to do justice, to love kindness, and to walk humbly with Him. In the Scriptures are found the standards and principles that guide the believer in this walk. These ethical imperatives, willingly accepted by the believer, enable us to be a part of God's purposes in the world. Moreover, in this we are called to an obedience that does not stop short of our willingness to suffer for righteousness' sake, even unto death.

Our life in Christ includes an unstinting devotion to deeds of kindness and mercy and a wholehearted participation in collective efforts to alleviate need and suffering. The believer will work for honesty, justice and equity in human affairs; all of which witness to inherent rights and a basic dignity common to all persons created in the image of God. Such contemporary issues as racism, housing, welfare, education, Marxism, Capitalism, hunger, crime, sexism, family relationships, aging, sexuality, drugs and alcohol, abortion, leisure, pornography, and related issues call for prayerful consideration, thoughtful analysis, and appropriate action from Christians, and must always be a matter of concern to the Church. Thus, we remember that faith without works is dead.

Postscript

In April, 1974 the Good News Board of Directors appointed a Theology and Doctrine Task Force to prepare an affirmative statement of Scriptural Christianity for Good News.

The task force was chaired by the Rev. Dr. Paul A. Mickey, Assistant Professor of Pastoral Theology, Divinity School, Duke University, Durham, North Carolina. Additional task force members included: the Rev. Riley Case, Pastor, Wesley UM Church, Union City, Indiana; the Rev. Dr. James V. Heidinger, Pastor, The UM Church, Cadiz, Ohio; the Rev. Dr. Charles V. Keysor, Editor, Good News, Wilmore,

Kentucky; the Rev. Dr. Dennis F. Kinlaw, President, Asbury College, Wilmore, Kentucky; Mr. Lawrence Souder, layman, Centerville, Ohio; the Rev. Dr. Frank B. Stanger, President, Asbury Theological Seminary, Wilmore, Kentucky; and initially, the Rev. Bob Stamps, Chaplain, Oral Roberts University, Tulsa, Oklahoma.

© 1975 Forum for Scriptural Christianity Within The United Methodist Church (Good News.) Permission is hereby granted to reproduce this document without alteration, providing credit is given to copyright holder.

Appendix B

The Houston Declaration

IN DECEMBER 1987, forty-eight leading United Methodist ministers from forty-two churches in eighteen states gathered in Houston to draft a strongly worded statement cautioning the United Methodist Church against a move away from traditional doctrine.

The pastors from some of the denomination's largest churches came on short notice and at their own expense at the invitation of seven prominent United Methodist pastors, including William H. Hinson, pastor of Houston's First United Methodist Church, who served as chairman of the group and host pastor for the gathering.

On December 15, the organizing pastors released the Houston Declaration to the media, a document carefully prepared by those present which affirmed their strong support of three key United Methodist positions: (1) the primacy of Scripture; (2) the traditional language of the Holy Trinity as "Father, Son and Holy Spirit"; and (3) the ban against the ordination of those practicing homosexuality.

In addition to Hinson, the other pastors who signed the letter of invitation for the gathering included James Buskirk, pastor of First UMC in Tulsa; Maxie D. Dunnam, pastor of Christ UMC in Memphis; Ira Gallaway, pastor of First UMC in Peoria; William H. Hinson, pastor of First UMC in Houston; J. Ellsworth Kalas, pastor of Church of the Savior in Cleveland;

John Ed Mathison, pastor of Frazer Memorial UMC in Montgomery; and O. Gerald Trigg, pastor of First UMC in Colorado Springs.

What did they think might result from the gathering and statement? Dr. Ira Gallaway, one of the key organizing pastors, said he believed the meeting will cause other United Methodist clergy and laity to stand up and be counted. "We are sounding a clear note for people to rally around and take hope in," said Gallaway.

All forty-eight clergy present signed the Houston Declaration.

The Houston Declaration

Out of love and concern for the United Methodist Church, 48 pastors from 18 states, from Massachusetts to California, from Illinois to Florida, representing large churches and small, came together in Houston, Texas, December 14–15, 1987. We came as pastors who baptize and marry, confirm and bury and live among our people. We came to reaffirm and promote the central certainties of our faith. In the face of actions by some boards and agencies and some caucus groups that tend to undermine these certainties, and in the fulfillment of our ordination vows, we feel compelled to speak to three crucial truths which are essential to the life, witness and scriptural integrity of the church: (1) the primacy of Scripture; (2) the nature and name of the one God, Father, Son, and Holy Spirit; and (3) the high and holy character of ordained ministry.

I. The Primacy of Scripture

We United Methodist pastors affirm the Wesleyan principle of the primacy of Scripture and recognize that we share a common heritage with Christians of every age and nation. We have witnessed the confusion and conflict resulting from the ambiguity of the present doctrinal statement as contained in Paragraph 69 of the 1984 *Discipline*.

We therefore endorse the following declaration regarding the primacy of Scripture, as included in the newly proposed doctrinal statement:

United Methodists share with other Christians the conviction that Scripture is the primary source and criterion for authentic Christian truth and witness. The Bible bears authoritative testimony to God's self-disclosure in the pilgrimage of Israel, in the life, death, and resurrection of Jesus Christ, and in the Holy Spirit's constant activity in human history, especially in the mission of early Christianity. As we open our minds and hearts to the Word of God through the words of human beings inspired by the Holy Spirit, faith is born and nourished, our understanding is deepened, and the possibilities for transforming the world become apparent to us.

The Bible is sacred canon for Christian people, formally acknowledged as such by historic ecumenical councils of the church. Our doctrinal standards identify as canonical thirty-nine books of the Old Testament and the twenty-seven books of the New Testament. Our standards affirm the Bible as the source of all that is "necessary and sufficient unto salvation" (Articles of Religion) and "the true rule and guide for faith and practice" (Confession of Faith).

We properly read Scripture within the believing community, informed by the tradition of that community. We interpret individual texts in light of their place in the Bible as a whole. We are aided by scholarly inquiry and personal insight, under the guidance of the Holy Spirit. Wesley's method of interpretation applied this rule: "The obscure text is to be interpreted by those which speak more plainly," and the more difficult passages understood in terms of the "analogy of faith," that is, "the whole scope and tenor of Scripture," the core witness of Scripture as a whole. The Bible serves both as a source of our faith and as the basic criterion by which the truth and fidelity of any interpretation of faith is measured.

II. The Trinity

We confess the historic Christian Faith in the one God, Father, Son, and Holy Spirit.

In Jesus Christ, the divine Son, God has been definitively revealed to humankind, and the world graciously reconciled to God. At the exaltation of Jesus, the one whom he consistently called Father sent forth the Holy Spirit to declare the things of Christ, so that the good news of our redemption might be proclaimed to all people. At least since the gospel of St. Matthew, the church has consistently baptized "in the name of the Father, the Son, and the Holy Spirit" those who accept the message (Matthew 28:19–20).

We deplore the effort in baptism, ordination, and the total liturgy of the Church to re-symbolize the Faith by abandoning the name of God, Father, Son and Holy Spirit or adopting inadequate substitutes. To do so is to deny the revelation attested in the Scriptures, transmitted by faithful men and women in the Christian tradition, and offered to the world for its salvation.

Formulas such as "Creator, Redeemer, Sustainer" or "Creator, Christ, Spirit" are inadequate substitutes. As to the first: God's richly personal being cannot be defined merely in functional terms. As to the second: Christ and the Spirit are not mere creatures.

We affirm equality and inclusive language in all human relationships.

III. The Ordained Ministry

The Church, on the authority of the Scriptures, has never viewed homosexuality as a part of God's diverse, good creation, but has always considered homosexual practices as a sin and a manifestation of the brokenness of God's fallen creation. Every scriptural reference to the practice of homosexuality is negative (Leviticus 18:22; 20:13; Romans 1:18–32; 1 Corinthians 6:9–10). Following the Old

Testament prohibitions, the apostle Paul sees homosexuality practices as a sign and consequence of a turning away from the Creator in order to worship the creature. Homosexual practices become an extreme expression of the turning in upon itself which is the essence of humankind's sin.

We repudiate all irrational fear of and contempt for homosexual persons. We affirm a ministry of Christian compassion, care and redirection for those who have engaged in homosexual practices as they seek help in overcoming temptation and changing their style of life. Persons may or may not be able to change their sexual orientation; persons can change their lifestyle. That possibility is the very essence of the gospel of Christ (I Corinthians 6).

It is not acceptable in the context of the Christian faith that persons engaging in homosexual practices should be ordained to the ministry or continue in representative positions within the Church.

Conclusion

We covenant together to proclaim these central truths of the Christian Faith and to invest our lives and ministry in the continuing renewal of our beloved church. We invite all, laity and clergy of the United Methodist Church, to join with us as persons who have been called to follow Christ and give our lives to advancing the gospel and the historic Christian Faith. The need is urgent—the time is now!

We stand as servants and disciples of Jesus Christ our Lord.

Organizing Ministers

Rev. James B. Buskirk, First United Methodist Church, Tulsa, OK

Rev. Maxie D. Dunnam, Christ United Methodist Church, Memphis, TN

Rev. Ira Gallaway, First United Methodist Church, Peoria, IL

Rev. William H. Hinson, First United Methodist Church, Houston, TX

Rev. J. Ellsworth Kalas, The Church of the Savior, Cleveland, OH

Rev. John Ed Mathison, Frazer Memorial United Methodist Church, Montgomery, AL

Rev. O. Gerald Trigg, First United Methodist Church, Colorado Springs, CO

Signatories to the Declaration

Rev. Barbara Brokhoff, Evangelist, Clearwater, FL

Rev. Joseph H. Bullington Jr., Cokesbury UMC, Pensacola, FL

Rev. Kirbyjon Caldwell, Windsor Village UMC, Houston, TX

Rev. Riley Case, District Superintendent, Marion, IN

Rev. Brad Dinsmore, Lake Magdalene UMC, Tampa, FL

Dr. Malone Dodson, Roswell UMC, Roswell, GA

Rev. Roy Dunn, Good Samaritan UMC, Cupertino, CA

Rev. P. Jackson Edwards, Wesley Memorial UMC, Cleveland, TN

Dr. Thomas E. Farmer, First UMC, Jacksonville, FL

Rev. Larry Goodpaster, Oxford University UMC, Oxford, MS

Dr.. C. W. Hancock, District Superintendent, Macon, GA

Rev. Don Harp, Gainesville UMC, Gainesville, GA

Rev. Carl Harris, St. Paul's UMC, Orangeburg, SC

Rev. Cornelius Henderson, District Superintendent, Atlanta, GA

Dr. J. William Jones, Grace UMC, Decatur, IL

Dr. Jimmy Jones, First UMC, Orlando, FL

Rev. William R. Key, Isle of Hope UMC, Savannah, GA

Dr. R. L. Kirk, St. Luke's UMC, Lubbock, TX

Dr. Arthur Landwehr, First UMC, Evanston, IL

Rev. Henry Matthews, Bon Air UMC, Richmond, VA

Rev. J. R. McCormick, Parkway Heights UMC, Hattiesburg, MS

Dr. William Morris, District Superintendent, Murfreesboro, TN

Dr. Raymond Owen, First UMC, Bartlesville, OK

Rev. John Patterson, Grace UMC, Indiana, PA

Rev. Ora Bell Peck, Bardwell UMC, Bardwell, KY

Rev. William Pickett, Pine Castle UMC, Orlando, FL

Rev. Joe A. Rand, People's UMC, Bradford, MA

Dr. Richard Rohrer, Hyde Park UMC, Tampa, FL

Rev. William W. Roughton, First UMC, Melbourne, FL

Dr. Charles Sayre, Haddonfield UMC, Haddonfield, NJ

Dr. David Seamands, Asbury Theological Seminary, Wilmore, KY

Dr. Charles Sineath, First UMC, Marietta, GA

Rev. Robert Snyder, Cardington First UMC, Cardington, OH

Rev. Robert Souders, St. Matthew's UMC, Belleville, IL

Dr. Robert H. Spain, Brentwood UMC, Brentwood, TN

Rev. Al Vom Steeg, St. Luke's UMC, Fresno, CA

Dr. Edd Templeton, First UMC, Tullahoma, TN

Dr. Vernon Tyson, Edenton Street UMC, Raleigh, NC

Rev. Charles D. Whittle, First UMC, Abilene, TX

Dr. Garnett Wilder, Snellville UMC, Snellville, GA

Dr. Charles W. Williams, Moody Memorial First UMC, Galveston, TX

Rev. Ruth M. Wood, Byhalia UMC, Byhalia, MS

Rev. E. R. Woolridge Jr., Virginia Beach UMC, Virginia Beach, VA

Appendix C

A Call to Action

ON FEBRUARY 27–28, 1988, forty-seven laypersons representing all jurisdictions of the United Methodist Church gathered in Chicago to support the Houston Declaration, believing it was time to issue a call to action. These laypersons believed that action in support of the Houston Declaration would help thrust their church to renewed effectiveness and spiritual power equal to the challenges of the day. They also affirmed support for church legislation that would make clear the basics of the faith as outlined in the Declaration.

The Steering Committee members for the Call to Action included the following United Methodist laypersons: Mr. David Dolsen, lay delegate, Rocky Mountain Conference; Mrs. June Parker Goldman, lay delegate, Iowa Conference; Mr. Gus Gustafson, lay delegate, North Georgia Conference; Dr. Jim Holsinger, leader, lay delegation, Virginia Conference; Mrs. Eve Kirk, lay delegate, Northern Illinois Conference; Mrs. June D. McCullough, chair, Southern New Jersey Delegation; and Mr. William Randolph Smith, lay delegate, Texas Conference.

A Call to Action

A Lay Response to the Houston Declaration

We, as concerned laity from every jurisdiction of the United Methodist Church, gathered in Chicago, Illinois, February 27–28, 1988, to support the Houston Declaration. At this time the issues addressed by this Declaration—the primacy of Scripture, the nature and name of the Trinity, and the character of the ordained ministry—are critical in the life of our church. Efforts to deviate from these historic principles violate our beliefs as United Methodist laity. It is for this reason that we have met and developed this document.

The Primacy of Scripture

We, as laity, welcome and endorse the Houston Declaration's clear statement on the primacy of Scripture. John Wesley declared that he was a man of one Book. It is clear from his life and words that John Wesley believed in and practiced a life that was rooted in the primacy of Scripture. Here we use the term primacy to mean in first place. We believe that Scripture is the basis for our faith and practice of Christianity. Without Scripture there would be no Christianity as we know it, since there would be no written revelation by God to the people of the world. Reason, tradition, and experience, under the guidance of the Holy Spirit, assist in the interpretation of the Scripture for every time and age. We find the primacy of Scripture to be within the traditions of Wesleyan Christianity. We stand fully committed to the primacy of Scripture as the basis of our Christian faith and practice.

The Trinity

We, as laity, appreciate and support the Houston Declaration's statement regarding the Trinity. We affirm the traditional names of "Father, Son, and Holy Spirit" for the Trinity. Jesus himself instructed us to baptize in the name of the Father, Son, and Holy Spirit. We believe that for ordination and the sacraments of the Church, Baptism and Communion, these names cannot be improved upon. We further believe we are invoking the power and blessings of God by using the names of the Father, Son, and Holy Spirit in our worship experience. We must guard against language that would devalue the Trinity and weaken our faith. God desires a personal relationship with us, and to substitute functional words does not adequately convey this relationship.

The Ordained Ministry

We, as laity, affirm the high character of ordained ministry and the historic Christian stand on the sin of homosexual practice as stated in the Houston Declaration. The Church, on the authority of Scripture, has set high standards for ordained ministry. We call upon Conference Boards of Ordained Ministry to maintain these high standards and uphold the *Discipline*. Although we support the United Methodist Church position on chargeable offenses (Par. 2621), we strongly urge action by the 1988 General Conference to strengthen and clarify standards for ordained individuals. We reaffirm the traditional Christian standard of sexual morality; celibacy in singleness and fidelity in marriage. We believe it is not acceptable in the context of the Christian faith that persons unwilling to maintain these high standards be accepted as candidates, ordained as ministers, or appointed to serve in the United Methodist Church. We affirm a ministry of Christian compassion, care, and redirection for clergy who have not maintained the standards set by the church.

A Call to Action

Let us respond now to the Houston Declaration in a spirit of prayer, hope, love, and commitment to our historic Christian Faith. For too long too many of us have remained silent, deeply concerned about the decline of our Church but uncertain what we should do. Now it is time for every concerned United Methodist to speak and act positively, while loving and respecting those who disagree with us.

We call on every United Methodist layperson who wants a vital, renewed, Christ-centered church to speak out now for the Houston Declaration and its principles. We invite laypersons to endorse this Laity Response. There is a great need for each person to state his or her views to pastors, delegates, members of Annual Conferences, bishops, and church agencies.

We call on every United Methodist pastor to present the Houston Declaration to his or her congregation, invite their study and response, and give an opportunity to sign an endorsement of the Houston Declaration.

We call on every local church Administrative Board or Council to endorse the Houston Declaration and send this endorsement to General and Jurisdictional Conference delegates.

We call on all delegates to the 1988 General and Jurisdictional Conferences and all members of Annual Conferences to take action and adopt specific legislation upholding the principles of the Houston Declaration.

We call on all United Methodists to make a personal commitment to join us in earnest prayer for the General Conference and its delegates during each day of the General Conference.

We believe the Holy Spirit speaks to us through the courageous pastors who wrote and signed the Houston Declaration. We believe the Holy Spirit now calls us to give our active support and help our church to be faithful to God's Word and our Wesleyan heritage.

This we do in the name of our Lord Jesus Christ.

Appendix D

The Louisville Declaration

IN JULY 1990, nearly one thousand people gathered at the Galt House Hotel in Louisville, Kentucky, for the Convocation on World Mission and Evangelism. The event was sponsored jointly by Good News, the Mission Society for United Methodists, a Foundation for Theological Education, and the National Association of United Methodist Evangelists.

Speakers at the national gathering included Bishop Richard B. Wilke, Bishop William R. Cannon, Bishop Earl G. Hunt Jr., Nigerian Bishop Ayo Ladigbolu, Dr. Ira Gallaway, Dr. Gerald Anderson, Dr. Walter Kimbrough, Dr. William Hinson, Dr. George G. Hunter III, Mrs. Julia McClean Williams, Dr. Geoffrey Wainwright (paper read by Dr. H. T. Maclin), and Dr. Ed Robb.

On the final morning of the convocation, participants were invited to stand, expressing their support by consensus of a statement that had been prepared and distributed the previous evening for reflection and feedback. The statement, called "The Louisville Declaration: A Call to Faithfulness in Mission" was drafted by a small committee, chaired by Dr. Dean Gilliland, director of the cross-cultural studies program and professor of contextualized theology and African studies at Fuller Theological Seminary.

The Louisville Declaration invited those present to join in embracing several concerns, which include in part: (1) to reaffirm that Jesus Christ is the only Savior of people everywhere; (2) to renew dedication to the evangelization of the world; (3) to evangelize children and youth; (4) to recognize that at the heart of our church's crisis is a defection from her essential Wesleyan doctrine; and (5) to pray for a bold new leadership in the church.

THE LOUISVILLE DECLARATION
A CALL TO FAITHFULNESS IN MISSION

Preamble

We have gathered in Louisville as United Methodists from thirty-eight states to reaffirm the Great Commission and to renew our vision for spreading the Gospel of Christ at home and abroad. Throughout the convocation we have rejoiced in our oneness and have faced our failures. In a spirit of repentance, we invite United Methodists to join us in embracing the following concerns:

I

We reaffirm that Jesus Christ is the only Savior of people everywhere, regardless of birth or religion. Jesus said, "Unless you are converted and become like children, you will never enter the Kingdom of Heaven" (Matthew 18:3). Today, when people of all religions live in close contact with each other, we must declare that the pre-eminent Christ is above any religious or social system. This leads us to work for the conversion of the nations as our Lord commanded (Matthew 28:19).

II

We dedicate ourselves anew to the evangelization of the world, praying that God would enhance our zeal for the greatest mission opportunity the church has ever known. Above all, this means verbal witness to non-Christians, planting churches where there are none and ministering in Christ's name to a wide range of human needs. Our homes must be "embassies for Christ" and our churches centers where members are called into tangible ministries among the people of all nations.

III

We call for the evangelization of children and youth—within and outside our churches—where substance abuse, broken homes, sexual immorality and suicide ruin vulnerable lives and breed hopelessness. Many are drawn into cults because of the absence of vital Christianity. Our United Methodist Church is ill-prepared to reach this neglected generation and to channel their energies toward the Kingdom of God.

IV

We acknowledge that Christ draws all his followers into lives of personal holiness which undergirds our witness in word and deed. The Holy Spirit empowers believers to manifest the gifts of the Spirit in service and the fruit of the Spirit in their character. The call to moral integrity and self-control is critical for the church's mission. Heterosexual promiscuity and homosexual involvement are both incompatible with the life of holiness and wholeness to which all disciples are called.

V

We deplore our church's defection from its essential Wesleyan Doctrine. The crisis of the United Methodist Church today is a lack of biblical authority and a flawed theology. We must resist imposing upon the church any agenda as a substitute for the central themes of the gospel. The church's preoccupation with the socio-political arena has diminished its credibility and the influence in the world. Our faith has come to us at the cost of the lives of saints and martyrs. We must not pass to succeeding generations a gospel which is distorted or defective.

VI

We pray for bold new leadership in the church. We reject the assumption that continued membership decline is inevitable, and we deplore easy rationalizations which evade the crisis. Two decades of decline is unacceptable and calls for church-wide repentance. Today's leadership must be characterized by spiritual maturity and apostolic vision. We call on leaders at every level—bishops, pastors, laity—to train our membership in serious Bible study and in tasks of missions and evangelism. The world is forever our parish!

Therefore, we offer this Declaration to all who love our church. We urge United Methodists everywhere to pray for renewal and faithfulness to the gospel. Because God has been gracious in bringing us to this moment of crisis and action, we commend these concerns to the church. We will work with the Spirit of God in any steps required for change.

Appendix E

The Memphis Declaration

ON JANUARY 24–25, 1992, more than one hundred United Methodist clergy and laity gathered in Memphis, Tennessee, to issue a declaration affirming the United Methodist Church's traditional stance on human sexuality and calling the church to a new emphasis on mission and world-wide evangelism.

The document, named the Memphis Declaration, was drafted on a Friday and Saturday at the Sheraton Airport Inn in Memphis. It became a rallying point for issues that would be addressed at United Methodism's upcoming General Conference to be held May 5–15 in Louisville, Kentucky.

Reverend Maxie Dunnam, senior minister at Christ United Methodist Church, Memphis, at the time of the gathering, served as host pastor and chairman of the Coordinating Committee. The May/June 1992 issue of Good News reported some 200,327 affirmative signatures to the Memphis Declaration, and total signatures finally exceeded 212,000, representing one of the largest grassroots expressions ever in United Methodist history. Max and June Goldman of Spirit Lake, Iowa, graciously took responsi-bility for receiving and counting signatures as they came in.

Speaking at a news conference at the 1992 General Conference in Louisville, Dunnam reported that they received signatures from churches of all sizes from every state in the union and every jurisdiction in United

Methodism. The Declaration was also endorsed by boards and committees of local churches. "They expressed the hope they see in this for the renewal of the church," said Dunnam.

David Stanley, a lay delegate from Iowa, said about those who had signed the Declaration, "These are people in the pews back home who love our church. They are deeply concerned about the direction of the church and are calling it to faithfulness to the Wesleyan tradition."

The Coordinating Committee for the Memphis Declaration included the following pastors and laypersons: Dr. Jim Buskirk, Mr. Phillip Connolly, Dr. Maxie Dunnam, Dr. Ira Gallaway, Mrs. June Parker Goldman, Mr. Gus Gustafson, Dr. William Hinson, Dr. James Holsinger Jr., Dr. J. William Jones, Dr. Evelyn Laycock, Dr. John Ed Mathison, Dr. Ed Robb Jr., Mr. David M. Stanley, and Mr. Paul D. White.

THE MEMPHIS DECLARATION

In his preface to the *Standard Sermons*, John Wesley wrote, "I design plain truth for plain people." Those of us gathered here today in Memphis, lay and clergy alike, seek to emulate Wesley and speak "plain words of truth" to affirm and live out the mandate of Jesus Christ to be his disciples and to call all persons of every race and nation to name and follow him as Savior and Lord.

In the tradition of The Houston Declaration, we come together to challenge United Methodists to live more faithfully as the body of Jesus Christ, under his lordship. This involves confessing, proclaiming and living the Apostolic faith.

In light of the authority of Scripture, we affirm that:

1. God revealed himself in Jesus Christ, the only way of divine salvation.
2. Holy living is the way for Christians to live out the mandate of discipleship given by Jesus Christ.

3. The local congregation is the center for mission and ministry to the world.

God's Revelation in Jesus Christ

Among the people called Christian—in many nations and among many peoples—including United Methodist, there has been a falling away from commitment to the basic truths and doctrines of the Christian faith.

If we are to be obedient to the teaching of Scripture and to our Wesleyan heritage, we must lift up Jesus Christ as God's gift of salvation offered to all humanity. There are doctrinal issues on which Christians may disagree. We dare not, however, deny our Lord in the name of a shallow pluralism or in a vain attempt to elevate tolerance above primary faith commitment to Jesus Christ. We must not surrender the uniqueness and centrality of Jesus Christ and our Christian heritage for the sake of an easy dialogue with those who are not yet Christian, or a false ecumenism with those who do not profess the fullness of the Christian faith.

Jesus of Nazareth was God in human flesh who lived on earth, suffered and died on the cross, was raised from the dead, lives as eternal Savior and Redeemer, present with us in the person of the Holy Spirit, and He will return again. He is God's only way of salvation. We are called to live out and share this faith personally and collectively as our primary purpose and commitment.

God's Call to Holy Living

We affirm the call of Jesus Christ, the teaching of holy Scripture, and the faithful witness of John Wesley, that as Christians we are called to holy living. We cannot be self-righteous, because our own personal lives fall far short of his standard of holy living, but the standard must be upheld.

The power of Jesus Christ is at work in the person of the Holy Spirit and can transform every life and overcome every sin. He calls his Church to transform the current culture, not conform to it.

We urge all United Methodists, including ourselves, to turn away from a consumer mentality, greed, and moral disintegration. We are called to be servants and witnesses to our neighbors in word and deed, leading the world to repent and accept Jesus Christ as Savior and Lord.

The Church must reach out in a ministry of love, compassion, and healing to all persons—married, single, children, one-parent homes, and broken families. We affirm marriage as the God-ordained pattern of relationship between men and women. God created us male and female, and the natural order of creation and procreation is the union of male and female as husband and wife. The Christian Church has always held this to be in accordance with God's will. We challenge the Church to be unequivocal in support of the Christian family, the sanctity of human life, and Christian sexual morality: fidelity in marriage and celibacy in singleness.

Scripture plainly identifies adultery, fornication and homosexual practice as sins of the flesh (signs and consequences of the fallen condition of humankind that needs redemption). Let us cease to debate homosexual practice as if the witness of the Scripture and the tradition of the Church were not clear from the beginning. A militant minority must not be allowed to control the direction of the Church of Jesus Christ.

It is time for us to move on to the central purpose of the Church: to serve the world in Jesus Christ's name and win the world for Him.

Local Congregation

The local church is the primary place where we encounter the risen Lord. It must again become, in doctrine and practice, the center of the mission and ministry of the Church. The purpose of the boards, agencies and seminaries must be focused on the equipping of the people of God to be in ministry where they worship and work.

Fiscal responsibility calls for the curtailment, reordering, and reduction of the bureaucracy of the Church so that more of our tithes and offerings will go directly into mission and ministry and *not* increasingly into general church staff and support for boards, agencies and study commissions.

We are concerned about ministerial leadership. We must be especially careful that a seminary education be consistent with our Wesleyan heritage and not dominated by a secular mind-set. Some of our seminaries are committed to both the teaching and modeling of our Wesleyan heritage, recognizing that seminaries are places where men and women are trained for Christian ministry. We celebrate their faithfulness to the Church and we pledge our loyalty and support to them.

Call to Action

We urge the 1992 General Conference to take these actions and pass necessary legislation to:

1. Reaffirm the use of Biblical language and images in our common life together; mandate the use of the name Father, Son, and Holy Spirit whenever we speak of the Trinity; and reject the replacement of Biblical language and images in the proposed *Book of Worship*, and in other church materials, with alternative language and images which alter the Apostolic faith.

2. Abolish the General Council on Ministries as an unnecessary and costly layer of bureaucracy. It is in direct conflict with the Constitution of the Church, which assigns to the Council of Bishops "the general oversight and promotion of the temporal and spiritual interest of the entire Church and for carrying into effect the rules, regulations, and responsibilities prescribed and enjoined by the General Conference" (Par. 50, Art. III, The Constitution).

3. Reduce the number, size, staff and costs of General Church boards and agencies.

4. Restore the Church's mission and evangelistic thrust. Establish a General Board of Evangelism, including the transfer of the section on church extension from the National Division of the Board of Global Ministries, so that reaching the world for Christ will again be central to the purpose and mission of the Church.

5. Approve the recommendation of the Study Commission and mandate the move of the General Board of Global Ministries out of New York, to enhance the mission and ministry of the Church.

6. Reaffirm Christian sexual morality and the current provisions of the United Methodist Discipline (Par. 71f., 402.2, 906.12). Homosexual persons are people of sacred worth to whom we are called to minister. Since the practice of homosexuality is, however, incompatible with Christian teaching, we call for the rejection of the report and recommendations of the Committee to Study Homosexuality, and oppose further official study. The Biblical witness and the unbroken tradition of the Church provide the foundation of our understanding.

7. Affirm that baptism is a means of God's grace, but that a personal decision to accept Jesus Christ as Savior and Lord is essential for salvation and for full membership in the Church.

Appendix F

An Invitation to the Church

ON APRIL 5-6, 1994, a group of ninety-two United Methodists gathered in Atlanta, Georgia, to consult about the future of the United Methodist Church. Those attending were evangelical, traditionalist, and moderate United Methodists all concerned about addressing the liberal trend they fear could split the denomination.

The three prominent United Methodist leaders who brought the group together included: Bishop William R. Cannon (retired) of Atlanta; Rev. Maxie Dunnam, pastor of Christ United Methodist Church in Memphis and president-elect of Asbury Theological Seminary; and Rev. Thomas C. Oden, professor of theology at Drew Theological School.

The ninety-two participants included bishops, seminary professors, pastors, some members of the World Methodist Council, and prominent laity from all five U.S. jurisdictions of the United Methodist Church. The group issued a statement, called "An Invitation to the Church," which said, in part, that only by recovering a biblically based historic faith that emphasizes the centrality of Christ can the church "avoid schism and prevent mass exodus."

Planners of the event said they expected to go beyond written documents to designing and implementing a grassroots strategy to affect the church directly. "In order to enact the Discipline's call to 'doctrinal reinvigoration,' and to avoid schism and prevent mass exodus, we intend to form a Confessing Movement within the United Methodist Church," the Invitation statement said. "By this we mean people and congregations who exalt the Lordship of Jesus Christ alone, and adhere to the doctrinal standards of our church."

Dr. Tom Oden, one of the three conveners, decried what he termed "already a profound division" in the church, and said the group wants to develop a broad coalition of "traditionalists and centrists who are unwilling to see the confession of Jesus Christ as Lord and Savior become neglected in our Christian teaching." Bishop Richard C. Looney of Macon, Georgia, expressed a concern of many about "how we hold ourselves accountable for what we've already decided in the Discipline. We work hard at coming to positions we feel good about, and then people go their own route."

In addition to Looney and Cannon, four other United Methodist bishops attended the meeting: Mack B. Stokes, retired, of Atlanta; Earl G. Hunt, retired, of Lake Junaluska, North Carolina; Felton M. May of Harrisburg, Pennsylvania; and William Morris of Montgomery, Alabama.

What follows is the full text of "An Invitation to the Church" released at the Atlanta meeting. The statement was distributed first to the Council of Bishops, then to the church's general agencies, and then to the church at large. United Methodists throughout the church were invited to sign it. Dr. John Ed Mathison was elected as chairman of the Steering Committee of the Confessing Movement. Other national gatherings have been held and the Confessing Movement within the United Methodist Church now has an office and full-time staff in Indianapolis, Indiana.

An Invitation to the Church

which led to

The Confessing Movement within the United Methodist Church

I

The United Methodist Church is at the crossroads. We face the peril of abandoning the Christian faith, thereby becoming unfaithful disciples of Jesus Christ, or we can embrace the promise of becoming God's instrument in a new awakening of vital Christianity. The causes of the crisis are complex and multiple. However, we believe that the central cause is our abandonment of the truth of the gospel of Jesus Christ as revealed in Scripture and asserted in the classic Christian tradition and historic ecumenical creeds. Specifically we have equivocated regarding the person of Jesus Christ and his atoning work as the unique Savior of the world. We have been distracted by false gospels, and compromised in our mission to declare the truth gospel to all people and spread scriptural holiness. For the sake of the Kingdom of God, it is now time for action.

II

The renewal, reform and healing of our church can come only through the life-giving power of the Holy Spirit. We cannot yet see clearly how God will lead us along this path. However, with John Wesley, we affirm the apostolic faith of the universal Church together with those Wesleyan distinctives which give form to our faith, as articulated in the doctrinal standards of our own church (vis., the Articles of Religion and Confession of Faith, Wesley's *Standard Sermons* and *Explanatory Notes*). These constitute the essential, unchangeable truths of our tradition. We gladly own this anew for ourselves and seek to reclaim it for our whole church.

III

Under God's judgment and by God's grace we covenant to participate in the Spirit's reconstruction of the church built upon the foundation of the faith once for all delivered to the saints. We covenant to engage in a revitalized mission which expresses our historic concern for social holiness and fidelity to the fulfillment of the Great Commission. To all United Methodists regardless of race or gender who desire to contend for this faith, we extend an invitation to join us in this endeavor.

In order to enact the *Discipline's* call to "doctrinal reinvigoration," and to avoid schism and prevent mass exodus, we intend to form a Confessing Movement within the United Methodist Church. By this we mean people and congregations who exalt the Lordship of Jesus Christ alone, and adhere to the doctrinal standards of our church.

We call upon all pastors and congregations to join with us in this Confessing Movement, and to challenge and equip their people as agents of God's Kingdom.

We look to the Council of Bishops for doctrinal oversight according to paragraph 514.2 "to guard, transmit, teach and proclaim corporately and individually the apostolic faith as it is expressed in Scripture and Tradition, and as they are led and endowed by the Spirit to interpret that faith evangelically and prophetically." In particular we ask the bishops to affirm their own teaching authority and to declare our church's commitment to Jesus Christ as the only Lord and Savior of the World.

We call upon seminaries of our church to transmit the historic Christian faith. We call upon the boards and agencies of the church to fulfill their primary role of being servants of the local church.

IV

The crisis we discern extends beyond our denomination. We witness similar strains and struggles among our sisters and brothers in all the churches of the West. Because we are baptized into the one universal Church, and because the problems we face will best be resolved by utilizing the gifts God gives to the whole community of faith, we rejoice in the stirrings for renewal that we see among other communions. We commit ourselves to praying with them for the coming of the kingdom in our midst.

Appendix G

Confessional Statement

We Confess Jesus Christ: The Son, The Savior, The Lord

PREAMBLE

DURING THE FIRST week of Easter, 1994, a group of 92 laity, clergy, bishops, and professors gathered to consult about the future of The United Methodist Church. We issued "An Invitation to the Church" for others to join us in exalting Jesus Christ as we confront the crisis of faith within The United Methodist Church. In love for the Church we [a gathering of over 800 United Methodists meeting in Atlanta, Georgia, April 28–29, 1995] now present this Confessional Statement for the renewal and reform of The United Methodist Church.

The crisis before us is this: Will The United Methodist Church confess, and be unified by, the apostolic faith in Jesus Christ; or will The United Methodist Church challenge the primacy of Scripture and justify the acceptance of beliefs incompatible with our Articles of Religion and Confession of Faith?

The United Methodist Church is now incapable of confessing with one voice the orthodox Trinitarian faith, particularly Jesus Christ as the Son of God, the Savior of the world, and the Lord of history and the Church. While giving assent to Jesus Christ as Lord, our denomination tolerates opinions that "strike at the root of Christianity" (John Wesley). Our Church suffers from private versions of the faith that do not find their root in Scripture.

The purpose of this Confessional Statement is to call The United Methodist Church, all laity and all clergy, to confess the person, work, and reign of Jesus Christ. This Statement confronts and repudiates teachings and practices in The United Methodist Church that currently challenge the truth of Jesus Christ—the Son of God, the Savior of the world, and the Lord of all. Aware of our own sinfulness, we who make this Confession submit our common witness and our lives to the judgment and mercy of God, as attested in Scripture, the written Word of God.

We Confess Jesus Christ

THE SON

"He (Jesus) . . . said to them, 'But who do you say that I am?' Simon Peter answered, 'You are the Messiah, the Son of the living God.' And Jesus answered him, 'Blessed are you, Simon son of Jonah! For flesh and blood has not revealed this to you, but my Father in heaven" (Matt. 16:15–17 NRSV).

We confess, in accordance with Holy Scripture and with the Holy Spirit's help, that Jesus Christ is the one and only Son of God. Confession of Jesus as the Son is essential, not a matter of personal opinion. It is a matter of revelation, which was given to Peter and to the Church by God whom Jesus called Father. With Peter and the other Apostles, we confess that Jesus is the Christ. We confess with John and the other Apostles that in Jesus of Nazareth, the Word made flesh, the eternal Son of God has come into the world to make known the fullness of God's glory in grace and truth (John 1). Therefore we confess, in continuity with the apostolic witness of the Church, that Jesus Christ is "true God from true God" (the Nicene Creed), the Second Person of the Holy Trinity: Father, Son, and Holy Spirit.

We repudiate teachings that claim the person of Jesus Christ is not adequate to reveal the fullness of God (Heb. 1:1–3). We reject the claim that the maleness of Jesus disqualifies him as the true revelation of God. We reject the claim that God can be fully known apart from Jesus Christ. According to the apostolic faith, such teachings are false and unfaithful to the Gospel.

THE SAVIOR

"There is salvation in no one else, for there is no other name under heaven given among mortals by which we must be saved" (Acts 4:12 NRSV).

We confess, in accordance with Holy Scripture and with the Holy Spirit's help, that Jesus Christ is the one and only Savior of the world. In him, we see not only the fullness and the glory of God, but also the model and power for our own freedom from the bondage of sin and death (Heb. 2:14–18). Through his obedient life, teaching, and ministry, his death on the cross for the sins of the world, and his bodily resurrection, he is the Savior of the world. God through Jesus Christ conquers sin and death, brings salvation to this rebellious world, and reconciles "the world to himself" (2 Cor. 5:18–21 NRSV).

We repudiate teachings that repress, turn away from, or offer substitutes for the atoning death and life-giving resurrection of Jesus. We oppose any redefinition of the Christian faith that diminishes or eliminates the saving work of Jesus Christ in order to make dialogue with others more agreeable. We reject any claim that regards the incarnation, crucifixion, and resurrection as merely one salvation among others. According to the apostolic faith, such teachings are false and unfaithful to the Gospel.

THE LORD

"As you therefore have received Christ Jesus the Lord, continue to live your lives in him, rooted and built up in him and established in the faith, just as you were taught, abounding in thanksgiving. See to it that no one takes you captive through philosophy and empty deceit, according to human tradition, according to the elemental spirits of the universe, and not according to Christ. For in him the whole fullness of deity dwells bodily, and you have come to fullness in him, who is the head of every ruler and authority" (Col. 2:6–10 NRSV).

We confess, in accordance with Holy Scripture and with the Holy Spirit's help, that Jesus Christ is the one and only Lord of creation and history. In the midst of many competing voices, the Church seeks to hear, trust, and obey Jesus the Lord and his commandments (1 Cor. 8:5–6). True authority in the Church derives from, and furthers obedience to this Lord. True authority in the Church holds the community accountable to this Lord, especially when teachings and practices arise that undermine or deny his Lordship.

We repudiate teachings and practices that MISUSE principles of inclusiveness and tolerance to distort the doctrine and discipline of the Church. We deny the claim that the individual is free to decide what is true and what is false, what is good and what is evil. We reject widespread and often unchallenged practices in and by the Church that rebel against the Lordship of Jesus Christ. For example:

- experimenting with pagan ritual and practice
- consuming the world's goods without regard for the poor
- accommodating the prevailing patterns of sexual promiscuity, serial marriage and divorce
- resigning ourselves to the injustices of racial and gender prejudice
- condoning homosexual practice
- ignoring the Church's long-standing protection of the unborn and the mother

Any new teachings in the Church that seek to set aside the biblical witness cannot be established by votes, or appeals to personal experience, or by responding to contemporary social pressures. According to the apostolic faith, such teachings and practices are false and unfaithful to the Gospel.

THE CONFESSIONAL CHARGE

This, then, is our confession: We confess that Jesus Christ is the Son, the Savior, and the Lord, according to the Scriptures. The United Methodist Church has never had an institutional guarantee of doctrinal diversity without boundaries. We implore other United Methodists, laity and clergy, to join us in this confession. Relying upon the power of the Holy Spirit, we vow to make this confession in the congregations, boards, divisions, agencies, seminaries, and conferences of our denomination.

We will faithfully support United Methodist activities, groups, programs, and publications that further this confession, and we will vigorously challenge and hold accountable those that undermine this confession. All the while, readying for the coming of Jesus Christ in power and glory, we welcome ecumenical partnerships in the advancement of this confession.

April 29, 1995

Notes

Introduction

1. *Call to Action Steering Team Report*, 2010, by the United Methodist Church. The full report is available at http://umc.org/calltoaction.
2. J. I. Packer, *"Fundamentalism" and the Word of God* (Grand Rapids: Eerdmans, 1958), 27.

Chapter 1: United Methodism's Forgotten Past

1. *Call to Action Steering Team Report*, 2010, by the United Methodist Church. The full report is available at http://umc.org/calltoaction. The final report on the Operational Assessment can be found in appendix 8 of the *Call to Action* report.
2. *The Book of Discipline of the United Methodist Church* (Nashville: United Methodist Publishing House, 1988), par. 69, sec. 4.
3. Mack B. Stokes, *The Bible in the Wesleyan Heritage* (Nashville: Mississippi Annual Conference, 1979), 69–70.
4. The term "evangelical" means much more historically than being warmhearted or evangelistic. Carl F. H. Henry, founding editor of *Christianity Today*, has this helpful definition: "Evangelical Christians are thus marked by their devotion to the sure Word of the Bible; they are committed to the inspired Scriptures as the divine rule of faith and practice. They affirm the fundamental doctrines of the Gospel, including the incarnation and virgin birth of Christ, his sinless life, substitutionary atonement, and bodily resurrection as the ground of God's forgiveness of sinners, justification by faith alone, and the spiritual regeneration of all who trust in the redemptive work of Jesus Christ." ("Evangelical,"

in *The New International Dictionary of the Christian Church*, J. D. Douglas, gen. ed., [Grand Rapids: Zondervan, 1974], 358–59.)

5. *The Book of Discipline of The United Methodist Church* (Nashville: United Methodist Publishing House, 2012), par. 336, 262.

6. When we speak of the mainline Protestant churches, we usually are referring to the Seven Sisters of American Protestantism: the American Baptist Church, the Episcopal Church, the Evangelical Lutheran Church in America, the Presbyterian Church (USA), the United Methodist Church, the United Church of Christ, and the Disciples of Christ.

7. Edwin Lewis, "The Fatal Apostasy of the Modern Church," *Religion in Life* 2 (Autumn 1933).

8. See Dean C. Curry, "Evangelical Amnesia," *First Things* (October 2007): 15–17.

9. J. Gresham Machen, *Christianity and Liberalism* (Grand Rapids: Eerdmans, 1922; repr., 1981), 2. Citations refer to the 1981 edition.

10. Curry, "Evangelical Amnesia," 17.

11. John Lawson, *An Evangelical Faith for Today* (Nashville: Abingdon, 1972), 10.

12. Alister E. McGrath, Studies in Doctrine (Grand Rapids, MI: Zondervan, 1997), 239–40.

Chapter 2: The Early 1900s

1. F. Ernest Johnson and Arthur E. Holt, *Christian Ideals in Industry* (New York: Methodist Book Concern, 1924), 12.

2. Ibid., 13.

3. George E. Vincent, "The Industrial Revolution," in *Social Ministry*, ed. Harry F. Ward (New York: Eaton & Mains, 1910), 81.

4. Ibid., 91.

5. Charles Howard Hopkins, *The Rise of the Social Gospel in American Protestantism* (New Haven, CT: Yale University Press, 1940), 99.

6. Aaron Ignatius Abell, *The Urban Impact on American Protestantism*, 1865–1900 (Hamden, CT: Archon, 1962), 3.

7. Vincent, "The Industrial Revolution," 94.

8. Robert Moats Miller, "Methodism and American Society, 1900–1939," in *The History of American Methodism*, ed. Emory Stevens Bucke, 3 vols. (New York: Abingdon, 1964), 346.

9. Ibid., 347.
10. Kenneth Cauthen, *The Impact of American Religious Liberalism* (New York: Harper & Row, 1962), 13.
11. Thomas C. Reeves, *The Empty Church: The Suicide of Liberal Christianity* (New York: Free Press, 1996), 81.
12. Hopkins, *The Rise of the Social Gospel in American Protestantism*, 123.
13. Cauthen, *The Impact of American Religious Liberalism*, 7.
14. Lloyd J. Averill, *American Theology in the Liberal Tradition* (Philadelphia: Westminster Press, 1967), 69.
15. Ibid., 23.
16. This remarkable statistic comes from *"Old Path Methodism" in a Modern World: Henry Clay Morrison's Campaign for the Evangelical Option in the Modern Period*, an unpublished doctoral dissertation by Ronald E. Smith for Drew University, June 2005, 289.
17. Albrecht Ritschl was a German systematic theologian who taught at Bonn and Gottingen. He was one of the most influential continental Protestant theologians during the period of 1875–1930, which was the formative period for liberal Protestantism.
18. Averill, *American Theology in the Liberal Tradition*, 32.
19. Sydney E. Ahlstrom, ed., *Theology in America: The Major Protestant Voices from Puritanism to Neo-Orthodoxy* (Indianapolis: Bobbs-Merrill, 1967), 532.
20. Hopkins, *The Rise of the Social Gospel in American Protestantism*, 206.
21. Reeves, *The Empty Church*, 86.
22. Ibid.
23. Ibid.
24. John Alfred Faulkner, *Modernism and the Christian Faith* (New York: Methodist Book Concern, 1921).
25. Ibid., 218.
26. Ibid.

Chapter 3: Methodist Theology in Transition

1. Leland H. Scott, "Methodist Theology in America in the Nineteenth Century," *Religion in Life* 25 (Winter 1955–56): 87. The article was a brief summary of his doctoral dissertation at Yale University.
2. Ibid., 88–89.
3. Ibid., 95.

4. Ibid.
5. Gerald O. McCulloh, "The Theology and Practices of Methodism, 1876–1919," in *The History of American Methodism*, ed. Emory Stevens Bucke, 3 vols. (New York: Abingdon, 1964), 592.
6. Quoted in Robert E. Chiles, *Theological Transition in American Methodism: 1790–1935* (New York: Abingdon, 1965), 65.
7. Ibid.
8. Scott, "Methodist Theology in America in the Nineteenth Century," 94.
9. McCulloh, "The Theology and Practices of Methodism, 1876–1919," 597.
10. S. Paul Schilling, *Methodism and Society in Theological Perspective*, Methodism and Society series, 4 vols. (New York: Abingdon, 1961), 3:24.
11. Quoted in Sidney E. Mead, *The Lively Experiment: The Shaping of Christianity in America* (New York: Harper & Row, 1963), 55.
12. Chiles, *Theological Transition in American Methodism*, 23.
13. Schilling, *Methodism and Society in Theological Perspective*, 29.
14. McCulloh, "The Theology and Practices of Methodism, 1876–1919," 600–6.
15. Scott, "Methodist Theology in America in the Nineteenth Century," 94.
16. Chiles, *Theological Transition in American Methodism*, 27; citing Colin Williams, *John Wesley's Theology Today* (Nashville: Abingdon, 1960), 16–17.
17. Schilling, *Methodism and Society in Theological Perspective*, 32.
18. *John Wesley's Sermons: An Anthology*, eds. Albert C. Outler and Richard P. Heitzenrater (Nashville: Abingdon, 1991), 300–9.
19. Thomas C. Oden, *Doctrinal Standards in the Wesleyan Tradition*, rev. ed. (Nashville: Abingdon, 2008), 112–14.
20. Ibid., 112.
21. Latitudinarianism is a position of being liberal in one's views, permitting free thought, especially in religious matters; one who cares little about particular creeds and forms. (*Webster's New World Dictionary of the American Language* [Cleveland and New York: World Publishing, 1959], 826.)
22. *John Wesley's Sermons*, 307.
23. Chiles, *Theological Transition in American Methodism*, 23.

24. Schilling, *Methodism and Society in Theological Perspective*, 33.
25. *The Book of Discipline of the United Methodist Church*, 2012, (Nashville: United Methodist Publishing House), sec. 3, "Restrictive Rules," par. 17, art. 1.
26. Schilling, *Methodist and Society in Theological Perspective*, 41.
27. Chiles, *Theological Transition in American Methodism*, 61.
28. Ibid.

Chapter 4: Charges of Theological Modification and Doctrinal Revision

1. Leland H. Scott, "Methodist Theology in America in the Nineteenth Century," *Religion in Life* 25 (Winter 1955–56): 93.
2. George W. Wilson, *Methodist Theology vs. Methodist Theologians* (Cincinnati: Jennings and Pye, 1904), 5.
3. Ibid., 6.
4. Ibid., 8.
5. Ibid., 329.
6. John A. Faulkner, "One Hundred Years of Episcopal Methodism," *New York Christian Advocate* (September 9, 1926): 1124, quoted in William J. McCutcheon, "American Methodist Thought and Theology, 1919–60," in *The History of American Methodism*, ed. Emory Stevens Bucke, 3 vols. (New York: Abingdon, 1964), 263.
7. John A. Faulkner, "William Newton Clarke in a New Role," *Methodist Review* 91 (January 1917): 75.
8. Ibid., 77.
9. Ibid., 78.
10. Ibid., 79.
11. Ibid.
12. Ibid., 78.
13. John Alfred Faulkner, *Modernism and the Christian Faith* (New York: Methodist Book Concern, 1921), 218.
14. Ibid., 222.
15. Harold Paul Sloan, "Course of Study," *New York Christian Advocate* 95.5 (January 29, 1920): 154. Cited in Howard Glen Spann, "Evangelicalism in Modern American Methodism: Theological Conservatives in the 'Great Deep' of the Church, 1900–1980" (PhD diss., Johns Hopkins University, 1994), 190. Spann's work

has major treatment of Sloan and other Methodist evangelicals involved in reform efforts during this period.

16. Howard Paul Sloan, "Historic Christianity," *Pentecostal Herald*, November 9, 1921, 4. Cited in Spann, "Evangelicalism in Modern American Methodism," 194.

17. From pamphlet, "The Occasion, Basis, Growth, and Purpose of the League," quoted in McCutcheon, "Methodist Thought and Theology," 271. For a comprehensive treatment of Sloan's influence, see William Bryant Lewis, "The Role of Harold Paul Sloan and the Methodist League for Faith and Life in the Fundamentalist-Modernist Controversy of the Methodist Episcopal Church" (diss., Vanderbilt University, 1963).

18. B. Smith Stull, "A Year of Progress," *The Call* 1.10 (February 1926): 166–67. Cited in Spann, "Evangelicalism in Modern American Methodism," 199.

19. "The Methodist League for Faith and Life," *New York Christian Advocate* 100.15 (April 9, 1925): 478. Cited in Spann, "Evangelicalism in Modern American Methodism," 199.

20. McCutcheon, "American Methodist Thought and Theology," 272.

21. Ibid., 272–73.

Chapter 5: Transition in Membership Standards and the Diminished Place of Doctrine and Creeds

1. Harold Paul Sloan, "The Course of Study and the Bishops," *The Call* 1.8 (December 1925): 125. Cited in Howard Glen Spann, "Evangelicalism in Modern American Methodism: Theological Conservatives in the 'Great Deep' of the Church, 1900–1980" (PhD diss., Johns Hopkins University, 1994), 200.

2. Ernest Fremont Tittle, "The Use and Abuse of Creeds," *Methodist Review* 89 (November 1917): 866–74.

3. Ibid., 866.

4. A. H. Goodenough, no title, *Methodist Review* 92, (November 1910): 973; quoted in Kenneth Edwin Barnart, "The Evolution of the Social Consciousness in Methodism" (unpublished PhD diss., University of Chicago, 1924), 89.

5. Harris Franklin Rall, "Not Intellectual Credence but Personal Trust," *Methodist Review* 108 (1924): 253ff.

6. Ibid., 56.

7. Philip O. Frick, "Why the Methodist Church Is So Little Disturbed by the Fundamentalist Controversy," *Methodist Review* 107 (1924): 421–26.

8. *Discipline of the Methodist Episcopal Church*, 1884, par. 118, quoted in Gerald O. McCulloh, "The Theology and Practices of Methodism, 1876–1919," in *The History of American Methodism*, ed. Emory Stevens Bucke, 3 vols. (New York: Abingdon, 1964), 600.

9. *Doctrines and Disciplines of the Methodist Episcopal Church*, 1920 (New York: Methodist Book Concern, 1920), pt. 9, chap. 1, par. 524, p. 470.

10. Robert E. Chiles, *Theological Transition in American Methodism: 1790–1935* (New York: Abingdon, 1965), 71.

11. S. Paul Schilling, *Methodism and Society in Theological Perspective*, Methodism and Society series, ed. the Board of Social and Economic Relations of the Methodist Church, 4 vols. (New York: Abingdon, 1961), 3:30.

12. Edwin Lewis, "The Fatal Apostasy of the Modern Church," *Religion in Life* 2 (Autumn 1933): 491.

13. The Social Creed of the Churches was a social manifesto subscribed to by the mainline denominations in America. It was first adopted by the Methodist Episcopal Church in 1908, and later that year by the Federal Council of Churches. Methodist leader Harry F. Ward was the chief drafter of the statement.

14. For an excellent account of this dramatic "theological conversion" in Lewis, including his controversial work, *A Christian Manifesto*, with reactions from various Methodist leaders, see William J. McCutcheon, "American Methodist Thought and Theology, 1919–60," in *The History of American Methodism*, ed. Emory Stevens Bucke, 3 vols. (New York: Abingdon, 1964), 304–15.

15. Chiles, *Theological Transition in American Methodism*, 66–67.

16. Ibid., 64.

17. Riley B. Case, *Evangelical and Methodist: A Popular History* (Nashville: Abingdon, 2004), 78.

18. Ibid.

19. George W. Wilson, *Methodist Theology vs. Methodist Theologians* (Cincinnati: Jennings and Pye, 1904), 122–23.

20. Chiles, *Theological Transition in American Methodism*, 64.

21. Ibid., 70.

22. Case, *Evangelical and Methodist*, 78–79.
23. William James, *Varieties of Religious Experience: A Study in Human Nature* (New York: Longmans, Green, 1902), 502; quoted in John Leland Peters, *Christian Perfection and American Methodism* (New York: Abingdon, 1956), 167.
24. Curtis K. Jones, "Personalism as Christian Philosophy" (unpublished PhD diss., Union Theological Seminary, 1944), 213; quoted in Chiles, *Theological Transition in Methodism*, 74.
25. Chiles, *Theological Transition in American Methodism*, 104.
26. McCulloh, "The Theology and Practices of Methodism," 597.
27. For a fuller statement of the charges and the essential portions of Bowne's testimony, see Francis J. McConnell, *Borden Parker Bowne: His Life and His Philosophy* (New York: Abingdon, 1929), 179–206.
28. Ibid.
29. Case, *Evangelical and Methodist*, 78.
30. Ibid., 79.
31. McCulloh, "The Theology and Practices of Methodism," 596–97.
32. Ibid., 597.

Chapter 6: Just What Was Theological Liberalism?

1. Alister McGrath, *A Passion for Truth: The Intellectual Coherence of Evangelicalism* (Downers Grove, IL: InterVarsity Press, 1996), 28.
2. Ibid., 31.
3. Ibid.
4. Richard John Neuhaus, "What Do Liberals Believe Today?" *Good News* (March/April 1991): 15.
5. Edwin Lewis, *A Christian Manifesto* (New York, Cincinnati, Chicago: Abingdon, 1934).
6. J. Gresham Machen, *Christianity and Liberalism* (Grand Rapids: Eerdmans, 1923).
7. "Liberalism and Conservatism in Theology" by J. I. Packer in *New Dictionary of Theology*, eds. Sinclair B. Ferguson, David F. Wright, and J. I. Packer (Downers Grove, IL: InterVarsity Press, 1988), 384–85.
8. Lewis, *A Christian Manifesto*, 18.
9. Ibid., 31.
10. Machen, *Christianity and Liberalism*, 7.
11. Ibid., 6.

12. Ibid., 7.
13. Lewis, *A Christian Manifesto,* 105.
14. Ibid.
15. Machen, *Christianity and Liberalism,* 109, emphasis mine.
16. Ibid.
17. Lewis, *A Christian Manifesto,* 17.
18. Ibid., 11.
19. Machen, *Christianity and Liberalism,* 17.
20. Packer, "Liberalism and Conservatism in Theology," 385.
21. Lewis, *A Christian Manifesto,* 19.
22. Ibid., 27.
23. Machen, *Christianity and Liberalism,* 113.
24. Packer, "Liberalism and Conservatism in Theology," 385.
25. Lewis, *A Christian Manifesto,* 175.
26. Machen, *Christianity and Liberalism,* 110.
27. Ibid.
28. Ibid., 112.
29. Ibid.
30. Packer, "Liberalism and Conservatism in Theology," 385.
31. Lewis, *A Christian Manifesto,* 142.
32. Ibid.
33. Machen, *Christianity and Liberalism,* 68.
34. Ibid.
35. Ibid., 108.
36. Packer, "Liberalism and Conservatism in Theology," 385.
37. Some of the following thoughts were included in my *Theological Malpractice? Essays in the Struggle for United Methodist Renewal* (Anderson, IN: Bristol Books, 2000), 64–65.
38. The account of Bonhoeffer's visit to America is from Eric Metaxas's *Bonhoeffer: Pastor, Martyr, Prophet, Spy: A Righteous Gentile vs. the Third Reich* (Nashville: Thomas Nelson, 2010), chap. 7, 99ff.
39. Ibid., 101.
40. Ibid.
41. Ibid., 102.
42. Ibid., 103.
43. Ibid., 104.
44. Ibid., 105.
45. Ibid., 106.

46. Ibid.
47. Ibid.
48. Ibid., 107.
49. Robert P. Shuler Sr., "Crucifying Christ Afresh" (editorial), *The Methodist Challenge* 13, no. 3 (August 1944): 3–4.
50. James Gordon Gilkey, *A Faith to Affirm* (New York: Macmillan, 1940).
51. Ibid., 11.
52. Ibid.
53. Ibid.
54. Ibid.
55. Ibid., 16.
56. J. I. Packer, *"Fundamentalism" and the Word of God* (Grand Rapids: Eerdmans, 1958), 27.

Chapter 7: Methodism and the Social Gospel

1. Mark A. Noll, "Social Gospel" in *New Dictionary of Theology*, eds. Sinclair B. Ferguson, David F. Wright, and J. I. Packer (Downers Grove, IL: InterVarsity Press, 1988), 647.
2. Robert Moats Miller, "Methodism and American Society, 1900–1939," in *The History of American Methodism*, ed. Emory Stevens Bucke, 3 vols. (New York: Abingdon Press, 1964), 389.
3. Charles Howard Hopkins, *The Rise of the Social Gospel in American Protestantism* (New Haven, CT: Yale University Press, 1940), 99.
4. Noll, "Social Gospel," 647.
5. Ibid.
6. Ibid.
7. Ibid.
8. Aaron Ignatius Abell, *The Urban Impact on American Protestantism, 1865–1900* (Hamden, CT: Archon, 1962), 159.
9. Ibid.
10. George M. Marsden and B. J. Longfield, "Fundamentalist-Modernist Controversy," *Dictionary of Christianity in America*, ed. Daniel G. Reid (Downers Grove, IL: InterVarsity Press, 1990), 466.
11. Ibid.
12. Hopkins, *The Rise of the Social Gospel in American Protestantism*, 221.
13. Levi Gilbert, "The Church and Social Problems," *Methodist Review* 90 (May–June 1908): 424.

14. Harris Franklin Rall, *The Coming Kingdom* (New York: Methodist Book Concern, 1924), 16.
15. Harry F. Ward, *The New Social Order* (New York: Macmillan, 1920), 9.
16. Ibid., 332.
17. Walter Rauschenbusch, *Christianity and the Social Crisis* (New York: Macmillan, 1907), 279.
18. Quoted in Kenneth Edwin Barnhart, "The Evolution of the Social Consciousness in Methodism" (unpublished PhD diss., University of Chicago, 1924), 99.
19. Walter Rauschenbusch, *Christianizing the Social Order* (New York: Macmillan, 1912), 127.
20. Ibid.
21. Ibid., 125.
22. Frank Mason North, "The City and the Kingdom," in *Social Ministry: An Introduction to the Study and Practice of Social Service*, ed. Harry F. Ward (New York: Eaton and Mains, 1910), 304.
23. Ibid., 305.
24. Francis J. McConnell, *Living Together: Studies in the Ministry of Reconciliation* (New York: Abingdon Press, 1923), 44.
25. William DeWitt Hyde, *Outlines of Social Theology* (New York: Macmillan, 1895), vi.
26. Lloyd J. Averill, *American Theology in the Liberal Tradition* (Philadelphia: Westminster Press, 1967), 129.
27. John G. Woolley, "The Voices of the Century," *Zion's Herald* 73 (July 1895): 435.
28. Ibid.
29. Hopkins, *The Rise of the Social Gospel in American Protestantism*, 101.
30. Robert T. Handy, *A Christian America: Protestant Hopes and Historical Realities* (New York: Oxford University Press, 1971), 166.
31. William M. Balch, "Social Salvation," *Methodist Review* 91 (September 1909): 745.
32. F. Ernest Johnson, *The Church and Society* (New York: Abingdon Press, 1935), 54.
33. Handy, *A Christian America*, 160.
34. John C. Bennett, *Social Salvation: A Religious Approach to the Problems of Social Change* (New York: Charles Scribner's Sons, 1935), 46.

35. Ibid., 53.
36. Ibid., 55.
37. Ibid., 61.
38. Herbert Welch, "The Church and Social Service," *Methodist Review* 90 (September–October, 1908): 714.
39. Francis J. McConnell, *Christian Citizenship: An Elective Course for Young People* (New York: Methodist Book Concern, 1922), 7.
40. Johnson, *The Church and Society*, 37.
41. Ibid., 38.
42. Ibid., 40.
43. Ernest Fremont Tittle, "The Use and Abuse of Creeds," *Methodist Review* 89 (November 1917): 874.
44. H. Richard Niebuhr, *The Kingdom of God in America* (Hamden, CT: Shoe String Press, 1956), 194.
45. Ibid., 193.
46. F. Ernest Johnson, *The Social Gospel Re-Examined* (New York: Harper & Brothers, 1940), 3.
47. Ibid., 73.
48. Colson, a chief counsel for President Nixon, went to prison during the Watergate controversy in 1973, during which time he was converted to Christ. He spent the remainder of his life establishing ministries to people in prison. He died in 2012. Colson lived his Christian life "under the sense of divine imperative."
49. Walter G. Muelder, *Methodism and Society in the Twentieth Century*, the Methodism and Society series, 4 vols. (New York: Abingdon, 1961), 2:34.
50. Richard M. Cameron, *Methodism and Society in Historical Perspective*, the Methodism and Society series, 4 vols. (New York: Abingdon, 1961), 1:289.
51. Riley B. Case, *Evangelical and Methodist: A Popular History* (Nashville: Abingdon, 2004), 81.
52. Ibid.
53. Thomas C. Reeves, *The Empty Church: The Suicide of Liberal Christianity* (New York: Free Press, 1996), 93.
54. Ibid., 99.

Chapter 8: Methodist Resistance

1. Albert Edward Day, "More Methodist Needs—a Voice from the Crowd," *Methodist Review* 106 (July 1923): 549–50.
2. Ibid., 550.
3. Ibid.
4. Ibid., 551.
5. Ibid., 551–52.
6. Borden Parker Bowne, *The Essence of Religion* (Boston: Houghton Mifflin, 1910), 165.
7. Francis J. McConnell, *Christian Citizenship: An Elective Course for Young People* (New York: Methodist Book Concern, 1922), 32.
8. Edwin Lewis, *A Christian Manifesto* (New York, Cincinnati, Chicago: Abingdon, 1934), 9.
9. Ibid.
10. Howard Glen Spann, "Evangelicalism in Modern American Methodism: Theological Conservatives in the 'Great Deep' of the Church, 1900–1980" (PhD diss., Johns Hopkins University, 1994), 52.
11. "What Is Disturbing the Methodists?" *Christian Century* (May 20, 1926): 637–40. Cited in Riley B. Case, *Evangelical and Methodist: A Popular History* (Nashville: Abingdon, 2004), 81–82. In chapter 4 of his work, Case provides numerous examples of the changes taking place in Methodist doctrine during this period.
12. George Herbert Betts, *The Beliefs of 700 Ministers and Their Meaning for Religious Education* (Nashville: Abingdon, 1929). The study was one of the Abingdon Religious Education Monographs with John W. Langdale, general editor, and George Herbert Betts, editor.
13. Ibid., 22.
14. Case, *Evangelical and Methodist*, 83.
15. Ibid.
16. Ibid., 84. Citing Betts's study, 43.
17. Ibid. Citing Betts's study, 57.
18. Ibid.
19. Ibid., 85.
20. Charles Clayton Morrison, *The Social Gospel and the Christian Cultus* (New York: Harper & Brothers, 1933), 31.
21. Ibid., 101.

22. Day, "More Methodist Needs—a Voice from the Crowd," 553.

23. Ibid., 554.

24. Harold Paul Sloan, "The League's Circular Letter and the Replies," *The Call* 2.2 (June 1926), cited in Spann, "Evangelicalism in Modern American Methodism," 160.

25. For a thorough and fair treatment of the Holiness Movement and the controversy within Methodist around the turn of the century, see John Leland Peters, *Christian Perfection and American Methodism* (New York: Abingdon, 1956).

26. Richard M. Cameron, *Methodism and Society in Historical Perspective*, the Methodism and Society series, 4 vols. (New York: Abingdon, 1961), 1:267.

27. William Warren Sweet, *The Story of Religion in America* (New York: Harper & Brothers, 1930), 355.

28. Peters, *Christian Perfection and American Methodism*, 138.

29. Ibid., 139.

30. Case, *Evangelical and Methodist*, 19–20.

31. Peters, *Christian Perfection and American Methodism*, 148.

32. Ibid.

33. Sweet, *The Story of Religion in America*, 353.

34. Vinson Synan, *The Holiness-Pentecostal Movement in the United States* (Grand Rapids: Eerdmans, 1971), 219. Cited in Spann, "Evangelicalism in Modern American Methodism," 84.

35. Delbert R. Rose, *A Theology of Christian Experience* (Minneapolis: Bethany Fellowship, 1965), 110.

36. Georgia D. Shelley, "Loyalty to the Master," *Pentecostal Herald* 20 (January 1904): 2–3.

37. Peters, *Christian Perfection and American Methodism*, 176.

38. Ibid.

39. Ibid., 176–77.

40. J. W. Mendenhall in *Methodist Quarterly Review* 71:476, cited in Peters, *Christian Perfection and American Methodism*, 177.

41. Ibid.

42. Ibid.

43. John J. Tigert, *Methodist Review* (September–October 1895): 120.

Chapter 9: A Remaining Evangelical Presence

1. Howard Glen Spann, "Evangelicalism in Modern American Methodism: Theological Conservatives in the 'Great Deep' of the Church," 1900–1980 (PhD diss., Johns Hopkins University, 1994), 4.
2. Charles W. Ferguson, *Methodists and the Making of America* (Austin: Eakin Press, 1983), 396; cited in Spann, "Evangelicalism in Modern American Methodism," 4.
3. Ibid.
4. Frederick A. Norwood, ed., *Sourcebook of American Methodism* (Nashville: Abingdon, 1982) introduction; cited in Spann, "Evangelicalism in Modern American Methodism," 4.
5. Ibid., 5.
6. Ibid.
7. Ibid.
8. Ronald E. Osborn, *The Spirit of American Christianity* (New York: Harper & Brothers, 1958), 143–44.
9. Ibid., 145.
10. Ibid., 144.
11. Ibid., 168, 170.
12. Spann, "Evangelicalism in Modern American Methodism," 7.
13. Ibid.
14. R. Michael Sigler, "Methodism Unmasked: Official Survey Reveals Membership Still Conservative," *Good News* (November–December 1990): 15.
15. Ibid., 16.
16. Ibid.
17. William R. Hutchison, ed., "Protestantism as Establishment," *Between the Times* (Cambridge: Cambridge University Press, 1989), 14.
18. John G. McEllhenney, ed., *Proclaiming Grace and Freedom: The Story of United Methodism in America* (Nashville: Abingdon, 1982), 99.
19. Percival A. Wesche, *Henry Clay Morrison: Crusader Saint* (Wilmore, KY: Asbury Theological Seminary, 1963), 62.
20. Spann, "Evangelicalism in Modern American Methodism," 106.
21. Ibid., 107.

22. Kenneth Cain Kinghorn, *The Story of Asbury Theological Seminary* (Lexington, KY: Emeth Press, 2010), 53. Kinghorn provides an excellent account of the events leading up to the founding of Asbury Theological Seminary in chapter 3 of this important work.

23. Henry Clay Morrison, "The Preachers of the Future," *Pentecostal Herald* (March 10, 1920): 1.

24. Henry Clay Morrison, "Is There Cause for Alarm?" *Pentecostal Herald* (March 8, 1922): 1.

25. Kinghorn, *The Story of Asbury Theological Seminary*, 57.

26. Henry Clay Morrison, "What Is the Matter with Methodism?" pt. 4, *Pentecostal Herald* (November 14, 1923): 2.

27. Ibid., 1.

28. Kinghorn, *The Story of Asbury Theological Seminary*, 56.

29. Ibid. For the account of Morrison's passing and the following four memorial citations, see pages 99–100 of Kinghorn's work.

30. Ibid., 67.

31. From a stenographic copy of Bishop Darlington's address, quoted in Percival A. Wesche, "The Life, Theology, and Influence of Henry Clay Morrison" (PhD thesis, the University of Oklahoma, 1954), 351.

32. Arthur J. Moore, "Personal Tribute," *Pentecostal Herald* (September 2, 1942): 3.

33. Roy Smith, "Henry Clay Morrison," *New York Christian Advocate* (April 9, 1942): 2.

34. "Dr. H. C. Morrison's Passing" (stenographic record of E. Stanley Jones's address at Asbury College May 8, 1942).

Chapter 10: A History of Protests and Calls for Reform

1. Robert Pierce Shuler had three sons who followed him into the ministry. His grandson, Robert P. Shuler III, is a graduate of Asbury Theological Seminary and has written an extensive biography about his grandfather, *"Fighting Bob" Shuler of Los Angeles: God's Man for the Issues of His Time* (Indianapolis: Dog Ear, 2011). In chapter 6, I cited Shuler's article about liberal theologian James Gordon Gilkey, who spoke at the Texas Pastors' School at Southern Methodist University. See pages 76–77.

2. For Keysor's full article, see Charles W. Keysor, "Methodism's Silent Minority," *Good News* (November/December 2007): 17. Keysor

served as executive secretary of *Good News* until his retirement in 1980. I was elected to head *Good News* beginning in April 1981, and served as president and publisher for twenty-eight years, until retiring in 2009.

3. Ibid.,14–15.

4. Ibid., 15.

5. Keysor was trained at the Medill School of Journalism at Northwestern University and had served as the managing editor of Methodism's *Together* magazine. Following his conversion at a Billy Graham crusade, he decided to enter the ministry and graduated from Garrett-Evangelical Theological Seminary in Evanston, Illinois, and became a clergy member of the Northern Illinois Conference of the Methodist Church.

6. For a fuller history of the ministry of Good News, see "40 Years of Vision for United Methodist Renewal and Reformation," by James V. Heidinger II, *Good News* (November/December 2007): 6–13.

7. Riley B. Case, *Evangelical and Methodist: A Popular History* (Nashville: Abingdon, 2004), 45ff. Riley Case was involved on Good News's behalf in conversations with the Curriculum Committee of the United Methodist Publishing House for many years. He documents here his experience and understanding of the controversy that existed around Sunday school materials.

8. Ibid., 46, citing *Teacher I and II* (Spring 1969); quoted in Charles Keysor, "Cyanide Revisited," *Good News* (July–September 1970): 19.

9. Ibid., 47. Riley Case's work *Evangelical and Methodist* has a more expanded treatment of Good News's efforts for reform and renewal. He began with the intention of writing a history of the Good News ministry, but as he was doing his research, his work went far beyond that original purpose.

10. The Confessing Movement chose Patricia Miller, state senator from Indianapolis, Indiana, to be the executive director of the movement. She continues in that capacity today.

Chapter 11: Doctrinal Problems in our Denominational Seminaries

1. The bishop made these remarks in his plenary address at the January meeting of the Congress on Evangelism in January 1993, an event sponsored by the Council on Evangelism.

2. John Lawson, *An Evangelical Faith for Today* (Nashville: Abingdon, 1972), 7–9.

3. Ibid., 7. Lawson may have been referencing Good News here. His faculty colleague at Candler, Dr. Claude Thompson, gave a major address at the first national Good News Convocation, held in Dallas in 1970.

4. Ibid., 8.

5. Ibid., 8–9.

6. Ibid., 8.

7. Ibid., 11.

8. Ibid., 12.

9. Ibid., 9.

10. Ibid., 12.

11. http://www.touchstonemag.com/archives/article.php?id=06-04-012-f

12. John Lawson, *Introduction to Christian Doctrine* (Wilmore, KY: Francis Asbury, 1980), 104–5. This is a reprint of his *Comprehensive Handbook of Christian Doctrine* (Englewood Cliffs, NJ: Prentice Hall, 1967).

13. Carl E. Braaten, "The Gospel Proviso: Lessons from Twentieth-Century Theology for the New Millennium," chapter 14 of *Ancient & Postmodern Christianity: Paleo-Orthodoxy in the 21st Century: Essays in Honor of Thomas C. Oden*, ed. Kenneth Tanner and Christopher A. Hall (Downers Grove, IL: InterVarsity Press, 2002), 202.

14. Ibid.

15. Ibid., 203.

16. "Social Reform: An Evangelical Imperative in the Crisis," Claude Thompson, *Good News* (October–December 1970): 73–78. This article was adapted from Thompson's address at the Good News Convocation in July 1970. His reference to "men" being trained reflects the fact that at the time, most seminarians were male.

17. Thomas C. Oden, *Systematic Theology*, 3 vols. (San Francisco: HarperSanFrancisco, 1992). Other of Oden's works related to this study are: *Requiem: A Lament in Three Movements* (Nashville: Abingdon, 1995); *The Rebirth of Orthodoxy: Signs of New Life in Christianity* (San Francisco: HarperSanFrancisco, 2003); *Turning around the Mainline: How Renewal Movements Are Changing the Church* (Grand Rapids: Baker Books, 2006); and *A Change of*

Heart: A Personal and Theological Memoir (Downers Grove, IL: InterVarsity Press, 2014).

18. Oden, *The Rebirth of Orthodoxy*, 85.
19. Ibid.
20. Ibid., 85–86.
21. Ibid., 87.
22. Ibid., 88.
23. Ibid.
24. See his new autobiography: *A Change of Heart: A Personal and Theological Memoir* (Downers Grove, IL: Intervarsity Press, 2014).
25. Oden, *The Rebirth of Orthodoxy*, 90.
26. Ibid., 90–91.
27. Ibid., 91.
28. Ibid., 93.
29. Ibid., 92.
30. Oden, *A Change of Heart*, 149.
31. Ibid.
32. Ibid.
33. Ibid.
34. Oden, *Requiem*.
35. Ibid., 36.
36. Ibid.
37. Ibid., 37.
38. Ibid., 40.
39. Ibid., 46.
40. Ibid.
41. Oden, *A Change of Heart*, 170.
42. Ibid.
43. Oden, *Requiem*, 22.
44. Ibid.
45. Ibid., 38.
46. Ibid., 14.
47. For the full text of Dr. Robb's address, go to the website of a Foundation for Theological Education at: www.aftesite.org /explore-the-foundation/about-the-foundation. See "The Crisis of Theological Education in the United Methodist Church," by Edmund Robb. The citations that follow are from that text.
48. Ibid.

49. For a fuller story about United's renaissance, see "Roadmap for Renewal," John Southwick, *Good News* (May/June 2014): 22–26.

Chapter 12: The Trivialization of Christian Doctrine

1. Alister McGrath, *Understanding Doctrine: Its Relevance and Purpose for Today* (Grand Rapids: Zondervan, 1990), 13.
2. For a thorough news report on the Re-Imagining Conference, see "United Methodist Women Get Taste of Sophia Worship," by Dottie Chase, *Good News* (January/February 1994): 36–38. Ms. Chase attended the conference. See also "Mainline Denial: How Our Churches Are Responding to 'Re-Imagining,'" by Susan Cyre, *Good News* (March/April 1994): 12–14.
3. Chase, "United Methodist Women Get Taste of Sophia Worship," 36–38.
4. Susan Cyre, "Mainline Denial," 12.
5. Bishop Mack Stokes's letter is on page 3 and the Canon and Hunt articles are on pages 16–17 of *Good News* (March/April 1994).
6. See news article in *Good News*, "Bishops Issue Statement on 'Biblical Wisdom'" (January/February 1995): 35–36, which is adapted from United Methodist News Service. The article contains the full text of the statement.
7. Most evangelicals believed that the radical doctrinal views expressed at Re-Imagining were not representative of most United Methodism women in our local church units. Many of them were also distressed by what they heard, but often found it difficult to believe their leadership in New York would be supportive of such a conference. Within two months, UMW leadership released "A Time of Hope—A Time of Threat," a statement boldly defending the Re-Imagining Conference and claiming critics were denying women the right to do theology.
8. See news article "Bishop Hearn Addresses 'Gnat-Camel Syndrome,'" *Good News* (January/February 1995): 37. The article is adapted from United Methodist News Service.
9. Tom Griffith, "Three Cheers for Our Evangelical Brothers and Sisters," *Open Hands* (Winter 1995).
10. Ibid.

11. I purposefully note the word "dissenting" as the bishop used this word specifically about his views in his book. See C. Joseph Sprague, *Affirmations of a Dissenter* (Nashville: Abingdon, 2002).

12. *Kane County Chronicle*, December 20, 1996. (Page number unknown.) Bishop Sprague was the bishop of the Northern Illinois Annual Conference at the time.

13. Marcus J. Borg, *Meeting Jesus Again for the First Time: The Historical Jesus and the Heart of Contemporary Faith* (New York: HarperOne, 1995).

14. Ibid., page unknown.

15. Ibid.

16. "And Can It Be That I Should Gain," by Charles Wesley, *The United Methodist Hymnal* (Nashville: United Methodist Publishing House 1989), no. 363.

17. Borg, *Meeting Jesus Again for the First Time*, page unknown.

18. *Kane County Chronicle*, no page number.

19. Ibid.

20. "The Role of Bishops and District Superintendents," *The Book of Discipline of the United Methodist Church* (Nashville: United Methodist Publishing House, 2012), par. 403, 316.

21. Sprague, *Affirmations of a Dissenter*, 16.

22. Thomas C. Reeves, *The Empty Church: The Suicide of Liberal Christianity* (New York: Free Press, 1996), 177.

23. Sprague, *Affirmations of a Dissenter*, 40.

24. Ibid.

25. Ibid., 41.

26. Ibid., 42.

27. Ibid., 43.

28. Ibid., 44.

29. Ibid., 45.

30. Ibid.

31. *The Book of Discipline of the United Methodist Church*, 64.

32. Ibid.

33. *Webster's New World Dictionary of the American Language: College Edition* (New York: World Publishing, 1957), 423.

34. *The Book of Discipline of the United Methodist Church*, "Chargeable Offenses and the Statute of Limitations," par. 2702, 776.

35. For a full news article about the complainants' response to the SRT dismissal of their complaint, see, "Lambrecht Responds to Dismissal of Sprague Complaint," by James V. Heidinger II, *Good News* (May/June 2003): 36–38. For the United Methodist News Service article about the filing of the complaint see, Kathy L. Gilbert, "Complaint Filed against Bishop Sprague," *Good News* (March/April 2003): 35–36.

36. Heidinger II, "Lambrecht Responds to Dismissal of Sprague Complaint," 37.

37. Peter C. Moore, ed., *Can a Bishop Be Wrong? Ten Scholars Challenge John Shelby Spong* (Harrisburg, PA: Moorehouse, 1998).

38. For further documentation about Spong's doctrinal error, see "Bishop Spong, the Theological Criminal: The Virtual Atheism of John Shelby Spong," UK Apologetics, accessed January 4, 2017, http://www.ukapologetics.net/08/spongintro.htm.

39. Walter Hooper, ed., *God in the Dock: Essays on Theology and Ethics* (Grand Rapids: Eerdmans, 1970), 89–103.

40. Ibid., 89.

41. Ibid., 89–90.

42. Ibid., 90.

43. Ibid.

44. Ibid.

Chapter 13: Getting the Gospel Right

1. George G. Hunter III, "Denominational Direction: Does the Call to Action Lead the Way?" *Good News* (March/April 2011): 13.

2. "Doctrinal Standards and Our Theological Task," *The Book of Discipline of the United Methodist Church* (Nashville: United Methodist Publishing House, 2012), par. 103, sec. 2, 54–63.

3. Ibid., 59.

4. Ibid.

5. Wolfhart Pannenberg, "How to Think about Secularism," *First Things*, no. 64 (June/July 1996): 31.

6. Ibid.

7. Ibid.

8. John Leland Peters, *Christian Perfection and American Methodism* (New York: Abingdon, 1956), 177.

9. For the introduction to the statement, go to: http://www
   .christianitytoday.com/ct/1999/june14/54.o.html. For the full text
   of "The Gospel of Jesus Christ" go to: http://christianitytoday.com
   /ct/1999/June14/53.o.html.
10. See note 9 for reference to the introductory statement.
11. Ibid.
12. See note 9 for reference to the full text of "An Evangelical
    Celebration."
13. Ibid.
14. Ibid.
15. Ibid.
16. The Barmen Declaration was a historic statement issued in 1934
    by German Protestant Christians in opposition to the German-
    Christian movement supported by the Nazis. Leaders in the
    Confessing Church movement included pastors Martin Niemoller
    and Dietrich Bonhoeffer.
17. See note 9, ibid.
18. Ibid.
19. Personal letter, Jonathan B. Hawk to Edwin Lewis, October 16,
    1934. Cited in *The History of American Methodism*, 3 vols. (New
    York: Abingdon, 1964), vol 3, pt. 5, "American Methodist Thought
    and Theology, 1919–60," by William J. McCutcheon, 309.
20. See note 9, ibid.
21. "The Divisions We Must Sustain," Robert P. George, *Touchstone:
    A Journal of Mere Christianity* (July/August 2003), http://www
    .touchstonemag.com/archives/article.php?id=16–06-050-f. George
    is the McCormick Professor of Jurisprudence and director of the
    James Madison Program in American Ideals and Institutions at
    Princeton University.
22. Ibid., 4.
23. Ibid., 5.
24. Ibid.
25. Philip Turner, "An Unworkable Theology," *First Things* (June/July
    2005): 10–12.
26. Ibid., 10.
27. Ibid.
28. Ibid.
29. Ibid., 10–11.

30. Ibid., 11.
31. Ibid.
32. Ibid.
33. Ibid.
34. Ibid., 12.
35. Ibid.
36. John R. W. Stott, *The Message of Galatians* (London: Inter-Varsity Press, 1968), 23.
37. See Lewis's comments on pages 63–64.
38. See Machen's comment on page 64.

Index